COMMUNITY ECONOMIC DEVELOPMENT

This book is published in cooperation with the National Welfare Grants Program, Human Resources Development Canada.

COMMUNITY ECONOMIC DEVELOPMENT

Perspectives on Research and Policy

Edited by Burt Galaway and Joe Hudson

THOMPSON EDUCATIONAL PUBLISHING, INC.
Toronto

Requests for permission to make copies of any part of the work should be directed to the publisher. Additional copies of this book may be obtained from the publisher.

Orders may be sent to:

Canada	*United States*
14 Ripley Avenue, Suite 105	240 Portage Road
Toronto, Ontario	Lewiston, New York
M6S 3N9	14092

For faster delivery, please send your order by telephone or fax to:
Tel (416) 766–2763 / Fax (416) 766–0398

Canadian Cataloguing in Publication Data

Main entry under title:

Community economic development : perspectives on research and policy

Includes bibliographical references.
ISBN 1-55077-061-6

1. Economic development.   2. Community development.
3. Poverty. 4. Canada - Economic policy.
I. Galaway, Burt, 1937-   . II. Hudson, Joe.

HC79.P6C65 1994   338.9   C94-930943-5

*Cover photo: Evening on the North Shore (1924); by Clarence Gagnon.
Oil on Canvas, 77.0 x 81.6 cm.; Collection: National Gallery of Canada.*

Printed and bound in Canada.
2   3   4   99 98 97

Table of Contents

    Principles and Conditions of Development Strategies   30
    The Validity Field of Neighbourhood Development
    Strategies   32
    A Few Last Questions   34

**4. Community Economic Development Organizations in
   Developing Countries   37**
Katherine Ichoya

    Role of CEDS   37
    Role of Non-Governmental Organizations in CED   40
    The Role of Women in CEDS   42
    Conclusions and Recommendations   43

PART 2:

**SCOPE AND CHARACTERISTICS OF COMMUNITY
ECONOMIC DEVELOPMENT**

   Development in Canada   48**
Mike Lewis

    The Growth Equity Model   50
    The Loan/Technical Assistance Model   52
    Human Resource and Employment Development Model   53
    Planning and Advisory Model   55
    Intermediary Organizations   56
        Technical Assistance to CED Initiatives   56
        Development Finance Intermediaries   56
    Concluding Comments   57

**6. Regional, Local and Community-Based Economic
   Development   59**
Tim J. O'Neill

    Definitional Issues   60
    Regional Development Policy   62
    Local Development Policies   66
    Community-Based Economic Development Initiatives   67
        Deficiencies in the Local Economy   68
        Current Approaches to Community Economic Development   69
        Current Programs of Support for Community Development   71

**7. An Integrated Development Model for Building
   Sustainable Communities in Canada   73**
Marcia L. Nozick

    Creating Local Wealth Through Economic Self-Reliance   74
        (i) Making More With Less   75
        (ii) Making the Dollars Go Around   76
        (iii) Building Collective Self-Reliance   78

PART 3:

ENVIRONMENTS CONDUCIVE TO EFFECTIVE COMMUNITY DEVELOPMENT

PART 6:
URGENT AND SPECIFIC NEEDS OF COMMUNITY ECONOMIC DEVELOPMENT

Acknowledgements

Earlier versions of the papers presented in this volume were developed for a Research and Policy Symposium funded by National Welfare Grants, formerly of Health and Welfare Canada and more recently Human Resources Development Canada. The symposium was co-sponsored by the University of Calgary Faculty of Social Work and the University of Manitoba Faculty of Social Work along with National Welfare Grants. We extend our deepest appreciation to Guy Brethour and David Thornton of National Welfare Grants for their support, encouragement, and assistance in planning both the Symposium and this publication. The book is only possible because of the hard work of the authors whose papers are presented here. We thank them for their efforts and appreciate the spirit of cooperation as we worked under tight timelines. A special word of thanks is due to many people whose hard work was essential to the production of this volume: Karen Braid and Barb Messenger, University of Calgary, Faculty of Social Work (Edmonton Division), prepared volumes of correspondence and other materials in preparation for the Symposium; Claudette Cormier and Val Thiessen of the University of Manitoba Faculty of Social Work were responsible for manuscript production; and Patricia Turenne did French/English translations for the work. Finally, we appreciate the assistance of Keith Thompson, Thompson Educational Publishing, who helped move this from manuscript to book form. This volume is a collaborative responsibility and would not have been possible without the assistance of many people. Ideas and points of view expressed in the chapters, however, are solely the responsibility of the various authors. Materials presented in this volume do not necessarily represent the policies or views of National Welfare Grants or the sponsoring organizations.

Foreword

An examination of community economic development (CED) in terms of both research and policy requirements is timely. Early in 1992, staff in the National Welfare Grants Program (NWG) began planning a national research and policy symposium. The event, held in Alberta, Canada, from March 30 to April 3, 1993, allowed researchers from Canada, the United States, France, and Kenya as well as decision makers from Canada to discuss the social and economic potential of CED. Decision and policy makers came from the Canadian federal and provincial governments, as well as from the non-government sector, including community economic development organizations, voluntary, and business organizations. Specific objectives of the Symposium were to identify and critically assess the current state of research on CED, to identify implications for current research for Canadian policy and programming, to develop a working agenda for Canadian research efforts, and to share information and promote dialogue among key Canadian and international researchers and senior policy decision makers. The research papers presented and conclusions reached at the Symposium provide the basis for this book.

The book reflects the objectives and theme areas covered during the symposium. A common thread throughout the symposium, and therefore this book, is the existing and potential link between the economic and social objectives of CED. In the wake of socio-economic restructuring, brought about, in part, by the globalization of economic activity, CED is increasingly perceived as a strategy in the fight against poverty which is complementary to more traditional approaches such as employment training, guaranteed income supplemention, and social assistance targeted at individuals rather than communities.

Successful examples of CED initiatives show that the right mix of resources, and support from different local partners, can make a difference. CED may not be a panacea but, under appropriate circumstances, it is an effective response to the economic and social difficulties of communities and concomitant impacts.

The practice of CED is well ahead of both research and policy. The lack of supportive research and documentation is especially evident as is the absence of systematic evaluation of this intervention. Sound evaluative research can help policy-makers, program developers, and practitioners better understand the conditions under which CED is most likely to succeed and when its implementation is preferable to a more traditional intervention model. The NWG Research and Policy Symposium on CED was a first attempt to assess the current state of systematic knowledge on CED in Canada as well as provide a research agenda for the immediate future.

I am delighted with the book's outcome and pleased to have been associated with this project. Sincere appreciation is extended to the Symposium's organizing committee members all of whom made a significant contribution to its success. Joe Hudson, Faculty of Social Work, The University of Calgary, and Burt Galaway, Faculty of Social Work, University of Manitoba, served co-directors of the Symposium and Guy Brethour of National Welfare Grants identified the researchers and policy makers who participated in the Symposium as well as the symposium themes and general topics of the papers presented.

This book will make a significant contribution to the development and promotion of CED in Canada. It will be of vital interest to a wide variety of audiences including decision makers in the government and non-government sectors, community developers and practitioners as well as researchers and students—in short, anyone who is concerned with the social and economic well-being of our Canadian communities. I commend all those associated with this book and the preceding symposium for their commitment and vision.

David Thornton, Ph.D.
Director, National Welfare Grants,
Human Resources Development Canada

Contributors

Alderson, Lucy. WomenFutures Community Economic Development Society, Vancouver, British Columbia.

Asselin, France. Program Development Consultant, National Welfare Grants, Human Resources Development, Ottawa, Ontario.

Brodhead, Dal. Chief Executive Officer, New Economy Development Group Inc., Ottawa, Ontario.

Bryant, Christopher R. Professor, Département de Géographie, Université de Montréal, Montréal, Québec.

Challen, Dave. Assistant Professor, Department of Social Work, Lakehead University, Thunder Bay, Ontario.

Coady, Nick. Associate Professor, Faculty of Social Work, The University of Calgary, Calgary, Alberta.

Conn, Melanie. WomenFutures Community Economic Development Society, Vancouver, British Columbia.

Coyle, Mary. Executive Director, Calmeadow Foundation, Toronto, Ontario.

Donald, Janet. WomenFutures Community Economic Development Society, Vancouver, British Columbia.

Dumaine, François. Assistant Executive Director, National Anti-Poverty Organization, Ottawa, Ontario.

Favreau, Louis. Professor of Social Work, Human Sciences Department, Université du Québec à Hull, Hull, Québec.

Fontan, Jean-Marc. Former coordinator of L'Institut de Formation en Développement ÉConomique Communautaire, Montréal, Québec. Sessional Lecturer in sociology at Université de Montréal and École des Hautes Études Commerciales. He is a freelance rerscher and writer on CED.

Frank, Flo. Laingsbrough Resource Group, Red Deer, Alberta.

Galaway, Burt. Professor, Faculty of Social Work, University of Manitoba, Winnipeg, Manitoba.

Hudson, Joe. Professor, Faculty of Social Work, The University of Calgary (Edmonton Division), Edmonton, Alberta.

Jacquier, Claude. Researcher, CIVIL-CNRS, Centre national de la recherche scientifique, Grenoble, France.

Kemp, Leslie. Senior Program Associate. Social Planning and Research Council of British Columbia, Vancouver, British Columbia.

Ichoya, Katherine. New Hampshire College, Manchester, New Hampshire, U.S.A.

Lamontagne, François. Director of Research, New Economy Development Group Inc., Ottawa, Ontario.

Lewis, Mike. Executive Director, Centre for Community Enterprises, Port Alberni, British Columbia.

Lockhart, R.A. (Sandy). Professor of Sociology and Native Studies, Trent University, Peterborough, Ontario.

Mason, Donald. Co-Director, Institute for Cooperative Community Development, Manchester, New Hampshire, U.S.A.

MacDonald, Dennis. Director, Community Development and Skills Adjustment, Employment and Immigration Canada, Hull, Québec.

MacNeil, Teresa. Director, Extension Department, St. Francis Xavier University, Antigonish, Nova Scotia.

McKnight, Michael. Project Officer, National Welfare Grants, Human Resources Development, Ottawa, Ontario.

McPherson, Dennis. Professor, Department of Social Work, Lakehead University, Thunder Bay, Ontario.

Ninacs, William. Head of Research, Corporation de développement communautaire des Bois-Francs, Victoriaville, Québec.

Nozick, Marcia. Winnipeg, Manitoba.

Nutter, Richard. Associate Professor, Faculty of Social Work, The University of Calgary (Edmonton Division), Edmonton, Alberta.

O'Neill, Tim. President, Atlantic Provinces Economic Council, Halifax, Nova Scotia.

Pell, David. Executive Director, Community Business Centre, George Brown College Foundation, Toronto, Ontario.

Polèse, Mario. Professor, INRS-Urbanisation, Université du Québec, Montréal, Québec.

Shragge, Eric. McGill University, School of Social Work, Montréal, Québec.

Swack, Michael. Director, Community Economic Development Program, New Hampshire College, Manchester, New Hampshire, U.S.A.

Tremblay, Diane-Gabrielle. Professor, Télé-université, Université du Québec, Montréal, Québec.

Watson, Kenneth. Rideau Research Associates Ltd., Ottawa, Ontario.

Introduction

Burt Galaway and Joe Hudson

This book contains a set of original papers dealing with the state of community economic development with particular reference to Canada. The first set of papers provide overviews of CED in Canada, the United States, Europe, and developing countries, followed by papers relating specifically to CED in Canada. These are organized in relation to five themes: scope and characteristics of CED, environments conducive to effective CED, evaluation of CED, partnerships with CED, and urgent and specific needs for CED. The final chapter by Dal Brodhead and François Lamontagne suggests directions for policy development and research. Taken together, the chapters constitute a state-of-the-art description of community economic development in Canada. They are largely descriptive of CED programs and are ideological in the sense that they lay out a set of beliefs regarding community economic development.

Several authors present descriptive information regarding the development of CED programs across Canada. Dal Brodhead examines CED on a province-by-province basis. Louis Favreau and Bill Ninacs report research regarding CED organizations in Québec, and Mike Lewis analyzes CED in Canada in relation to four models—equity, loan technical assistance, resource employment and development model, and planning and advisory. There is very little research reported other than Ken Watson's review of evaluations of several federally funded initiatives which suggest that they have been largely ineffective in job creation. The papers by Bill Ninacs and Louis Favreau and by Jean-Marc Fontan and Eric Schragge are directed towards providing more systematic descriptions of CED programs. The materials in this book represent work of current CED experts and will provide a basis for more systematic conceptual work regarding CED and for more rigorous research to test the propositions on which CED rests as well as to assess the outcomes and effectiveness of CED programs.

Four key concepts reoccur through the chapters. First, CED blends together interest in accomplishing economic development and social development goals. Second, CED occurs at a local or community level which often refers to rural communities and/or neighbourhoods within urban areas. Third, CED involves participation of citizens, especially traditionally disadvantaged groups. Fourth, CED requires partnership—both internal partnerships among organizations in the area being served as well as partnerships with external organizations. These four concepts provide a starting point for specifying the nature of CED and identifying some of the areas to which research may be directed.

The process of problem solving, as developed by John Dewey (1933), has provided a framework that has been widely adopted in human services (Perlman, 1957; Compton and Galaway, 1994; Brody, 1982; Reid, 1978; Epstein, 1988) and is useful for CED. Problem solving includes problem identification or definition, determining goals or objectives, considering alternative ways of accomplishing goals, selecting an alternative, action or intervention to accomplish the goal, and evaluation. Except for François Lamontagne and Christopher Bryant, the chapters in this volume do not explicitly place CED within the problem-solving framework, although in context it is clear that they are considering CED as a form of community problem solving. Lamontagne suggests five stages of development planning that are consistent with other formulations of the problem-solving process— assessing the community situation, setting priorities and developing goals, identifying activities to meet these goals, implementing the development activities, and monitoring and evaluating the results. Bryant defines CED as a process of addressing community needs through setting goals and objectives, identification of strategies and implementation of appropriate initiatives.

Problem Definition and Specification

The first step in the problem-solving process involves the dual activities of engaging the community and defining the problem to be addressed through the CED process. The chapters in this volume identify general problem areas to which CED may be a useful response with little attention to the process by which the CED practitioner engages communities and arrives at a joint understanding of the problem to be addressed by a CED initiative.

Most of the work is confined to general discussions of the types of problems for which CED is thought to be an appropriate response. A range of problem areas are identified including social alienation (Brodhead; Jacquier), social and economic stagnation of marginalized neighborhoods (Favreau, Ninacs), inability of communities to regenerate and sustain themselves (Nozick), a need to revitalize the local economy (O'Neill), unemployment (Pell; Fontan & Schragge), economic decline or stagnation (O'Neill), unemployment (Tremblay), economic crises in communities such as mill closures (Brodhead), environmental degradation (Pell), and the flow of capital out of communities (Swack & Mason; Nozick). Claude Jacquier emphasizes the condition of neighborhood alienation in European cities coming about because of the uncoupling of social and economic factors as the most important circumstance leading to the need for community economic development; he sees many CED initiatives as growing out of violent incidents in which groups of people within neighborhoods fight among themselves.

The prevailing view among authors represented in this book is that CED attempts to address both problems of economic development, especially unemployment, and problems of social alienation and disintegration within communities. Favreau and Ninacs suggest that CED organizations in Québec wage a war against poverty and disintegration of the social fabric from structures that are democratically controlled by the members of the community.

While there is general agreement on the idea of addressing both social and economic problems, these chapters are remarkably silent on how the CED practitioner engages communities in the process of defining the problems to be addressed. Research addressed to understanding how these processes occur and how they can be replicated is necessary for CED to continue developing in a systematic way.

Setting Goals and Objectives

The next step, after defining the problem, is to formulate goals and objectives. Goals and objectives are designed so that, if they are accomplished, the initial problem condition will be alleviated. The work represented in this volume tends to focus on the nature of CED goals and objectives, including tension between simultaneously trying to accomplish social and economic objectives rather than on the process of formulating the goals. Given the consistent emphasis upon participation, most authors would probably agree with Claude Jacquier's position that residents of the area subject to CED should have a major say in developing the goals and programs. Further, the papers dealing with the nature of partnership, especially partnerships with organizations external to the CED area, caution that one of the dangers is that the external partner will impose goals on the neighborhood or community residents. Many CED organizations have not developed mission statements or mandates tied to specific problems and objectives and, thus, simply reflect the goals of a government program or are very general (Pell).

The nature of CED goals must necessarily relate to the nature of the problem being addressed. Just as there is tension as to whether CED efforts should be directed towards problems of social alienation or economic decline, so there is tension as to which goal area should be emphasized. A minority of the authors have resolved this unequivocally. Mario Polèse, for example, argues that the success of any CED initiative must be judged by its capacity to bring more money into the community than goes out; Fontan and Schragge note that one of the central goals of CED is to generate employment in communities that face chronic unemployment but they also link CED efforts to accomplishing social objectives. Others argue that CED efforts must be directed to both market and non-market activity and account for social, economic, spiritual and cultural aspects of life (Lamontagne; Nozick; Challen & McPherson; Anderson, Conn, Donald & Kemp). Sandy Lockhart argues that economic measures are more conceptual than empirical artifacts and reflect a particular conceptual paradigm. Jacquier suggests that the scope of goals is defined by answering the question: "What is a developed neighborhood or community?". The research by Favreau and Ninacs on CED organizations in Québec suggests that there are two different sets of organizations each with a different focus; Community Economic Development Corporations are likely to cluster activities around the economic pole whereas Community Development Corporations are likely to center around problems of social disintegration of communities.

Most of the writers agree that CED should accomplish both social and economic goals. Tension, however, may exist between the social and economic goals of CED (Fontan & Schragge; Brodhead; O'Neill) and merging economic and social goals is not straightforward and easy (O'Neill). Dal Brodhead suggests that combining social and economic development objectives has at times stimulated creative approaches but that sometimes the two objectives have proved irreconcilable. Tim O'Neill believes that the focus should be on fostering economic development and that social indicators will improve when the emphasis is upon economic measures. No one presents a convincing argument or evidence, however, as to why one should attempt to simultaneously accomplish economic and social goals and there is disagreement as to the relative importance of each set of objectives. Fontan and Schragge, for example, argue that CED cannot be a large scale job creation strategy but rather a process of community and local empowerment. O'Neill suggests that economic goals are the more important although the accomplishment of social objectives may flow from accomplishment of economic objectives. Polèse indicates that CED initiatives are subject to the same economic truths as conventional business ventures and wonders if the conditions necessary for successful CED ventures are any different than those necessary for other business ventures. Further work is needed to articulate a rationale for linking economic and social goals, explaining how this can be done, and defining the relationship of the two sets of goals. A number of research questions would then follow. What are the actual processes used to link the two sets of goals? Do social benefits flow from accomplishing economic goals? Are the two sets of goals compatible? Or, does accomplishing one set of goals tend to deter from accomplishing the other? What are the costs associated with attempting to simultaneously accomplish both economic and social goals?

Selecting Alternatives

After defining the problem and determining objectives or goals, the third step in the problem-solving process is to select an alternative form of active intervention designed to accomplish the goals. This presumes that one is not locked in to a particular form of intervention but, rather, that several alternatives are considered with the most appropriate intervention selected taking into consideration the local situation, strengths of the community as well as any outside resources, the nature of the problem definition, and the goals.

A number of alternative ways of accomplishing CED goals are identified by the authors including local ownership of businesses and housing to retain capital in communities (Swack & Mason; Pell; Nozick), micro-enterprise programs (Swack & Mason; Ichoya), borrowing groups (Swack & Mason; Ichoya), local self-help and collective self reliance (Ichoya; Nozick), fostering an entrepreneurial culture (O'Neill; Pell), investing in infrastructure (O'Neill), provision of information (O'Neill, Lewis), provision of capital for both debt and equity financing (O'Neill, Pell), training (Tremblay, Frank), community loan funds (Nozick; Swack & Mason), and employment placement services and job training (Swack & Mason).

Mike Lewis identifies four models of community economic development each focusing on a different set of approaches. The loan and technical assistance model focuses on debt financing to worker cooperatives and other forms of community owned businesses and projects; the human resources and development model places emphasis on human resources planning, training, job readiness, client advocacy, outreach to community businesses and institutions, job placement and self-employment training; the planning and advisory model places emphasis on providing planning and technical assistance; and the growth equity model emphasizes building equity or wealth generating assets within communities. Mario Polèse notes that the wide range of community development activities makes it possible for both the left and the right to find common ground; persons on the left will emphasize alternatives to developed models and community solidarity whereas persons on the right will probably welcome CED initiatives with references to the importance of self-reliance and entrepreneurship.

While a number of community development activities are identified as contributing to accomplishing community development goals and objectives, the papers do not provide an analysis of how to match particular CED activities to a particular community, define problems, and select goals. There is also little evidence of systematically sorting through and considering alternative courses of action although, of course, this may occur in practice. There is agreement, however, that community development activities and interventions occur at a very local level in small communities, reserves, or urban neighborhoods. Focus on local communities is one of the common themes running these papers. Lockhart, for example, argues that CED emphasizes localized, participatory economic planning as the most effective alternative to the insecurity, dependency, and vulnerability of large scale, remote, socially detached and politically non-accountable economic organizations.

This vision of CED as one of economic and social development activities at a very local, community level runs through the chapters. Lockhart sees community integrity, stability, and value orientations as fundamental prerequisites to success of an economic development plan. The impetus towards CED stems from the inability to control globalized markets so that community and social needs are recognized; he draws a parallel between the effects of the industrial revolution when national governments deliberately destroyed local controls to provide national markets and suggests that the same thing is now happening as national sovereignty is being reduced in favour of global markets. O'Neill differentiates among regional development, local development, and community development. Various definitions of community are advanced, but they all seem to involve defined geographic areas such as a neighbourhood, a small town, or reserve. This appears to remove from consideration the concept of a community of interest although one of the case illustrations is of this nature. Fontan and Schragge, for example, describe a courier service designed to provide employment and learning opportunities for chronic mentally ill persons. This CED example is bounded by persons with common characteristics—a common interest— rather than a common geographic boundary. But this illustration is not typical of the examples and concepts of community discussed in the book, all of which focus on local geographically defined units.

Work needs to be done at further defining the concept of community and at advancing a rationale to explain why local communities are more likely to enhance social and economic goals than larger units. An implicit assumption in most of the work is that local units will be more responsive to the needs of individuals, especially disadvantaged individuals, than larger units. But what is the evidence to support the assumption? How does one assure that power structures within local communities are any more benign or beneficial than power structures in larger communities? History suggests that larger units of government, whether provincial or federal, may be more effective at protecting individuals from the tyrannies of local despots than local communities. The increasing power of local rulers, for example, was one of the influences that plunged Europe into the dark ages in the eighth and ninth centuries. The Charter of Rights is a federal document. Social and economic development may well be able to be carried out at the local community level in a way that is effective and recognizes the human rights of all people, including newcomers to the community. But a more explicit rational needs to be developed and tested to explain how this can happen.

A related matter has to do with the argument that benefits of community economic development should flow to the community. This of course requires a definition of community and an explanation as to how benefits can flow to the community at large. Do not benefits flow to individuals who exercise discretion as to how they use these benefits? Benefits might well be in the form of wages to workers, consulting fees to CED and other experts, jobs and power for civil servants, and so forth. Does the concept of benefits flowing to the community mean that the benefits flow to individuals within the defined geographical area contrasted with benefits flowing to individuals outside that defined geographic area? If so, this needs to be made clear and a rationale advanced as to why individuals within the community should receive the benefits instead of individuals outside of the community. Absentee landlords and business owners are often criticized but what about absentee human service providers including CED practitioners?

> The current remote and bureaucratized systems must be changed in order to end the economic mistargeting of our existing human-service spending. In any poor urban neighborhood, tens of millions of dollars are spent each year on human needs—health services, foster care, recreation, environmental clean-up, drug education and treatment, nutrition, and housing improve-ments. Almost every dollar of this investment currently goes to teachers, police officers, day care providers, nurses, outreach workers, probation officers, foster families, social workers, health care professionals, planners, managers, landlords, administrators, and service contractors who live some place else. The second time these dollars are spent, they are spent somewhere else.

> We are used to decrying the problems of absentee landlords and absentee merchants, but we have largely ignored the absentee human-service system we have so consistently sustained. Community-planned and community-man-aged human-service systems would not only work better for clients, they would also contribute jobs, enterprise, and development to the neighbor-hoods that need them most. (Annie E. Casey Foundation, 1994, p. 3.)

Having benefits flow to persons within the community rather than outside the community may partially plug the problem of capital leakage noted by Swack and Mason as well as Nozick, assuming, of course, that these individuals reinvest the benefits within the communities.

Action to Accomplish Goals

The action or intervention phase of the problem-solving process involves activities undertaken to implement the alternative course of action that has been selected to accomplish the goals. The chapters in this book tend to describe CED programs rather than discussing the steps that might be taken to implement them. There is agreement, however, that two key concepts underlie the action phase—participation and partnership.

Swack and Mason argue that an individual's well-being is identified in terms of the collective identification of community needs and wants and that underdeveloped communities remain poor because the people who live in the communities do not have control over the resources of their community. Nozick notes that participation requires a shift in powers from government bureaucracies to grassroots management and from outside ownership and control of capital to local ownership and control. Others argue for an increase in responsibility for local, municipal governments (Pell) and for an expanded role for non-governmental organizations (Ichoya). MacNeil notes that the role of government in CED may be as a stage-setter and enabler rather than a doer and that past expectations of government action may be counterproductive as this results in a condition of learned helplessness in which communities take no action on their own. Bryant notes that CED aimed exclusively at marginalized or underprivileged segments of the community will itself be marginalized if these people are not included in the decision-making process. Challen and McPherson suggest that social service agencies within the community can bring their expertise to play in terms of involving people. Favreau and Ninacs note that CED organizations in Québec wage a war against poverty and disintegration of the social fabric from organizations that are democratically controlled by the members of local communities. Participation in cooperative relationships within communities is necessary for the success of the CED effort, to strengthen community autonomy, and to develop mutual benefits for persons within the communities (Ichoya; Brodhead; Nozick; Anderson, Conn, Donald & Kemp).

The view is that community economic development can best occur under conditions of broad-based participation by all groups within the community, including traditionally disadvantaged groups. There has been little discussion, however, about how to secure community participation and awareness, although Frank indicates that this requires a training effort. There needs to be considerable conceptual work done to explain both why broad-based participation is necessary and how it can occur. What are reasonable costs to secure broad-based participation? What are the rights of groups of individuals who wish to opt out to pursue their own particular economic and social goals? What constitutes broad-based participation?

Partnership is another concept that occurs across many papers. There is general agreement that partnership among groups within the community is essential, partly to secure broad-based participation. Further, partnership is necessary between communities and external partners who can contribute resources such as money and expertise necessary for the local community development effort. Different types of partnerships are envisioned. Some will be among different levels of government agencies (MacNeil), some between government agencies and neighborhood group organizations (MacNeil, Brodhead). Brodhead, for example, identifies partnership between those affected by underdevelopment and those who represent their interest in government as necessary. Others note the need for partnership between the corporate sector and voluntary organizations who often represent the interest of disadvantaged groups (Bryant). Watson finds from an evaluation of 20 community employment strategies, a tendency of these organizations to bypass existing organizations and the failure of most to involve local business elements in the planning process.

The concern has been how to retain some degree of equality in the partnership so that interests of the external partner do not dominate (Bryant; MacNeil). Thus there is concern that external partners may exploit or take advantage of the community. Interestingly none of the chapters consider the other possibility—that the community may exploit the external partner. For example, does exploitation of the external partner occur if communities accept resources and then do not use them for the intended purpose or do not follow through and meet the commitments made to secure the external resources? Research could focus on the nature of partnerships that contribute to community economic development, those that detract from it, the efficient types of partnership arrangements, and both benefits and cost of partnerships.

The concepts of participation in partnership seem to be predicated on the need for holistic approaches (Brodhead) to development, an integrated development strategy (Nozick) that creates wealth through economic self-reliance and gaining community control, and approaches that break down departmentalization services and bring players together (Jacquier). Most of the material presents a conceptual approach of what needs to be done but does not provide guidance about how to do it. Thus another clear area for future research is to identify how CED experts actually carry out their work—what is the nature of the process used to actually implement a CED program?

Evaluation is the final phase of the problem-solving process. In carrying out evaluation efforts one learns whether or not the goals have been accomplished as well as information as to whether the CED program has been implemented as planned. Authors report very limited evaluations of CED programs in Canada (Pell; Swack & Mason; Fontan & Schragge).

Several cautions and considerations are also raised in regards to evaluation. Swack and Mason note that micro enterprises need to be evaluated in relation to the knowledge that most small businesses fail within three years; questions also need to be raised as to whether this is an appropriate approach given that entrepreneurs typically spend long hours at low wages and must consider the impact of this on families. Second, programs need to be described and implemented in ways that are replicable (Watson; O'Neill). The time necessary for communities to develop CED projects must be considered (Watson). Diversity of Canadian local development organizations makes it difficult to evaluate their programs (Polèse; O'Neill). Lamontagne notes that we have no agreement on evaluation measures and need to work at designing appropriate development indicators. Fontan and Schragge suggest that it is important to determine whether the emphasis is to be on unemployed persons or the employment needs of communities and argue that CED must become a political force for disenfranchised communities.

Finally, evaluation must also take into consideration the possibility of unintended consequences; Watson, for example, notes that displacement of jobs within communities and inter-community displacements are consequences that need to be considered in evaluating CED.

Conclusions

The authors, most of whom are Canadian experts in community economic development, provide a useful overview of community economic development in Canada and a basis for vigorous conceptual work and research for this emerging field. Community economic development may hold promise for communities and neighbourhoods across Canada. But the promises will not be realized unless we move towards clearer conceptual work and quality research to guide and direct CED efforts.

CED conceptual and research work may focus in two general areas. The first is to provide a convincing rationale and logic, as well as testing of the logic, for the assumptions underlying CED; these assumptions include the linking of social and economic needs, simultaneously trying to accomplish holistic goals in both social and economic areas, local community control, widespread participation, and the importance of partnership.

A second area has to do with research directed towards documenting and understanding the nature of CED work. How do CED practitioners engage communities, define problems in a way that integrates both social and economic interests, select goals to be accomplished through holistic integrated approaches, determine the most useful way to accomplish the goals, and implement CED programs? A number of the authors have suggested the importance of training (Lockhart; Kemp; Tremblay) and some have noted that there is generally a lack of formalized training programs for CED practitioners in Canada. Establishment of training programs, however, may be premature until one can first document what it is people are to be trained to do. This requires clear documentation and understanding of the nature of CED work. Hopefully, this book will contribute to the advancement of practice and research on this important and timely topic.

PART 1

OVERVIEWS OF COMMUNITY ECONOMIC DEVELOPMENT

1

Community Economic Development Practice in Canada

Dal Brodhead

T he history of the community economic development movement in Canada has been haunted by attempts to invent a perfect definition of CED. However, its diversity continues to unfold at the community level.

The debate sets a framework for comprehending the scope and characteristics of CED initiatives in Canada and has implications for practice and policy. Although there are many variations, two contrasting views are sufficient to make the point.

Blakely (1989) embraces what Fontan (1993) refers to as the "liberal local development" approach:

> Local economic development refers to the process in which local governments of community-based organizations engage to stimulate or maintain business activity and/or employment. The principal goal of local economic development is to develop local employment opportunities in sectors that improve the community using existing human, natural and institutional resources (p.223).

Fontan suggests that this approach is neither "alternative nor reformist" and is oriented solely to economic growth. In contrast he quotes Swack and Mason (1987) who define community economic development as:

> ... an effective and unique strategy for dealing with the problems of poor people, powerless people, and underdeveloped communities. As an intervention strategy in an underdeveloped community it does not seek to make the existing conditions in the community more bearable. Instead, community economic development seeks to change the structure of the community and build permanent institutions within a community. As a result, the community begins to play a more active role vis-à-vis the institutions outside the community, and the residents of the community become more active in the control of the community's resources (p.327).

Fontan refers to this definition as progressive, "where notions of social solidarity, individual and collective empowerment and actual control over local resources and their development are at the heart of the desired change."

Whereas the "liberal" approach emphasizes business and employment development, the "progressive" approach stresses community empowerment and institution building.

Another way to approach the issue of definition, given the lack of a commonly agreed upon terminology, is to see if a particular policy, program or project qualifies as a comprehensive CED effort when measured against a checklist of key elements. A CED initiative, policy or organization should include some or, preferably, most of the following characteristics:

- be a response *to* or emerge *from* underdevelopment and marginalization at the community level;
- pursue economic development as a way of empowering people and increasing local self reliance;
- *seek to build local capacity* to plan, design, control, manage and evaluate initiatives aimed at revitalizing the community;
- incorporate *a comprehensive development approach* which aims at linking economic, social, cultural, environmental and other sectors of the community;
- *be inclusive* (not exclusive) in its outreach—enabling disadvantaged and disempowered groups in the community to create partnerships with others interested in a sustainable future for the community;
- *favour* medium and longer-term approaches over short-term quick fixes typical of early job creation schemes in Canada;
- ensure that benefit accrues *directly to the community* at large rather than primarily to individuals within the community;
- endeavour *to initiate partnerships* (and joint ventures) between the marginalized segments of the population and the rest of the community.

The "progressive" theme for CED holds more promise than does the liberal approach because of its explicit integration of social and economic objectives. The building of accountable institutions and local control over resources is directly concerned with the use of CED as a means of reducing disparity between various groups within society. CED-style economics must be concerned not only with the production of wealth (economic growth), but also with how wealth is managed and distributed within the community.

The Nature and Scope of Canadian CED Experience

Canadian CED examples discussed here will be put in the same categories that were used in the Economic Council's Local Development Paper #19 (Brodhead, Lamontagne, & Pierce). In this study, a local development organization (LDO) is defined as an "organization, sharing certain characteristics of both the public and private sectors, designed to benefit the community as a whole over the long term … Its goals are both socio-cultural and economic; it has a community purpose and yet it may establish strong commercial links with the private sector." Although not all of the examples referred to possess the full range of characteristics noted above, they do contain at least some key elements of the CED approach to development.

Three general categories of LDOs were identified in the ECC paper referred to above: the community development corporation (CDC); local financial institutions (LFIs); and local training institutions (LTIs). Some examples cited here may overlap categories or may simply have contributed to the later development of other forms of LDOs. No pure form exists, as many development initiatives or projects are shaped by the community which has generated them. A more comprehensive overview of regional and national CED should, of course, include examples from the Northwest Territories, the Yukon and Ontario as well as taking a closer look at national policies and programs which have affected the field of CED.

British Columbia

B.C. has had a rich and varied history of community action/development (CD) and CED experience. It continues to be a centre of innovation. The cooperative and labour movements have a long record of initiating community action in the province reaching back many years. The Sointula Co-Operative was a unique community organizing venture in the 1930s and the Prince Rupert Fishermen's Co-Operative is a continuing example of the longevity and vitality of an LDO. The Native Brotherhood of B.C. was an early advocate of aboriginal rights, especially those associated with the fishery, and in more recent years, has supported a wide range of economic and social projects.

In the 60s and 70s, aboriginal and urban initiatives were prominent and provided many valuable lessons about the development process. Economic development corporations were created by many Band Councils, including those of the Squamish, Bella Bella, Nimpkish, and Duncan. Housing and neighbourhood re-development issues were focal points in urban areas such as in Gastown in downtown Vancouver and in New Westminster. The federally (CMHC) inspired effort to create a mixed use environment and community on Granville Island, with substantial local resident and business input, is a model with urban CED. Mill closures in rural areas provided early examples of citizen-based collective action to overcome economic downturns and disruptions. The unsuccessful attempt to create a newly diversified economic base for Ocean Falls effectively meant its disappearance. Conversely, for the town of Chemanus, a plant shutdown served as a springboard for local action which ultimately led to the development of a unique tourist attraction as an economic revitalization strategy.

More recently, in the 1970s and 1980s, community development corporations (CDCs) such as the Northern Fisheries Development Corporation were created to facilitate increased aboriginal ownership in the fishing fleet. The Community Employment Program (CEP) of the Salmonid Enhancement Program (Fisheries and Oceans Canada) was a largely unrecognized effort designed to enable aboriginal communities to enter the promising aquaculture industry on the west coast. The needs and experiences of practitioners and community groups also led to the subsequent creation of some important CED-oriented local training institutions (LTIs). The Westcoast Development Co-Operative was originally formed to provide training resources and has gone on to develop the most up to date and focused CED training material used in Canada today. The Nicola Valley Institute of Technology has responded to the demand for trained aboriginal economic development officers and now offers a range of CED-oriented business and development courses. A number of women's groups have also been active in the CED field and have undertaken relevant research, provided training and support, as well as starting some business enterprises. Over the years, the Social Planning and Research Council of B.C. has documented and supported CED activities across the province and it has lobbied the various levels of government on the issue of CED.

The inaccessibility of capital to finance CED projects has been identified as a major obstacle in the development process. The Colville Investment Corporation a wholly owned subsidiary of the Nanaimo Community Employment Advisory Society (NCEAS) is an excellent example of an organization meeting community level capital needs. Evaluations by government funding agencies and a case study by the Economic Council (1990) affirm the growing viability and the benefits the NCEAS provides to the Nanaimo community. The parent organization of NCEAS (a CDC), was formed in the early 1980s to combat community economic decline and received funding through the Community Employment Strategy—a short-lived program of Employment and Immigration Canada (EIC). NCEAS utilized CES seed funding and subsequently EIC Community Futures funding to support small business ideas initiated by persons unable to obtain credit from the traditional banking system.

One of the most important LFIs in B.C. is the Vancity Credit Union. Its support for CED projects, as well as its creation of the Vancity Foundation are examples of the potential for financial institutions to innovate. These are examples of the vitality of the CED movement in British Columbia. The current provincial government has indicated its interest in the potential of CED as a component in its revamping of community and regional development policy in British Columbia. Government policy making can refer back to the history of CED experience in the province to chart a socio-economic course for the future.

Alberta

The breadth and depth of the community-based development approach in Alberta in the 60s and 70s is much thinner than in the case of B.C. The experience of the federally-financed ARDA projects in central and northern Alberta, such as Alberta Newstart in the Fort McMurray area, contributed to some of the early CED capacity building. Sizable investments were made in the training and mobilization of aboriginal peoples and the unemployed. Innovative training linked to business development resulted in creative lease purchase arrangements supported by Newstart which enabled individuals to enter a variety of economic sectors.

Subsequent to the Newstart experience, aboriginal organizations such as the Alberta Indian Association and the provincial Métis organization became active in rights advocacy and the provision of basic community services. These organizations began to create and experiment with their own development corporations as economic issues came to the fore. Viable and visible models were absent and, thus, the early history of these development vehicles was difficult and often unsuccessful. The transition to arm's length relationships, creation of more local and tribal development corporations and a move to a more supportive technical assistance role for the provincial bodies were all beneficial to the development process. These experiences contributed to the recognition by some aboriginal groups of the need for their own local financial institutions. An example is the Peace Hill Trust Company chartered in 1980. Later, large scale federal programs (NEDP and the Aboriginal Capital Corporations component of the Canadian Aboriginal Economic Development Strategy/CAEDS) drew on the institutional capacity building lessons provided by these initiatives.

At the same time, the federally-funded Company of Young Canadians (CYC) had a strong influence on the practice of development activities in the country. At its height it had 200 projects across Canada and 400 field workers. Local citizens groups came together in Calgary with the assistance of the CYC to address housing, zoning and poverty issues. In the north, the CYC worked with aboriginal groups in the Lesser Slave Lake area to mobilize, obtain resources, and positively influence development policies.

Other noteworthy Alberta development initiatives include the well-documented experience of the East Central Economic Development Association (ECEDA)—a multi-community initiative in the Drumheller area. ECEDA, one of the Economic Council's Local Development Series case studies, was a regional development organization representing the interests of a number of contiguous communities. It grew out of local organizing efforts and received some support from the provincial government. The case illustrates the negative impact of intermittent, ad hoc, and sometimes inappropriately designed government assistance on a promising local self-help initiative and also demonstrated how a lack of access to locally-controlled capital funds can hamper the performance of a promising development organization.

Saskatchewan

Historically, Saskatchewan has been a base for extensive local development activities initially undertaken by the cooperative movement. The prairie wheat pools are still major players in the provincial economy. The University of Saskatchewan supports human resource development in the cooperative sector by providing training, research, policy, and evaluation expertise across Saskatchewan and Canada. Its vision of development stretched beyond the co-op sector and contributed to CED thinking and development policy nationally.

Federal and provincial initiatives, such as those financed by ARDA (e.g., Newstart) were pursued particularly in central and northern areas of the province. Extensive work at the community level acted as a springboard for many of the innovative economic ideas and activities currently practised in the aboriginal communities. The Kitsaki Development Corporation in the Lac La Ronge area is one of the most successful aboriginal owned CDCs in the country. The Lac La Ronge Indian Band, through the Corporation, has become one of the key players in the regional economy of northern Saskatchewan. Kitsaki now possesses significant holdings and equity and has the resources to support its core organizational requirements. It can legitimately be viewed as a sustainable Aboriginal CDC.

Manitoba

Some of the earliest Canadian examples of community development workers being recruited, trained and deployed took place in Manitoba during the 1960s. The province continued to invest in a community-based approach to development throughout the 1970s with the creation of a number of northern programs and community development funds. During the same time period, joint federal-provincial cooperation resulted in one of the most successful rural development schemes in Canada financed by the Fund for Rural Economic Development Agreement, 1967–1977. This integrated resource management, human resource development, and infrastructure project, introduced profound changes in the Interlake Region. The Agreement and the project were largely shaped by the active involvement of community-based planning boards (Economic Council of Canada, Local Development Paper #18).

The Winnipeg Core Area Initiative (CAI) was also a well-documented project focused on problems of underdevelopment in the inner city. Three levels of government jointly designed, managed and supported this unique project, which was delivered by an umbrella corporation with a clear mandate, resources and staff. CAI levered other program resources, private investment, and innovation in the areas covered by the project. Although not a community development corporation itself, it was flexible and facilitated the creation of a number of community-specific development corporations (e.g., North Portage) and projects. CAI demonstrated the potential benefits of inter- and intra-government cooperation, effective use of CDCs, the need for training linked to development, and the importance of ready access to investment capital within the framework of a 10 year strategy.

The Urban Institute of the University of Winnipeg (an LTI), has over the years, contributed research, training and support to Community Development and CED initiatives. The production by the Institute of the Vulnerability Checklist in conjunction with the Canadian Association of Single Industry Towns (CASIT), added a useful training and self-assessment tool for CED. The more recent Development Indicators Guidebook (Development Indicators Project Steering Committee, 1991) built upon the CASIT and University of Winnipeg work.

Quebec

With its long history of community activism, the province of Quebec offers a wealth of experience in, and documentation of, community development efforts. One of the earliest concerted attempts to rethink and reshape the future of rural communities in Canada took place in the Gaspé region of Quebec. The policies and practices of the Bureau d'aménagement de l'est du Quebec (BAEQ) forced the depopulation and closure of rural communities in the Gaspé region and inspired enormous province-wide and national debate on rural development policy. It also led to the creation of some of the earliest citizen's movements determined to resist government policies and revitalize the area. By 1973, the JAL (St. Juste, Auclair, Lejeune) regional development project had been established in the Temiscouata region and was involved in the formation of small development corporations that focused on local issues such as farming, woodlot development, roads, housing etc. JAL involved local people directly through committees designed to identify and implement development priorities. Organizations such as the Jeunesse ouvrière catholique (JOC) emerged in the late 1960s from the social action committees of the Roman Catholic Church to work in poverty stricken areas. The JOC's legacy is clearly visible in the Bois Franc experience in the Victoriaville area east of Montreal.

Community mobilization was also underway in the 1960s and 1970s in the urban areas of the Province. The eastern and southwestern "quartiers" of Montreal were early centres of community action and animation. Collective actions were undertaken by groups such as the *comité de citoyens, organismes communautaires, organizations de lutte, groupes populaires, associations bénévoles,* and the *movements sociaux et fronts communs.* Their strategies were often militant and were characterized by marches and occupations. Their solidarity was impressive in demanding respect for rights, access to programs and fairness. They questioned the development policies and priorities—as well as the bureaucratic practices—

of governments. The deteriorating economic and social conditions in Montreal during the mid-seventies and onward [OPDQ, 1979, la Chambre de Commerce du district de Montreal (1983), and others] inspired local organizations to further evolve and to place more emphasis upon economic and other planning activities.

Ad hoc funding of local citizens groups by the OPDQ and the federal Secretary of State were re-configured in the late 80s and early 1990s. More significant resourcing became available as the importance and capacity of local community groups became recognized and accepted. In late 1990, the City of Montreal committed six million dollars to a five year plan in support of six CDCs working in the most disadvantaged areas of the city. Montreal has been a vital center of extensive urban CED innovation. A wide range of highly developed CED and CED-related organizations now operate in the city. The Quebec experience has been pivotal in determining the course of CED in Canada and in demonstrating its potential for the future.

The Atlantic Region

Community-based self help initiatives have played a major role in the development history of Atlantic Canada. The early cooperatives in north-eastern New Brunswick and the Coady-inspired fishermen's cooperative and union movements in Newfoundland were examples of citizen action in response to the severe conditions of socio-economic marginalization. The potential of citizen action to affect policy was demonstrated in the opposition to the relocation policies of the Newfoundland Government in the 1940s. The Extension Division of Memorial University, where the focus was on animating rural communities, was at the leading edge of development thinking at the time.

The Newfoundland and Labrador Government, partly in response to the pressure from the grass roots level, created a province-wide network of Rural Development Associations (RDAs) as focal points for development services and short-term job creation projects. A number of RDAs banded together several years ago to form a CDC—the Great Northern Peninsula Development Corporation—to pursue longer-term CED. It created several large enterprises including a fish plant which has suffered with the decline of the industry. However, a wood chip business subsidiary of the GNPDC has been profitable and helps sustain the organization in the face of government programs which fail to substantively address the Corporation's long-term needs. In spite of scarce resources, the GNPDC continues to undertake research and development initiatives aimed at creating innovative opportunities where the private and public sectors are unwilling or unable to act.

Basic survival in Cape Breton has always required cooperative community action whether by unions or local groups. In this difficult environment, New Dawn Enterprises was born in Sydney and is now one of the most sustainable CDC's in Canada. It effectively combines social and economic priorities and has built an equity base which is used to lever other private and public sector investment dollars and partners.

Urban community-based development initiatives are not lacking in the region. Halifax was a key centre of community development and urban renewal activity in the mid 1960s. The Black United Front organized across Nova Scotia at approximately the same time and aboriginal people in places such as Eskasoni began to mobilize at both the community and provincial levels. A number of CED projects emerged in the 1980s. One project, the Human Resources Development Association (HRDA), sought to create training programs linked to employment for the disadvantaged in Halifax. HRDA has successfully moved away from its original status as a heavily subsidized organization employing only low skilled labour and now operates a number of profitable businesses employing both low and high skill labour. Sustainability was one of HRDA's goals and it is now nearly a reality.

Local financial and training institutions were also developed in the region. The Eagle River Credit Union in Labrador illustrated the necessity of providing a local banking facility after one of the major banks left the area. Local training institutions have long operated in the Atlantic and a number of them have played important roles in the CED field. In addition to the Memorial University Extension Department, the Coady Institute in Antigonish was also an early player. Latterly, the University College of Cape Breton and the Rural and Small Town Research and Studies Program of Mount Allison University in New Brunswick have offered training in rural development and CED.

The Socio-Economic Potential of CED

The tools and diverse strategies of CED have been used by communities across the country to achieve a wide range of social and economic developmental goals. Although the current emphasis of CED tends to be primarily on the economic challenges confronting communities, there are also many instances in which CED has been adapted to achieve social objectives through the comprehensive implementation of bottom-up development strategies. The eroding social base within the community is often what first motivates practitioners within the CED community to get involved in the process of change and development from within.

The combination of social and economic development objectives within one framework results in a tension which, at best, has proven dynamic and has led to creative approaches to overcoming underdevelopment. But the different emphases and distinct activities of social and economic development have sometimes proven irreconcilable. Economic growth can take place without stimulating social development and, in fact, in some cases can be detrimental to social development. But it is rare for social development to occur without a simultaneous improvement in economic conditions.

CED is unique amongst the growth and development approaches because it insists on advancing social goals while pursuing economic development. Most conventional approaches to economic development do not include a clear position on social goals. CED, as a holistic approach to development, insists on the inclusion of both social and economic objectives.

The worsening of Canada's fiscal climate has affected the CED community. Government restraint has had the obvious effect of limiting sources of support for CED initiatives, and it has also had a more subtle impact on the way that CED is practised. Increasingly, local development organizations (LDOs) have involved themselves with profit making ventures and activities in order to ensure a secure revenue base that does not draw exclusively on government resources for the financing and operations of CED initiatives.

CED has emerged and gained currency as a tool intended to reverse the unwanted effects of social and economic decay at the community level. It is possible, therefore, to view it as a response born of necessity and used in times of dislocation and relative crisis. Increasingly, however, CED is perceived as having potential as a proactive strategy with potential for socio-economic planning and development in good times and in bad times. The complex challenges posed by a global economy require clear policy responses from communities and broadly based coalitions to develop strategies which simultaneously address local needs and realistically factor in global constraints and opportunities.

Conclusion

CED does not offer a panacea to the myriad of ailments plaguing the Canadian economy. But in many cases it has been a most effective way of creating developmental opportunities for marginalized groups or communities under difficult conditions. Although each community utilizes CED strategies in distinctively unique ways, there are certain common ingredients to successful CED projects. Integration of historical, cultural, environmental, economic, and community elements is central to CED ability to overcome significant socio-economic problems. CED's uniqueness is also its emphasis on the meaningful involvement of marginalized or disadvantaged community members. CED is premised on the belief that community members are the most knowledgeable about local conditions. Thus, it makes sense to harness local human resources and knowledge in creating development strategies which address community issues. Although the core of its strength comes from within the community, CED also recognizes an important role for external resources—whether they be financial, human or otherwise. Effective CED combines the knowledge and commitment of community members with the careful incorporation of outside resources.

Supportive government policy and program environments are critical to the effective use of CED as an approach to development. CED is a strategy designed to respond to and engage marginalized groups and underdeveloped areas in tackling their own development problems. A partnership between those directly affected by underdevelopment and those who represent their interests in government is necessary for CED to fully realize its potential. Much more needs to be done by governments if CED's prospective usefulness is to be maximized.

Policies and programs must stress cooperative rather than competitive approaches. The practice of setting up new committees to service new programs with separate bank accounts to administer each project and separate reporting formats and data bases, has undermined the continuity and efficacy of long-term local initiatives. Competing provincial and federal programs with similar goals, serving the same areas with separate bureaucracies, have sometimes proven to be well-intentioned efforts gone awry. They consume resources that could be used more efficiently to support comprehensive, long-term, local development initiatives.

Marginal program changes are not sufficient. Comprehensive and linked policy initiatives are needed across a number of sectors such as housing, finance, cooperatives, local and regional development as well as in the social service field. Improved documentation is needed on current and recent CED experience. Public policy advocacy of CED values and strategies needs to be undertaken to promote its vision of development for the future. Examples of supportive policies and programs such as the Community Development Block Grants Program and the Community Reinvestment Act can be drawn from the experience of other countries, the United States in particular.

In Canada, governments have tended to act in a piecemeal fashion with the consequence that a comprehensive CED policy and program environment continues to be glaringly absent. There are no national framework policies linked to the provincial and municipal levels of government. CED is a significant trend in Canada and it is relevant to current economic and social difficulties. It deserves attention and investment. A partnership between communities and groups experiencing social, economic, cultural and environmental marginalization and their governments is a vital step that needs to be taken to augment the range of development policies required to move closer to a sustainable Canadian society. CED can and should become an important additional socio-economic strategy that contributes to the revitalization of current local, regional and national development policies and programs.

2

Community Economic Development: An Overview of the U.S. Experience

Michael Swack and Donald Mason

Political talk shows trotted out scores of experts who preached the virtues of community development in the inner city, as the black plumes of smoke billowed over the skies of Los Angeles in April 1992. The community development blueprints ranged from creation of enterprise zones, tenant owned housing, to the development of small enterprises in distressed communities. CED was hot for a short period of time. As the turmoil in Los Angeles subsided, and the populations of the United States and Canada turned their attention to the World Series, the pundits moved to other topics. But, what was learned from this brief period of CED in the sun? Did the varied and often conflicting economic development strategies presented by the experts demonstrate anything that can be of value to those who have worked in the field of CED for years? What we did learn is that there is not agreement on a fully articulated definition of CED. The various approaches taken or suggested are often at odds with each other. Many are pursued as a sporadic approach to economic development, rather than part of an integrated plan necessary for the economic development of underdeveloped communities.

There are many American models of CED to draw upon and possibly adapt for utilization in other countries. S. Perry (1987) discusses the history of CED and its range of organizations, activities, and models. This chapter will focus on the definition of CED, access to capital for CED efforts, and job creation and business development. Four models—community development corporations, micro-enterprise development, community development financial institutions, and flexible manufacturing networks—demonstrate both the strengths and weaknesses of the CED approach in the United States.

Lack of Community Control and Capital Leakage

CED is quite different from traditional economic development strategies because CED emphasizes models of development that address issues of ownership and control of community resources. Traditional models of economic development identify individual well-being in terms of corporate interests and measures of economic growth such as GNP and per capita income. CED identifies an individual's well-being in terms of the collective identification of community needs and wants. The fundamental CED premise is that underdeveloped communities remain poor because the people who live in the communities do not have control over the resources of their community. The residents of an underdeveloped community do not have the means to control the resource of land and housing stock. They lack the ability to recirculate capital within the community because they do not control the institutions that put capital into the community, nor do they control the institutions that provide capital to assist in the growth of a community. This lack of control over community resources stifles the development of the community and dooms it to a marginal level of development (Swack and Mason, 1987).

Large amounts of capital in the form of wages, government transfer payments, and public and private investment flow into even the poorest communities. But this capital flows into the community, immediately rushes back out, and is not available to the community for use to further develop that community. Capital leakage is primarily caused by a community's lack of ownership of the institutions necessary to capture and re-cycle capital for the community's benefit.

Housing stock is one of the major resources in any community. Fewer and fewer housing units are owned by members of the community as a community begins to deteriorate economically. Rental property predominates, and these rental properties are generally owned by individuals or corporations who do not live in the community. Profits generated by rental income flow to outside owners and are used for investment elsewhere. This occurs whether the ownership is private or government. In poor communities, 30–40% of individual income is expended for housing, usually for rent. Since very little of the housing stock is owned by either the community, or individuals living in the community, the money spent for housing leaves the community very quickly. Discussions of CED in Canada tend to focus on enterprise development and often exclude the housing sector as a CED activity. But, in the United States, housing development by local non-profit organizations is often identified as the major form of CED undertaken by a community.

Underdeveloped communities also lack traditional financial institutions tied to the community and that provide needed capital for both business growth and housing development. Banks have closed and left neighbourhoods in economic decline. Financial institutions, once they no longer have any community ties, intentionally stop investing in these communities. The risk is thought to be too great to justify limited returns. Businesses cannot expand without capital and many are driven from the community into safer neighbourhoods in order to survive. Businesses close, jobs are lost, and neighbourhood residents must then travel great distances to purchase goods and services that were traditionally found in their own community. Economic viability declines as the resources of a community pass from the control of the community or its members.

Traditional economic development pursued by government generally focuses on methods for convincing outside capital to move into distressed neighbourhoods. This approach recognizes that lack of capital investment in a community leads to economic harm, but the cure continues the cycle of capital leakage from the community. Projects, such as manufacturers set up in an enterprise zone or low-income housing projects built through tax-credits, do not address the problem of control by the community over its resources. The manufacturer may provide jobs over the short term. When the tax benefits are exhausted, the firm can just as easily relocate to take advantage of other incentives. Low-income housing relieves a major problem but outside ownership of this resources does nothing to prevent the leakage of capital from the community.

Government can mandate that traditional financial institutions invest in economically depressed communities. The level of investment in underdeveloped communities by financial institutions, however, has not been significant, compared to the needs of those communities, notwithstanding the U.S. Community Reinvestment Act's requirements. Too often, financial institutions use minimal compliance with laws as proof of commitment to poor communities. Government should not withdraw support of community development efforts. Rather government needs to re-think the approach and formulate policies to enhance a CED strategy that facilitates community control of resources. Strategic government support could enhance the viability of each of the four models of CED.

Community Development Corporations

Community Development Corporations (CDCs) have played a role in community economic development for over twenty years. Many successful CDCs in the United States emerged from the civil rights struggle and the war on poverty. Some of the early CDCs emphasized enterprise development in distressed neighbourhoods most concentrated on housing development (Vidal, 1992). Over the years their role has expanded to include commercial real estate ventures, provision of technical assistance to small businesses, and even the operation of businesses.

CDCs are generally operated as non-profit corporations that draw membership from a specific geographic area. CDCs in rural areas may cover several counties, while inner city CDCs may only encompass several blocks.

A CDC's strength lies in its community roots, and the participation of the residents in its affairs. The formation of most CDCs is sparked by one individual or a small group of community people. CDCs often grow out of other community-based activities such as tenant organizing or bank challenges under the Community Reinvestment Act. Availability of public or private funding also influences the formation of CDCs (Vidal, 1992).

The track record of CDCs in the United States has been much stronger in housing than in commercial development or business development due to the fact that housing, by its nature, is a less risky enterprise. Government subsidies that make housing affordable help to assure high occupancy rates and successful projects. CDCs have been successful in forging partnerships with local and state governments to undertake specific real estate projects in distressed neighbourhoods, and have benefited from specific government funding ear-marked for CDCs. Many CDCs have branched out to undertake a wide range of CED projects, but this diversification has led some into difficulty. Inability to attract trained staff from the local community to fit the needs of expanding projects has forced many CDCs to rely upon others to fill these roles. In some cases, the original community base of support has become nothing more than a reminder of past participation.

A look at both the successful models and those that have failed is necessary to better understand the role of CDCs within community economic development. Has success has been achieved at the expense the community's voice in the affairs of the organization? How does the organizational structure continually encourage community participation in CDCs where success has not lead to a decline in community participation? The Dudley Street Neighbourhood Initiative (DSNI) in Boston, Massachusetts, has been particularly successful at maintaining active community participation. DSNI has maintained an active staff of community organizers and has created a separate corporation to carry out development activities. Viable and participatory CDCs can present the voice of the residents to the outside world, as well as be the leading institution in a plan to regain control over a community's resources. Further research and study needs to be conducted to determine how far a CDC can go in taking on development projects without losing a sense of being owned by the community.

The range of tools for community economic development has expanded over the years; many CDCs have broadened their mission to utilize those tools. Some CDCs have commercial real estate ventures, as well as low-income housing projects, under their roof. Many combine job-training efforts with self-employment training, as well as revolving loan funds to assist small businesses with accessing capital. There is a continuing need for research on these fully developed CDCs to determine whether this structure is an appropriate and effective structure for all of these wide-ranging CED tools. As a CDC gets larger and more complex, can it maintain its community base? As CDCs get more experienced and sophisticated do they retain the ability to represent community interests? Are CDC ventures different from traditional for-profit developments? Does local ownership of business, in itself, insure community and social benefits? There have been very few evaluations of CDCs, and most of those evaluations assume that CDC development automatically serves a community purpose and that CDCs simply need more support in order to expand their influence and impact.

Micro-Enterprise Development

Micro-enterprise programs work with entrepreneurial individuals seeking to start or expand small businesses. Micro-enterprises range from self-employment businesses to businesses employing five people. These businesses usually require small amounts of capital—typically between $250-$10,000—in order to operate or expand. Micro-enterprise programs represent a community-based economic development strategy for business development and job creation among those traditionally left out of the economic mainstream. They provide individuals with the capital and skills needed to turn businesses or business ideas into reality. The individuals served by micro-enterprise programs are predominantly women, often people of color, and almost all are welfare recipients, unemployed, or the working poor. The creation of small businesses is just one goal of micro-enterprise programs; they are also designed to increase incomes, stabilize families, raise self-esteem and self-confidence, develop skills, create role models, and spark a process of community renewal. Over 150 micro-enterprise development programs are represented nationally by the Association for Enterprise Opportunity (AEO) in Chicago (1993).

Many micro-enterprise programs include loan funds or offer financial services through partnerships with local banks or credit unions. Micro-loan funds usually are capitalized with grants or loans from foundations or government agencies. But micro-enterprises face many barriers. The loan sizes required by micro-enterprises are too small to be considered by traditional financial intermediaries. The cost of transacting such loans is unprofitable for these traditional intermediaries. Additionally, the borrowers are considered to be too risky—they do not have much equity to put into the businesses, they have very little collateral, and they do not have histories of running profitable businesses.

Many community-based organizations have successfully loaned to micro-enterprises even though the loans are considered too risky by traditional intermediaries. Working Capital, a program of the Institute for Cooperative Community Development in Manchester, New Hampshire, has made over 500 loans in New England since its inception two years ago. Working Capital utilizes a peer model of lending, a model utilized extensively overseas in places like Bangladesh and throughout Latin America. In this model, people join borrowing groups. Members start out by borrowing small amounts of money for their businesses. If any member of the group fails to repay his or her loan, other members or the group must either make this payment or they will be denied access to further credit. Working Capital has enjoyed a 98% repayment rate over the life of the program.

Many micro-enterprise programs provide training, technical assistance, and support services such as child care and transportation to borrowers in addition to providing capital. The provision of these non-fee generating services, combined with the small loan sizes, means that micro-enterprise programs are not able to support themselves on fee and interest income.

Micro-enterprise programs face barriers other than the barrier of access to capital. The government must eliminate barriers and penalties for transfer payment and public assistance recipients who pursue self-employment for micro-enterprise programs to succeed. Recipients of Aid to Families With Dependent Children (AFDC) should be allowed to accumulate business assets and deduct business related expenses in calculating net income. Unemployment insurance laws must be changed to exempt recipients from looking for work while starting a business. Public housing rent provisions should be changed to minimize increases for residents generating wage or self-employment income.

Two main approaches have been developed to assist micro-enterprise development. The first approach emphasizes self-employment training for low-income individuals who want to open their own small business, or expand an existing one. The second pursues an access to capital strategy as its primary goal, with training as an ancillary function. Both approaches assume that self-employment through small businesses will substantially contribute to the overall economic health of a community. Self-employment training programs are usually directed at a specific segment of the population. This segment can either be low-income women, minorities, or recently arrived refugees. The training is not limited to providing business skills, but most often also includes self-esteem techniques, personal and family organization, and job acquisition skills. While the ultimate goal of the training may be development of a small business, the success of the training is not usually measured in business start-ups alone. Building self-esteem and receiving permanent employment are considered equally significant in measuring success. Micro-enterprise projects that focus on access to capital proceed from the assumption that micro-businesses need capital to start or to expand, and that providing this capital quickly and easily is their primary mission. These programs are usually designed in such a way as to assist micro-businesses in securing capital. They might approach the problem in different ways, such as peer lending models, or training and then lending, but their primary goal is to get capital into the hands of micro-businesses as soon as possible. Both of these models have demonstrated success in the United States and through out the world.

Micro-enterprise development is a fast growing tool of CED organizations. But, it is a tool that needs to be evaluated carefully. Any enterprise development program must confront the fact that most new businesses do not survive for more than three years. Are self-employment training programs and micro-lending funds moving poor people into situations that will result in their eventual failure? We do not yet know the long-term effects of self-employment on low-income participants. The second sobering fact with respect to micro-enterprise programs concerns the wages and hours worked by those attempting to make their living through self-employment. Generally, self-employment means long hours at work, and, in the early stages, a low hourly wage. What negative impact do these two facts have on family structure, particularly if the self-employed worker is a single parent? This is an area that requires further research before one can completely endorse micro-enterprise development as a strategy for healing communities.

Should limited resources be invested into programs that support self-employment or invested in job training or education for the chronically unemployed? This decision should only be made on the basis of sufficient data to answer the fundamental questions raised by investment in self-employment. CED policy makers must still look deeper into the underlying values from which CED springs even if the data demonstrate that the dollars invested in self-employment models are justified through increased opportunities and the creation of wealth in a community. One of the premises of CED involves the need for the community as a whole to gain control over its own resources. Does self-employment development foster a psychology of community? Do some micro-enterprise development programs, through their models, do a better job at achieving this objective than others? If so, what are the critical components of those models?

Community Development Financial Institutions

Community development financial institutions (CDFI) such as development banks, community development loan funds and community development credit unions address the lack of access to capital problems occurring in underdeveloped communities. The United States has seen the development of a CDFI industry over the last 15 years. In some communities, a community loan fund provides needed capital for both businesses and housing development. In others, a community development bank, such as the South Shore Bank in Chicago, encourages deposits and savings from the community, as well as targeting that community for investment. Finally, Community Development Credit Unions (CDCU), such as the Self-Help Credit Union in North Carolina, are making development loans for home purchases, housing rehabilitation, and small business development and expansion. All of these models attempt to fill the capital gaps found in underdeveloped communities, as well as develop community-based financial institutions to assist in CED.

CDFIs play different roles in a community. Some take on the more traditional role of providing loan funds to expanding or start-up businesses, while other serve as vital links in raising capital for large scale housing or commercial development. The structure of the CDFI usually reflects the role that it has undertaken. Development banks, such as the South Shore Bank, tend to play more traditional roles in a community due to the regulatory environment in which they are forced to operate. Even these more traditional models, however, have recognized that certain capital needs can not be met through the traditional bank approach and have developed specialized subsidiaries. These subsidiaries provide equity capital to ventures, specialized micro-enterprise loans, and business training.

The wide range of CDFIs operating in numerous communities throughout the United States demonstrate that flexibility is a key ingredient for success in this field. Can one single financial institution deliver all of the capital services a developing community needs? Is it better to develop several specialized community financial institutions in order to fill specialized niches? Many different types of community development financial institutions are operating and developing in the United States and are molded by economic conditions and the regulatory environment. But many questions remain. Can a network of alternative institutions provide substantial amounts of capital in areas not served by the traditional capital markets? Can they reach appropriate scale? How can government best support these initiatives? What is the role of the traditional capital markets and how should traditional financial intermediaries support these non-traditional models?

Flexible Manufacturing Networks

Flexible manufacturing networks (FMNs) are relatively new to the CED portfolio in North America but have been successfully demonstrated in Italy and Denmark. Legislation has been passed in Oregon to encourage and assist their creation. Other efforts are underway through out the United States. FMNs bring together small manufacturers to cooperate in the development, creation, and marketing of a specific product. None of these small manufactures could have produced the product individually, but working together as a network, they can bring the product to market. Members of a network must share information, coordinate production, and place long-term gain over short-term profits to achieve success. The underlying premise behind FMNs is that cooperation provides a competitive advantage. Most FMN experiments taking place across the country have not addressed the capital needs of the members of the network. Oregon provides minimal financial support for development of the network and has no special program to supply capital for the members of the network. Capital Networks, a project of the Institute for Cooperative Community Development, in New Hampshire, is the only flexible manufacturing network project in the United States that focuses on the capital needs of the network members. This project is barely eight months old.

Presently, there are too few FMNs operating in the United States to judge the success of this model. Over the next several years, however, additional attempts to form FMNs will be undertaken. Interest in FMNs is based on the belief that the long-term economic health of a community, as well as that of a nation, is directly tied to the development of manufacturing jobs. Traditionally, manufacturing jobs have been those that pay the most and provide the most security, but the last decade has seen a marked decrease in manufacturing jobs. Long-term economic development of communities have suffered as manufacturers have closed plants and moved.

FMNs seem to point in the right direction but many questions surround this model. Can this model be an effective CED strategy if it is not tied to job training and job creation in low-income communities? What will the various small manufacturers participating in a FMN give back to the community? Can FMNs be tied to ownership issues which enhance community control over the process?

Conclusion

There is much innovative thinking taking place in the field of CED in the United States. Although all four models have demonstrated varying degrees of success, many questions remain to be answered for each of the models. The final bench mark that must be used in designing evaluations and research protocols is whether these various strategies contribute to the ability of a community to control its own resources. Failing to test against that standard fails the community in the long run.

3

Neighbourhood Development in the European Community

Claude Jacquier

The concept of community has been getting bad press in Europe except for the United Kingdom and Ireland. This term has a pejorative connotation as it is often associated with ethnicity, minorities, even the resurgence of local idiosyncrasies, when it is not being considered as opening the door to religious fundamentalism. It is often tarnished by the idea of communitarianism. Most European countries have been built on the classic ideal of nation-state, which negates local identities and cultural particularities. France represents the archetype of this phenomenon with its one and indivisible republic and secular structure. The consequences of this can be devastating for, though it is the minorities that are being ethnicized in the United States, in France and throughout Europe the majority that is being ethnicized as illustrated by the debates on French identity and now on European identity.

The problem with the community paradigm also lies in an inaccurate translation of the English term community and perhaps with the fact that the definition of this term is rather vague. A community, in the Anglo-Saxon meaning of the word, is not limited to the idea of ethnic minority. It designates "a place, the people living in that place, the interaction between these people, the feelings that stem from that interaction, the life these people share and the institutions that govern their lives, all at once." (Medard, 1969, p.58) *(Our translation)*. Community therefore refers to the idea of neighbourhood but, whereas this has a physical and geographic connotation, the idea of community also focuses on social and institutional content, giving it another operational dimension. According to Peter Wilmott (1984), a place has a sense of being a community if it combines the factors of interaction among residents, some shared interests, and identification with a place.

Nevertheless, the concept of community does not lack for interest in this ethnicized version. A modern conception of development must call into question the role communities have played in moulding citizens. The process of integrating immigrants from within or from outside has not been reduced, in European countries, to a mythical dialectic between state and individual in which various institutions, schools being one of them, have played a significant role. Underestimating the role these institutions play is futile, but it would be rewriting the history of the building of nation-states to force the issue. Institutions have not been the only operators in changing cultural diversity into today's national oneness. The traditional community structures of newcomers on city territories have contributed to this change every bit as much by creating the conditions that are conducive to this integration. Immigrants have had to rely most heavily on support from the communities to which they belonged to survive in the chinks in industrial societies at a time when the welfare state mechanisms were not what they are today. They needed the compensating support of their original communities, structured by family and neighbourhood ties, to withstand the assault of the assimilation process. More often than not, the brutal separation from the original communities was, with few exceptions, dearly paid for by the failure to integrate.

Discussing what may have been and what still is the role of the original communities in the task of integration is not being reactionary; it is attempting to take account of the diverse and multiple mediations at work in passage to a national identity. Raymond Boudon draws from his observations on the integration of Poles in France:

> the attachment to Polish traditions and integration into French society work in the same direction ...; all studies show that one of the essential factors of assimilation in the host society lies in the support immigrants are given by the primary groups surrounding them (family, friends, etc.). Yet this support is only effective when the primary groups themselves are not disorganized and disoriented. However, the fact that an individual may be attached to Polish traditions is precisely the sign that he or she belongs to primary groups whose solidarity has not been weakened and were therefore in a position to support the individual's efforts to integrate into the host society (1984, p.18) *(Our translation)*.

This complex process, which gives both the original community and the host society a part to play, must be taken into account all the more since the host society is far from having its identity entrenched; it is the result of a continuous building process that will never end. How can one raise something up as being the identifying standard when it is only temporary and subject to new additions, most often in tense situations? Successful societies and cities attract the most underprivileged; in future, this success will continue to draw in destitute people from all directions. We have clearly not seen the end of worsening tensions in cities where poor ghettos are traded off for rich ghettos.[*]

---

[*] The term "ghetto" is used only as a figure of speech for problem neighbourhoods are anything but ghettos

This concept of community referent, makes it possible to find ways of designing assessment procedures and formulating development projects that are not exogenous (what can be *done for* the neighbourhoods), but endogenous (what can be *done with* the inhabitants who live there or, even better, what they can *do for themselves*). This is no mere war of words but rather an approach that runs counter to urban reality. Such a referent would make it possible to avoid becoming caught up in the vain debate opposing residential and working-class neighbourhoods and to engage in a process that focuses on reconstructing the components of urban citizenship in these neighbourhoods. These components include respecting the dignity of the residents, recognizing their ability to manage the city's affairs, avoiding policies based on benevolence and aid, implementing a true decentralization of powers, and providing technical assistance for the emergence of projects initiated by the residents (Power, 1991; Jacquier, 1993). One can only criticize the way policies against alienation are being implemented, especially the shift towards administrative procedures, when it is the development process that should be given an impetus.

Do Community Development Strategies Exist in Europe?

Community development strategies exist in Europe, although they may not necessarily be called that. In Europe this type of approach is not distinguished from concepts of regional and local development, except for the United Kingdom and Ireland where this expression, community development, is used. In France and some other EEC countries, this concept was reformulated under the label of neighbourhood social development or urban social development. In the European cooperation program, the term "integrated approaches to urban development" is most often used. But this label does not quite cover all of community development. Most often it is a matter of approaches initiated by national, regional, or local authorities. They are usually top-down policies, while the dynamics of community development favours a bottom-up approach based on the characteristics of local societies.

Nevertheless, the integrated approaches to development in Europe have brought to the fore the need to develop resources and local potential and to involve members of grassroots communities. The most successful neighbourhood experiments are those that have linked top-down and bottom-up approaches, emphasizing strategic planning principles, analyzing the

---

as they feature neither religious or cultural homogeneity nor strict social organization. The main problem lies in the very fact that they are highly heterogeneous, being a mixture of people of all origins having nothing in common except their status of being poor. This creates phenomena of cohabitation that can become quite explosive. Nor do these neighbourhoods have the homogeneity of the old working-class neighbourhoods that are structured on capital-labour relationships. It might be better if these neighbourhoods were actually ghettos, for then one would find conditions favourable to development (de Rudder, 1987; Vieillard-Baron, 1990).

strengths and weaknesses of urban territories and identifying the threats and opportunities on which to act to create a development dynamic.

These integrated approaches to development focus on the economic question in two different ways. First, there can be no grassroots community development when communities are too dependent on the outside for their resources and there is no opportunity to capitalize locally on the resources they do have. Conditions must be created so that the money that is circulating in communities and neighbourhoods remains there. Second, economic development implies upgrading the local environment at all levels, especially by creating a local economic culture. The quality of a territory, the skills and qualifications of its residents, and the web of relationships that are established among them are the vital components of local wealth, even more important than natural resources or geographic factors of location.

Integrated approaches to development focus on the potential synergism between all the components of local communities. They pose the problem, so damaging to society today, of the increasing externalization of social life through economics and business (particularly training, mechanisms of solidarity, and alienation). The increasing volatility of businesses and their capacity to destroy the local socioeconomic fabric now work against them insofar as they are no longer able to find qualified staff, conditions favourable for expansion, or even communities with the resources to buy goods and services. Integrated approaches also stress development's ecological dimension as well as the need to save the environment and value it as a scarce natural resource.

Community Economic Development, Integrated Approaches to Development

The Crisis in Cities and Neighbourhoods

In Europe, most of the initiatives in this field grew out of violent neighbourhood incidents in which groups of people fought among themselves, against other groups, or against the police. These incidents are often indications of a much deeper crisis in society, or rather of a number of crises related to each other. They show a shift in the issues and major conflicts of post-industrial societies. The contradiction no longer lies with business, with the traditional capital-labour relationship, but with urban territories where there is a confrontation between those who are part of society and those who are alienated from it.

This contradiction represents an increased uncoupling of social and economic factors, a heightened segmentation of society that translates through the whole territory (two-speed cities), a lasting welfare-state crisis, and a social control crisis characterized by the growing inability of political-administrative management systems to adapt which has the effect of exacerbating alienation phenomena. As a result, society's outcasts become more visible, not because there are more of them, but because their social ties (family ties, neighbourhood ties, etc.) have been destroyed, placing them in the care of public systems, which puts them at the forefront of the social and political arena.

In this arena, the alienated minority (10% to 20% of the population) rarely finds suitable responses, as this would imply that the current system of resource and power sharing has undergone profound changes, changes that the overwhelming majority of those who own something and have some degree of power (the remaining 80 to 90%) would be against. Added to this are the facts that the neighbourhoods to which people alienated from the economic world are relegated are often under-represented in local political bodies; traditional social and political leaders no longer live there, and the police, justice and educational system no longer find the support needed to implement effective action there. In short, the pillars of democratic societies have been eroded.

Conditions do not seem propitious for community development. This situation creates the need for a society that is at a standstill to rise above its condition, but the seeds of renewal imply putting aside technical approaches to development. Community development strategies are not merely a matter of techniques and methods. If that were the case, development would have taken place long ago and the problems posed by phenomena of alienation would be solved. Community development actually stems from a political process. It involves formulating and implementing policies that overturn a certain established order.

Poverty and alienation are mostly urban phenomena. Cities have become the place in European societies where people who have the most problems integrating converge. Some city neighbourhoods bring together highly heterogeneous populations that have the peculiarity of cumulating a number of disabilities. This concentration of difficulties on well-defined urban territories generates a cycle of poverty and alienation. In short, it is in the heart of our large cities that the main threat of future social tension is located. These territories of alienation in the heart of our cities are the result of various processes that reinforce each other. Cities are the natural hosts of the most underprivileged populations from Europe's rural areas as well as from eastern Europe and the south Mediterranean. Migrations toward the European Community, the oasis of prosperity in the world, will not cease and, in future, it is the less developed of cities' neighbourhoods that will be destined to absorb them. Moreover, cities are constantly secreting territories of alienation and concentrating on these territories people no one else wants, since the mechanisms of urban segregation are the result of both the real estate market game and urban management policies. Lastly, these neighbourhoods in a state of crisis tend to be self-maintaining as they stigmatize the people living there. A culture of welfare and dependence is developed on the weakening of family and community solidarity structures. A cycle of erosion endangers the foundations of citizenship and democracy.

European Neighbourhoods in a State of Crisis: Similarities and Differences

A quick comparison of the features of these neighbourhoods shows above all that the situations are distinct from three different viewpoints. First, all differences in spatial and architectural features of places of alienation illustrated by the old neighbourhoods at Cureghem (Anderlecht), Ciutat Vella (Barcelona), Nordstadt (Dortmund), or even Dublin and Lisbon; urban areas built between the wars at Korreveg (Groningen) in the city of Charleroi or Fergualie Park (Paisley); newer neighbourhoods of single-family dwellings at Woensel West (Eindhoven) and Ardoyne Old Park (Belfast) or huge complexes at Fort Nieulay (Calais), Tenever (Bremen), Brossolette (Mulhouse) or yet again in Turin.

Second, all differences in political-administrative systems of city management and in levels of political impetus. There is no single management system for these neighbourhoods. Some are wholly owned by public agencies; others are made up entirely of privately-owned dwellings. Central government initiative is dominant in France, Holland, and to a lesser extent in Great Britain; local initiative prevails in Germany, Belgium, Portugal, Spain, Greece and Italy. Elsewhere, everything takes place in a subtle game being played between regional governments and local officials, as is the case in Ireland, Northern Ireland, and Scotland. Communal balkanization is the characteristic trait in France and in most southern European countries, while almost all northern European countries have undergone a redefinition of their political-administrative geography, without having succeeded in controlling the processes of segregation.

Third, all differences in behaviour and work habits in various cities. The participation tradition and communitarian movement characteristic of the Anglo-Saxon reality contrasts with the democracy by delegation that is often the dominant trait of continental European societies. The involvement of private economic players in those countries is evident, while in other European countries they are given only a very modest part to play.

Despite these significant differences, everywhere chunks of cities are being relinquished to the fringe of an urban area's operations to become a gathering point for the most underprivileged (the unemployed, unskilled youths, single-parent families, drug addicts, immigrant populations and so forth). Even more important than the contrast of these urban realities from one country to another is the relative position of these neighbourhoods in each city as special places where problems are concentrated. One does not feel less alienated even if one finds oneself in a less critical situation than other people in other cities or countries.

False Determinants and the Real Causes

Having briefly outlined the situation, we can call into question three determinants that are all too often accepted as self-evident truths when taken individually. First, there is no architectural and urbanistic determinant to phenomena of alienation, as the differentiation and social ranking of urban spaces do not have an impact on well-entrenched conflicts. They are built on signs that become more and more fragile as the urban forms become more homogeneous. It is often the smallest things that can make the biggest difference. Huge complexes are not European archetypes of neighbourhoods in a state of crisis. The erosion of this architectural and urbanistic form is, in France, a phenomenon that is historically dated and localized. It is no more dramatic now than it was in the old slum neighbourhoods twenty years ago. There is nothing to indicate what its fate will be over time with urbanization, the parameters of which we are far from having grasped.

Second, there is no ethnic determinant to alienation. In many neighbourhoods, the percentage of people originating from immigration is minute, even in countries which, at one time, built their development on importing foreign labour. Not one foreigner is to be found, in Belfast, Dublin and Paisley, not even a British citizen from abroad. In Glasgow, it is dyed-in-the-malt Scots who are being alienated. Such was also the case until recently in the cities of southern Europe. It is also true of France where immigrants are considered to be the root of all problems. In Fort Nieulay (Calais), the proportion of immigrants is negligible (.5%), even lower than it is for the city overall. The distinction can be made of signs and behaviours that are very closely related and variable in time and space (religious affiliation, social practices); each society has an infinite capacity to raise the spectre of the person who is different, the other, the scapegoat, enabling it to be structured and strengthened.

Lastly, there is no determinant linked to the single-functionality of space. In France and abroad, the districts that are most inhabited are all single-function residential districts, seeking to protect themselves from all nuisances. The people who live in these districts have no particular problem reaching even distant services, unlike those who live in neighbourhoods that are in a state of crisis.

Clearly, the conjunction of these determinants contributes to a certain fragility of neighbourhoods, but it does not explain everything. Most of these neighbourhoods, occupy a specific place in the spatial structure of urban areas that, at some moment in the city's history, made it a favourite gathering spot for people in trouble. Thus, all these neighbourhoods are ecologically stigmatized zones (near a railroad, a freeway or a busy thoroughfare, an industrial park, or a polluting facility such as an incineration plant or high-voltage wires) and kept at a safe distance away from the rest of the city (by distance, physical barriers, lack of public transportation). The condition of being alienated may be a long-standing one or it may be a rather recent phenomenon, permanent or reversible, but relationship to the whole of the urban structure is more important to the fate of these neighbourhoods than their intrinsic characteristics.

These neighbourhoods and their condition must therefore be examined in relation to the entire urban reality. They appears to be a functional necessity for urban areas to create marginal territories. The question of the intervention is not related to their intrinsic characteristics. At some time or other these neighbourhoods represented a stumbling block to urban dynamics either because they resisted the redeployment of the urban fabric, or, more often, because they were a threat to the social balance of cities. There will be no real renewal of these territories until they are seen to be crucial to reconstructing the urban space and a substitute space is found to which the residents can be relegated. These territories, which have gradually latched on to the rest of the city as the gaps were built up and filled in, are not devoid of assets including large dwellings, vacant viable spaces at a time when this urban commodity is scarce, green areas, parking, sunshine and quiet. What is considered a nuisance today (for instance, proximity to arterial roads and railway rights-of-way) could well become an asset in a not-too-distant future. Large companies and financial groups are beginning to be interested in these areas and are not doing so from the goodness of their hearts. They know that these areas have land and building development potential, with reserves of cheap properties that make it possible to anticipate development fifteen years ahead. But development in these neighbourhoods will take place at the expense of the current residents.

Strategies of Integrated Approaches to Urban Development

The tendency for dealing with these alienating situations has generally been to multiply local, national, and even European policies that are general, narrowly regionalized, and aimed at target populations. These policies have a limited impact on the problems they are supposed to be dealing with and they often clash with each other. Moreover, sector-based policies rarely challenge the division of powers, the forms of government, and the way services responsible for handling these problems do things. Compartmentalization and bureaucratic practices go a long way to perpetuate or even exacerbate problems.

The cities involved in the European development program were chosen because they were in the process of implementing or sought to implement development strategies that were a departure from this trend. Despite the various contexts, the problems were closely related. The focus was on a diversity of subjects (training and employment, health, housing, culture, etc.) that were opportunities and pretexts to approach neighbourhood management in different ways. Strategies called integrated approaches were devised to influence socioeconomic or institutional logic by trying to change the way cities are built and the people who live there are governed.

Principles and Conditions of Development Strategies

Two principles and three conditions can be identified. Development strategies are comprehensive approaches that take account of the diversity and complexity of the processes of change at work in urban societies. Thus the struggle against youth unemployment cannot be approached merely in terms of education. We must intervene in every aspect of the world in which these young people live, learn and work. Juvenile delinquency is no longer the sole responsibility of an increasingly more specialized staff; it is the symptom of deep-seated problems that require mobilizing all the players in young people's environments. Improving housing is not simply a matter of techniques and funding; it involves accurately analyzing residents' expectations and should strive to change the image of the city's neighbourhoods. Moreover, all these actions (fighting unemployment, preventing delinquency, improving housing) are interwoven and must be synergized so that they have a greater effect than if they were merely implemented individually.

Development strategies are transversal and interpartnerial approaches. Synergizing these actions implies being able to make players who are specialized in their own field of expertise work together simultaneously. This means that it should be possible to break down the compartmentalization of services that was created during a relatively linear production period in the city based on a certain degree of division of labour. The goal of integrated approaches is to bring together players who had not known each other previously, to change their ways of thinking and acting, and to promote renovating management systems to make them more suitable for the complexity of the problems encountered. This partnership must be built with the residents, the partners most concerned by the programs being implemented. It is they who will make the actions undertaken more enduring and compel management systems to adapt the services being delivered.

Territorializing these approaches is one prerequisite to successful action. Promoting a synergy among the partners signifies acting within a well-defined territorial framework (the neighbourhood) in order to take advantage of the effects of proximity and complementarity. This does not mean that all solutions must be found within this territorial framework, but that the neighbourhood is the appropriate locus for conducting a relevant, dynamic diagnosis of the problems people are facing and for mobilizing all the family, community, and institutional systems capable of taking advantage of the opportunities that arise. Integrated approaches to revitalization must hinge on more comprehensive city policies so that the initiatives taken at this level of management do not counteract the strategies being carried out in the neighbourhoods.

Developing concrete projects is the second condition to successful integrated approaches. Partnership, i.e., consensus-seeking among players and resident involvement, cannot be built in the abstract. Joint project development by various partners, some of whom are residents, makes possible a constructive mobilization able to enhance a neighbourhood's vitality. It involves paying a great deal of attention to the time it takes to implement changes and the pace of this implementation, since the pace of intervention is different for politicians and technicians than it is for residents. It is necessary possible to go beyond the logic of the spiral of disparate demands which so often translates into grants being wasted and to fight against the welfare mentality by teaching residents to take their problems and the management of their neighbourhood in hand. Running a project is somewhat like taking an introductory course in citizenship.

Lastly, integrated approaches must be the subject of contracting with various officials and funding agencies. Contracts are the manifestation of the partners' commitment to specific objectives, and a schedule of achievements that give credibility to the program under consideration. Moreover, the contract process makes it possible to define clearly the management system for the revitalization policy by placing control of the process into the hands of a partnerial steering committee and technical leadership into the hands of an operational team. The steering committee and the operational team are components of a laboratory for renewal of the city's political-administrative management systems which often exacerbates the crisis in neighbourhoods. This notion of laboratory is important as it gives these neighbourhoods the reputation of being a locus, not for dealing with problems of alienation, but for uncovering dysfunctional regulatory mechanisms and carrying out the renovation of institutions. This renovation can be applied generally throughout the city by networking innovative players within the government apparatus (Lemieux, 1992). Without being outrageously cynical, one could say that the fight against alienation is, at best, a consensual topic used to mobilize resources, a facilitating figure of political speech that makes it possible to deal with problems that are impossible to tackle head on, especially anything that has to do with changing political-administrative management systems and vested interests. In this area, one should proceed covertly to allow those whom Pierre Grémion (1987) called the "conspirators of renovation" to act.

These principles of integrated approaches to neighbourhood revitalization grew out of the experiments we have been able to examine over these past few years. The most convincing successes in the struggle against alienation and poverty can be credited to those cities that have been able to make the most of the various facets of this development strategy. However, implementing this strategy is not so simple and it did not come about naturally. It was the result of trial and error and the patient work of professionals backed by politicians who were particularly aware of the issues

European cities had to face. In some countries, such as France, Great Britain, and the Netherlands, these integrated approaches to revitalization have been the subject of national policies that greatly favoured their implementation and the transfer of expertise and methods. In other countries (Germany, Belgium, Spain, Ireland, and Italy) such a strategy was able to be carried out at the initiative of cities or small groups of professionals.

The Validity Field of Neighbourhood Development Strategies

To be relevant, the strategies being implemented must be included in a referential field with several key elements. First is the question of the nature of the assessment made of the realities of life in these neighbourhoods. The quality of the assessment is subject to caution. Most often, they are statistical descriptions of a few variables merely making it possible to fine-tune one's knowledge of a situation that has already been identified. Sometimes, when a framework already exists (for instance, a national policy such as the Neighbourhood Social Development (DSQ) policy in France or one for Social Renewal as in the Netherlands) the assessment is carried out merely to justify including the neighbourhood for ad hoc funding. Only rarely, as in the case of Bremen, are all the neighbourhoods of a city canvassed periodically to determine the priority sites for intervention based on a range of criteria that have been determined independently of the procedure to be used. It is also unusual for the assessment to result from comparing the outlooks of various players on the local scene (partnerial dynamic assessment).

Assessments are generally rather stereotyped. The categories used have very little relevance when reporting on the social reality of neighbourhoods, especially socioprofessional categories, while a good number of residents do not fall within this class as they are often excluded from the economic and social system. Often they give little significance to exploring the processes that have made these neighbourhoods what they are, and even less to analyzing the social and institutional mechanisms of alienation or yet again to a comparative analysis of budgets allowed to these neighbourhoods. The assessments that come closest to doing this are those developed under programs initiated by local professionals, outside predetermined procedures; very often this kind of study is essential to their strategy of justifying the process in the eyes of the various services and politicians.

The second key element has to do with the system of goals on which development programs are based. In great part, this system of referentials determines the nature of the assessment and controls how the actions selected will be formulated (their nature, their content, the partners to be called upon). The scope of the goals is defined by the reply to the question, *What is a developed neighbourhood or community?* While the question may be a simple, or even simplistic one, the answer is not quite as straightforward. Surveys carried out among people in charge in France and abroad provide a multiplicity of answers. This multiplicity is easily understood when one considers the diversity of cases. What is at issue are the goals that determine the practices of development players (professional, social, cultural, ideological and corporate goals), for very often these goals are not an endogenous product of the neighbourhoods, but rather models that have been imposed from outside. Thus, a socially developed neighbourhood could be defined as being a neighbourhood that has become just like the others; but is there really a general standard of what a good neighbourhood is? The socially developed neighbourhood might be defined as a restored neighbourhood, a socially readjusted neighbourhood, a pacified neighbourhood, etc. While not claiming to be exhaustive, Jacquier (1992) identified nine referents of action in urban social development: the new-technocratic-ruse type of development, the political-pacification-enterprise type of development, the improvement type of development, the social-improvement type of development, the process type of development, the standard type of development, the skimming-off type of development, the community-strategy type of development, and the political-strategy type of development.

The issue of imported goals brings out the problem of the realities of life in these neighbourhoods and the interventions directed at them. One of the lessons drawn from the European program pertains to the importance residents have or should have in development programs. Everywhere, at least in the discourse, the *doing for* so characteristic of past urban policies tends to give way to *doing with* neighbourhoods and, of course, with residents. It would be a contradiction in terms to think that social development could ignore residents and be effective without their taking part in these projects as players and full-fledged partners. As Xavier Greffe pointed out, development is "a process of diversifying and enriching economic and social activities on a given territory based on the mobilization and coordination of its resources and energies" (1984).

In France, practices in this field are relatively hesitant due to the residents' lack of skills and involvement in the city's operations. In the context of democracy by delegation, politicians actually have little interest in sharing the decision-making process. Moreover, decentralization has merely enhanced the power of local politicians, especially of mayors who have done little that is new to decentralize powers within neighbourhoods. In contrast, a number of cities in the European program have done a great deal by setting up new spaces within neighbourhoods where negotiations and decision-making can unfold and in which residents can have a place. Elected neighbourhood councils have been set up in Germany at Dortmund and Bremen. Elsewhere, local multipartner bodies have joined neighbourhood residents. In the Netherlands, the country that gave foreigners the right to vote in local elections in the early eighties, structures for technical aid are supported through public funds and made available to neighbourhood residents so that they may develop alternative projects and negotiate with municipal technicians and politicians; 60 professionals have been made available to neighbourhood associations in the city of Rotterdam. Significant work has been done in Great Britain to train neighbourhood leaders and foster the emergence of intervention tools in communities (community economic development corporations, resource centres). In Spain—Barcelona, for instance—neighbourhood youths are given assistance to create their own rehabilitation firms. In Italy, in the context of a total disintegration of powers, districts within large cities are being endowed with social action skills that sometimes lead to community development strategies calling for volunteer work. A backdrop to these approaches is the question of the image we have of the neighbourhoods and the people who live in them, and, ultimately, of urban citizenship. These neighbourhoods and their residents arc only rarely considered as potential resources to be enhanced and energized. There is a referent missing that could help one to imagine the reality of these territories, one that is found in Anglo-Saxon countries under the label of community, provided that it can shake off its negative connotations in Europe and on the condition that Anglo-Saxon countries not ascribe every virtue to it.

A Few Last Questions

In closing, we explore a few of the paradigms that shape the projects and practices of neighbourhood social development players. It is especially important to call into question the urban problematics that have become established over the past few years and that go back to a consensual model of cities from which conflicts, and struggles over territory, have been rooted out. The theme of urban struggles that was in vogue in the seventies may have given way to a softer formulation in terms of specialization and differentiation; but this should be seen not as the invalidation of the Marxist discourse but rather as the emergence of a new social cleavage within cities. This cleavage now divides the overwhelming majority of those who have something (jobs, houses, status, etc.) and the minority (those who live in insecurity); those who have access to resources (financial and cultural) and power (political, legal, media), and the minority of outcasts. These alienated people are not represented in political, labour or organizational bodies. They are second-class citizens have never had access to a share in the resources except by proxy (through social work specialists) or through violence (riots, theft, petty crime such as drug-pushing). Neighbourhood development programs are granted to them, either through guilt-ridden technocratism, or in the well-understood interest of keeping a social peace that is under threat. They may not continue as it will be very difficult in future for these programs to gain political legitimacy in the eyes of the electorate.

Have these neighbourhoods become out-and-out functional necessities in this new social division of labour and space? Is not the thinking that advocates reintroducing the middle-class strata into these neighbourhoods the product of wizardry? Otherwise it would not be done at the cost of evicting the people who are living there. Pressed by demands for housing in inner cities and the migratory flow from the European hinterland, are we not about to see new versions of the old slums spring up again on cities' outskirts? This cannot help but dislocate neighbourhoods now considered to be components of the urban fringes. The effect would be a positive one, but it would simply be shifting the problem elsewhere. Does the issue of alienation of neighbourhoods extend to the mechanisms that produce rich ghettos, or pockets of prosperity in cities?

Neighbourhoods said to be in a state of crisis may not be loci for a potential social renaissance, but they most certainly are places where futures can be built. In Europe, it is precisely in those neighbourhoods, that are the favourite refuges of alienated people and of newcomers to the member states of the European community, that a European culture is being developed. This culture will doubtless have very little to do with what we are now familiar with, or with what the technocrats in Brussels imagine it will be. If these neighbourhoods, and their residents, are the most advanced points in Europe, what a vindication that would be for these neighbourhoods said to be in a state of crisis.

However, we must be wary of fostering a naïve vision of things, a vision of a society in which conflicts would be rooted out, where common sense and a certain degree of intimism would prevail. It is well known that life in neighbourhoods is made up of tensions, confrontations, and power struggles. The importance and role of neighbourhoods and their residents are largely determined by mechanisms of power allocation working at the city level. The phenomena of rejection and alienation have nothing to do with fate. They can be blamed in great part on the way civil and political society works. Development, inasmuch as it leads to an effective struggle against the mechanisms of relegation and allocation, is carried out through a political strategy designed to make the residents of these neighbourhoods full-fledged citizens by acknowledging their freedom of conscience and not, as a secular tradition postulates, by referring to their skills and ability to understand.

We must also be wary of a certain angelism and humanism that usually results in neo-welfare. This recognition cannot be bestowed; it must be built on the basis of the characteristics of the residents in these housing complexes who, though financially poor, are not necessarily poor in spirit. The art of ruse, the tactical practices for dealing with institutional strategies, the diversion tactics and techniques of doing the exact opposite of what is asked are very political ways of making the best of situations and of doing things that some citizen groups have fully mastered. Let us not fool ourselves. Surviving in these neighbourhoods and in society when you have nothing is an art of living that requires a knowledge worthy of respect, even if it does border on illegality.

Acknowledging this reality and integrating it into a development strategy clearly constitutes a departure from traditional practices of social and community work. Until now, these neighbourhoods have all too often been considered territories where there was nothing at stake, spaces that were beyond the reach of politics, even apolitical. For politicians, services do not give one much room to manoeuvre for position and, in any event, they do not hold much prospect for political and professional advancement. These neighbourhoods, the millstones around the necks of municipal administrators, can be found less and less often in the heart of election campaigns, which is not to say that they do not influence the debate.

The time has come to return to an affirmative political approach to these neighbourhoods. Such a change in attitudes is the very foundation of the partnership with residents which, until now, could not be created because it seemed too much of a travesty. The need must still be felt for this to become reality. The events that erupt in the suburbs from time to time now act as a stimulus to creating the partnership, but we should be concerned that only extremists may take advantage of this necessity.

The issues of urbanity and civility lie at the heart of the neighbourhood development problematic. What should be included in these rather out-moded terms that are being given a harder and harder time in Europe? The current meaning of urbanity is a respect of others and of oneself, while civility consists in treating others as if they were strangers and in forging social ties with them while maintaining some distance. Respect and distance are two qualities that are often lacking in the neighbourhoods involved and in cities in general, whereas they are the two faces of urban solidarity. The notions of urbanity and civility, which are characteristics of city dwellers, are bourgeois virtues in the true meaning of the term and are in sharp contrast to rural cultural references, which are often those that still govern approaches to urban management. One of the problems European cities are having stems from the fact that the people in charge of running them feel only revulsion and fear of urban realities. The rural dream is a common thread throughout the whole political arena. Cities, the symbols of the emancipation of old allegiances and of freedom, also symbolize the forced refuge for those who, from time immemorial, have had to leave their native soil. The need for a rural exodus does not make cities a virtue. Through the old German adage that "city air is emancipating" may be true, it erases neither the pain nor the memories of the original uprooting.

If the goal of community development is urban solidarity, what is the possibility of thinking and building urbanity and civility? And what is the significance of making the urban social field an objective and technical one as propounded by the notion of development strategy?

4

Community Economic Development Organizations in Developing Countries

Katherine Ichoya

Poverty alleviation has no quick fixes and expectations must, therefore, be realistic. The dynamic interaction between rapid population growth, poverty, degradation of the natural environment and resource base, debt burden, capital flight, brain drain, adverse terms of trade, weak administrative capacities, and low levels of economic growth will have very profound negative effects in the developing countries. Governments must continue to rely on CED organizations for help because they cannot cope with these problems alone. This chapter will discuss the general situation of CED in developing countries, citing examples from Africa, and will examine the current status of CEDs, identify major gaps in knowledge, show how these gaps can be addressed, identify critical areas for further research, and suggest appropriate research approaches.

Role of CEDS

CEDs plan, implement, manage and monitor grassroots projects which compliment government development and intervention initiatives for the provision of basic human needs. They operate at local and national levels. Regional non-governmental organizations (NGOs) such as Economic Commission for West African States (ECOWAS), cover groups of countries with similar problems under geo-political boundaries and economic blocks. CEDs are successful because they are flexible, action oriented, adaptive, and sensitive to local needs in solving problems by using locally available human and material resources.

A traditional CED model called Harambee, meaning pulling together, is a system of communally helping neighbours or friends and was in place in Kenya before colonization by the British. This model became even stronger during the Colonial Era because husbands were required to be away from home either as freedom fighters or in detention camps. The British, to cope with the Mau-Mau Uprising (1952–54), forced the people to move into hastily constructed villages where they were required to observe a night curfew. The villagers relied on each other to cope with these new demands. The Harambee tradition has remained alive and active since Independence. The late President of Kenya, Jomo Kenyatta, used the Harambee slogan in all his public speeches to inform and encourage Kenyans to pull together in order to achieve self-reliance. The Harambee spirit is embodied in national development plans and in mobilization of human and material resources for development projects such as schools, water, sanitation, and community centers.

The Harambee model is in resonance with a project's social responsibility and community organization, especially individual roles and responsibilities. For example, individual land ownership through land adjudication and registration has not been able to eradicate social and community responsibility because families can censor land sales by individuals. Further, individual effort gives participating group members self-esteem and reassurance of their place and role in traditional and political groups at the grass roots level. Decision making is participatory and sensitive to available human and material resources as well as to the prevailing socio-economic and environmental conditions. Community priorities are realistic, achievable, and cost effective. The Harambee movement has been successfully applied by many CEDs. A CED project cycle is accepted and planned by members of a local community; an implicit understanding exists in communities as to how a project works. This community understanding is a factor which planners often overlook. This CED model could be replicable in many developing countries.

Research in developing countries has singled out the informal sector as the fastest growing part of the private sector. Income-generating activities in rural areas, generally categorized as off-farm activities, are expected to range from 19% to 23% in countries like India, Sierra-Leone, and Columbia, from 28% to 38% percent in Indonesia, Pakistan, Kenya and the Philippines, and as high as 49% percent in Malaysia (Ashe & Cosslett, 1989). Those engaged in these activities are often the landless in poor local communities.

In the urban areas, such as in Lagos, Nigeria, 50% of the employment is in the informal sector; in Bombay, the figure is 55%; and in Latin America and the Caribbean some 30 million people or up to a third of the economically active population are in the informal sector. In Lima, Peru, it is estimated that 78% of the furniture and 90% of the clothing is produced in the informal sector, and 85% of the bus transportation is informal. In San Salvador, 85% of the houses in the poorest barrios are home to a business. These businesses are projected to generate up to 120,000 jobs a day in the developing world by the year 2000. They will create a demand for related goods and services while they attract more urban migrants to the cities (Ashe & Cosslett, 1989).

More and more development projects are taking advantage of local knowledge about how to manage the environment. For example, people in the tropical rain forests of the Amazon and Southeast Asia have accumulated a valuable understanding of local ecosystems and African pastoralists, such as Masai and Samburu of Kenya, know their environment and how to use it to the greatest advantage without degradation. Building on local strengths requires care, expertise, and patience. But development projects that do not take existing practices into account often fail. For example, a particularly costly instance of neglecting local practices occurred in Bali, Indonesia. For centuries the traditional Balinese irrigation calendar had provided a highly efficient way of making the most of water resources, soil testing, and pest control. A sudden increase in insect pests, followed by declining crop yields, occurred when a large, traditionally financed agricultural project tried to replace traditional with high-input imported rice varieties. A subsequent project that built on the indigenous production system has been more successful. Community transformations and cultural changes often result from lack of awareness of local conditions. Planners, by ignoring local conditions, fail to consider strengths in the way of life of those they are promoting by their projects.

Projects are more successful if they are participatory from the initial stages of identification of objectives to design, implementation, and evaluation stages. For example, the National Irrigation Authority Project in the Philippines illustrates the need to involve community groups in planning construction and in finding ways to avoid the silting of channels and drains. Careful attention has brought about better maintenance of irrigation works and higher agricultural yields. In Jakarta, neighbourhoods have organized the collection of solid wastes by collecting monthly dues that are used to buy a cart and hire a local garbage collector. A volunteer from each household assists in collecting garbage and cleaning the neighbourhood drainage systems on a monthly basis. The wastes are then taken to a transfer station where they are picked up by municipal authorities. This combination of community collection and centralized disposal has allowed Jarkata to achieve an 80% waste collection rate—high by developing country standards and demonstrates the need for collaboration between the government and the local communities.

The ACCION Projects in Latin America have demonstrated that simple infusions of small amounts of credit ($10 to $500) over a period of one to twelve months, coupled with appropriate training, orientation, and encouragement can lead to significant increases in income, production, and employment. Thirty-five ACCION International affiliated micro-enterprise credit projects exist through Latin America. The programs disburse over two million dollars monthly to more than 40,000 participating tailors, cobblers, mechanics, street vendors, and so forth; they report a repayment rate of nearly 100% (Ashe & Cosslett, 1989, p.19).

Successful lessons have also been learned from Grameen Bank in Bangladesh, Badan Kredit Kecamatan, Bank Rakyat Indonesia unit, Desa in Indonesia, and the Agriculture and Agricultural Cooperatives in Thailand. A review of the overall performance of these four rural financial institutions has found that the projects must become self-sustainable and have a high level of outreach among the targeted population to be successful (Yaron, 1991). The project successes can be attributed to the use of a participatory development approach because they worked directly with the local communities. The two Indonesian banks use the existing social structure, "the authentic and official leadership in the village, to help achieve adequate selection of loan applicants and prompt loan collection" (Yaron, 1991). They rely on the local leadership who command good reputation, authority, and official and social status within the village community. The Grameen Bank offers simplified application procedures, extends credit quickly, avoids books and complex business plans initially, and avoids complex and complicated guarantees. The Bank works with existing economic activities, no matter how small; the focus is initially on the local market. The Bank extends small, short-term loans primarily for working capital, encourages savings mobilization, and charges interest rates at the market rate or higher. The high interest rates ensure accessibility of short-term money for small loans, and most importantly ensures group social security. For example, if a woman falls sick, another woman within her borrowing group takes responsibility for the sick woman's children, thereby ensuring care for the children and eventual repayment of the loan. The Bank encourages network relationships of the local communities and promotes informal coordination and collaboration with local banks and involved participants. All four countries have relied on self-help groups in credit delivery mechanisms that link the institutions and the individual borrowers. All projects have demonstrated the possibility of lending to the very poor, using components of mobile banking as an innovative means of providing low cost savings and lending services to the very poor. The projects have demonstrated that poor communities have the ability to work hard and raise their standings of living while using limited resources.

Role of Non-Governmental Organizations in CED

Mounting evidence of development failure during the decade of the 1980s has led development donors and governments throughout the world to a growing interest in non-governmental organizations (NGOs). NGOs have contributed recognition of the reality that an increasing number of the people are living in poverty and fast deteriorating living conditions. They have started anti-poverty programs designed to deliver welfare services, and have provided productive assets and projects that have created employment for the poor. NGOs reach the poor better than governments by encouraging participation of the local community, flexibility in implementation projects, and better cost effectiveness in project implementation. They deliver more services, especially in health related projects, than governments and have a more informal set-up which accommodates the poor.

The NGOs have been successful in establishing pilot projects for trade groups in both rural and urban informal sectors in Third World countries and have achieved significant results. Key examples are the Self-Employed Women's Association in Gujarat, India, and the Working Women's Forum in Tamil Maeh. In Latin America, NGOs have succeeded in training the urban informal sector women's groups in marketing and quality control. In Africa, they have succeeded in providing management training skills to women and in contributing to promotional skills in community development work. The Business and Professional Women's Club in Kenya has played a vital role in assisting rural women in businesses by providing informal training in simple business management skills. The Club has shared ideas and experiences through brainstorming sessions, seminars, workshops, and counselling sessions held in their rural towns. The Women in Service Development Organization Management (WISDOM) in Gambia has facilitated access to credit for rural and urban women in the informal sector through rotating savings and credit groups.

Promotion of the Rural Initiatives and Development Enterprise (PRIDE) is another example of a successful NGO with a high volume, high repayment, sustainable credit program that provides non-collateralized credit and savings facilities to micro- enterprises which are unable to obtain financial services from commercial banks. The PRIDE model is based on the principles of the Grameen Bank of Bangladesh and the Kenyan Harambee; and multiple group guarantees are used in lieu of traditional collateral. It operates in Kenya, Guinea, and Tanzania. By December 1992, PRIDE had extended a total of 3,500 loans valued at more than $715,000. The MUDZI Fund, a credit scheme in Malawi which also operates on the principles of the Grameen Bank, had distributed average credit of $100 (US) to 841 beneficiaries by November 1991. The loans were given mostly to women for income-generating activities. The experiences of credit schemes in Africa demonstrate that demand for credit accompanies high participation in community economic activities.

Church NGOs have played a key role in promoting activities of local CEDs in Africa. One church-run hospital in Malawi has successfully begun to work with the local church to encourage groups of poor women to save. The Young Women's Christian Association in Zambia has promoted income-generating activities of women's groups in vegetable growing, food processing, and primary health care. NGOs, such as World Vision, Action Aid, and Save the Children, have specifically contributed to promoting income-generating activities in most African countries, including Malawi, Zambia, Gambia, Burkina, Faso, and Kenya.

There are many NGO weaknesses despite their successes. NGOs have limited capacity to develop many successful projects because of limited funds. Some projects are uncompleted and some are not replicable. Soft budgets, poor technology, lack of management, and lack of capacity limits ability to handle projects as they grow and become more complex. NGOs do not, in most cases, do follow-up evaluations of projects.

Governments and NGOs often experience difficulty working with each other because of suspicion. Some governments see NGOs as intruders and argue that NGOs contribute to unequal development because they do not adhere to the government's national plan. Unequal distribution of resources through such projects creates competition and unrest in some countries. Some governments have actually de-registered NGOs from operating in their countries while others have been banned from some countries due to ideological and political differences. Differences between governments and NGOs could be avoided by ensuring that CED objectives and goals are clearly identified and understood by the local participating communities. NGOs can complement government projects by adopting certain government projects and collaborating with the government in dividing the tasks. NGOs can influence government programs by giving supportive parallel services where the governments have left a gap.

In 1984 and 1985, Gesellshaft Technischen Zussammerianbeit (GTZ), together with the Government of Malawi, established a program to provide cash loans to rural women in income generating activities. Over 100 Women's Clubs were established and the credit was used to trade in maize, brew beer, and prepare food for sale. The Kiondo Women's Association in Kenya collaborates with the government to assure quality control and international marketing of local Kenyan baskets. NGOs have assisted governments to mobilize grassroots support by organizing communities into manageable groups to enable the government to deliver services especially marketing services, credit, and cooperative groups.

The Role of Women in CEDS

Women in most Third World countries are disadvantaged by tradition, law, and policy. Their access to jobs and business opportunities, living conditions, involvement in development programs, time control, and human and material resources is limited. The subjective socio-cultural designation of science and technology as a male only field has been blind to the fact that nomadic women build most houses as well as contribute to agricultural development. Evidence in most developing countries suggests that women contribute heavily to the economy and family, usually far more than it is reflected in official labour force and national income statistics. Women produce most of the developing world's food crops, feed most of the households, contribute to fuel and water, care for children and meet basic needs. A United Nations report estimates that women's share in family food production is 80% in Africa, 60% in Asia, and 40% in Latin America. In Africa, women are mainly farmers and labourers in the informal sector and marketing businesses. A study by the Economic Commission for Africa shows the heavy burden undertaken by women. Women in subsistence communities perform 95% of cooking and family care, 90% of carrying water and fuel wood, 90% of crop processing, 80% of crop transportation to home and markets, 70% of weeding and hoeing, 60% of harvesting, 60% of marketing, and 50% of planting. Very few women, however, are enroled in architectural, engineering, and agricultural institutes in developing countries. These constraints limit the supply of information, resources, and opportunity to benefit economic growth. Women have moved beyond agriculture and home-based activities and now account for one-quarter of the developing world's industrial labour force.

Unaccountable numbers of women work as self-employed entrepreneurs in the fast growing informal manufacturing, trading, and service sectors. Women's participation has increased, however, with participatory development approach through CED initiatives. CEDs have, therefore, played a key role in promoting the status of women.

Conclusions and Recommendations

The Colonial ties and dependency have continued to hamper socio-economic development in most African countries because of manipulation of the development process by the former colonial powers and their local protegees.

Leaders and policy makers responsible for policy formulation often design plans, programs, and implementation strategies that apply Western models of development which are not in line with African traditions, values, experiences and environment. This has resulted in the failure of many CEDs. There is a need to review investments, codes, and both government and private sector policies in order to accommodate the needs of the local communities. Review of legal policies at all sectors is necessary, specifically policies affecting women's rights to possess and inherit land and property. Development policies should highlight the impact of women's economic well-being. Women's ministries should convince policy and decision makers of the need to strengthen the income-earning capacity of women as well as to guarantee the success of projects in health, population, and nutrition.

Ethnic differences, and the resulting conflicts currently being experienced in many African countries, may be resolved through use of existing CED community networks. Leaders and members of various CED committees should be encouraged to hold brainstorming sessions, workshops and seminars at the national, district, and local levels. Building regional networks through various CED representatives can provide exposure and promote regional marketing ties. Corruption has been cited as a major development problem in projects in many developing countries. Peer pressure can have a profound influence in minimizing and controlling corruption at the grassroots level; however, there is a need to intensify training in financial management to promote efficient management and financial accountability.

Colonial legacies have continued to clash with many diverse cultural systems in most developing countries by encouraging individualism at the expense of community-based societies. This has had a negative impact on CEDs. The formal financial lending institution systems, for example, are based on individual ownership, whereas the collateral is held in common, although registered through individuals. CED development projects must be sensitive to local socio-economic and political conditions. This can be achieved through the involvement of local and national elites, by networking with relevant organizations as well as political groups to enlist their support to tap both human and material resources. Any opposition must be dealt with through accommodation to guarantee project continuity. Donors should avoid overburdening host countries with unrealistic demands. An understanding of the social-cultural environments and beliefs of different ethnic groups is necessary to avoid imposing un-implementable projects which will end up failing.

CEDs can play a critical role in national development through collaborative public participation. The stakeholders, donors, contractors and government agencies must be involved at all stages of the project cycle. Projects which adapt to the local environmental and traditional structures have been successful. CEDs should avoid designing inflexible blueprint projects which are insensitive to local needs. Donor field officers must be allowed to vary project plans to meet unforseen circumstances as they arise.

Successful project management depends on participants who focus on project goals and performance by involving top management and others. Team building must guard against exclusion of larger political issues by focusing only on priority problems. Data collection, analysis, and evaluation procedures should be designed to improve project performance by local managers and inform beneficiaries about the results. Procedures must be simple and easily understood by all participants to ensure meaningful collaborative learning.

CED methodology is surely the most appropriate means for improving the quality of life of the urban and rural poor. In key areas there is a need to:

1. Review the policy environment in all CED sectors, especially those affecting women's legal rights in property ownership, inheritance, and minimum wage.

2. Review and promote appropriate training programs which are sensitive to gender issues and constraints.

3. Review and encourage the use of appropriate technology, specifically in the provision of basic human needs through exchange programs.

4. Review and promote credit policies for CED programs.

5. Review and promote tailored training programs based on the existing traditional community participatory models and the use of local languages.

6. Promote and respect traditional leadership selection process.

7. Promote informal communication channels through seminars, workshops, and informal social gatherings.

8. Research local traditional values and beliefs which have hindered the application of certain technologies.

9. Use formal and informal networks to address the issue of corruption which will be difficult to eradicate.

10. Design strategic marketing linkages between local, national, and international producers and consumers.

PART 2

SCOPE AND CHARACTERISTICS OF COMMUNITY ECONOMIC DEVELOPMENT

5

The Scope and Characteristics of Community Economic Development in Canada

Mike Lewis

How can one understand the range of initiatives in Canada that exist under the rubric of CED? What is the reach or sphere of CED action in Canada? What are the central characteristics of recent CED experience in this country? And finally, when the field is examined as a whole, are there policy issues that emerge which warrant further discussion? These are the questions that this chapter seeks to address.

There is no right way to classify CED initiatives in Canada. But models have emerged in Canadian CED that represent a useful starting point. They correspond with four key ingredients, summarized in Figure 5-1, that must be part of the mix if CED is to succeed. Few CED organizations have the resources in-house to supply all four ingredients. Furthermore, public policy and programs that have been put in place have generally not been designed with these central ingredients in mind. As a result, CED organizations have been shaped by government program criteria or by availability of resources, towards specializing in functions related to one or two of the key ingredients. In some cases, they have also sought ways to help create other organizations to fill in the gaps.

Figure 5-2 outlines four CED models in terms of missions, central roles, key goals, major functions, and the skills required from a general manager. Depending on the context and available resources, elements of the four can be blended in a variety of ways in any particular organization. The boundaries between these models are akin to elastic bands, capable of being stretched to be inclusive of one or more additional models. A combination of appropriate resources and organizational capacity to strategically manage a broadly based process of community revitalization is required for any stretch towards comprehensiveness. All four models are in operation in Canada. There are also several initiatives that combine two or more of the

Figure 5-1

Building An Economic Base: Four Key Ingredients

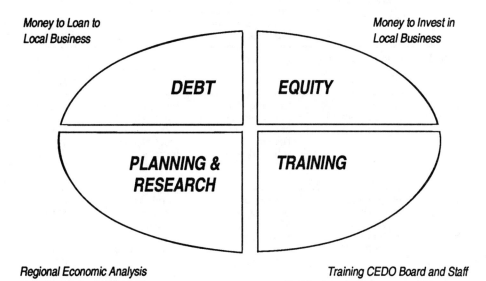

Money to Loan to
Local Business

Money to Invest in
Local Business

DEBT   EQUITY

PLANNING &
RESEARCH   TRAINING

Regional Economic Analysis
Defining Goals and Objectives
Research Specific to the Mission

Training CEDO Board and Staff
Training Local Employees and Managers

Source: WESTCOAST DEVELOPMENT GROUP
@ The Centre for Community Enterprise
Strategic Planning for the CED Practitioner (1992)

models. Each model must maintain a research and planning capacity, the focus of which will vary depending on mission and goals.

Most of these four models summarized in Figure 5-2 operate at the community or regional level. Another category of organizations, known as intermediaries, provide training, technical assistance, networking and brokerage services to CED organizations and initiatives. Intermediaries operate primarily at the regional level, although there are a few Canadian organizations that have some national reach. Lastly, there are the beginnings in Canada of development finance intermediaries. The potential for these becoming part of the CED portrait in Canada is not yet clear, but some interesting experiments have begun. These four models as well as the intermediaries will be used to roughly define and illustrate the scope of CED initiatives in Canada.

Figure 5-2
Basic Community Economic Development Models

	Growth/Equity	Loan/Technical Assistance	Employment Development	Planning & Advisory Services
Mission	Build an economic base	Development finance & business support to new & existing business	Human resource development Job creation	Support of businesses, development organizations, & local government
Central Role	Owner/Partner	Financier	Trainer/ Co-ordinator	Advice & technical assistance
Key Goals	1. Profits 2. Management 3. Jobs	Creating viable businesses at community level Becoming self-sufficient	Increased literacy Life skills Job readiness Occupational skills Increased employment	Depends on constituency & priorities, e.g., a Tribal Council that helps businesses to plan & get financing
Functions	Planning & research Investment Training (sometimes)	Assessing business plans Making loans Providing business counselling	Needs assessment Program development & management Organizing & financing Outreach & job placement Self-employment training	Advice to entrepreneurs Technical assistance & training for board members Research services Information, referral, & networking services Assistance to access funding
CEO Skills	Investor & deal-maker who understands CED	Experienced lender	Experienced community organization executive	Usually an Economic Development Officer

The Growth Equity Model

The growth/equity model emphasizes building equity or wealth generating assets. It is concerned with establishing, usually through a community
owned development corporation and less commonly through a network of
cooperatives, a direct ownership stake in the economy. The central mission
is to build an economic base which is more accountable to community goals
and priorities. Goals focus on generating profits for reinvestment (a pre-requisite to building an economic base), developing management capacity and
influence, and creation of jobs. This model is much more prevalent in the
aboriginal community than elsewhere.

There are at least 180 development corporations in aboriginal communities and tribal regions. They are usually owned by First Nation governments or regional tribal councils and the range of activity cuts across all sectors of the economy. The Kitsaki Development Corporation, for example, is owned by the La Ronge Indian Band and has, since 1985, utilized a joint venture strategy to vest itself as an owner in every major sector of northern Saskatchewan economy. Thirteen ventures, yielding about $17 million in annual gross revenues, have created 500 jobs—ventures range from manufacturing to trucking to catering and insurance. Kitsaki uses an investment approach which it supplements by skills training to maximize the capture of job benefits for the La Ronge membership. In other settings, more modest examples abound such as a grocery outlets or construction companies that operate as subsidiaries to aboriginal development corporations.

Application of this model outside of aboriginal communities is more limited because there is generally no public policy context or programs to support it. The affordable housing sector, which can be an asset building strategy, has been an exception to this general condition, although most of the cooperative and non-profit initiatives do not have explicit CED dimensions to their activities. New Dawn Enterprises in Sydney, Cape Breton was the first Community Development Corporation (CDC) in Canada. Since 1975 New Dawn Enterprises has focused on building an asset base in the housing sector and the creation and management of eight businesses and non-profit ventures. It is currently managing about $12 million in housing and other real estate assets. New Dawn has helped establish Sydney Ventures, a Business Development Centre, and another CDC in an adjacent community. Lastly, New Dawn organizes and manages a variety of training programs as well as an ongoing and systematic research and development program focused on new venture/project development.

Homes First Society in Toronto focuses on housing, employment development, and empowerment of the city's most marginalized—the homeless, pregnant adolescents and displaced families. It developed 324 housing units to date and with more under development based on a strategy of individual and collective empowerment and building a community of interest. Training and job benefits for marginalized people are integrated into construction, maintenance, renovation, and management. Homes First has been very innovative in housing the homeless; the Street City project reclaimed an abandoned industrial plant and converted it into a resident governed village complete with some basic commercial services (food, cheque cashing, and so forth) which employ residents. This approach to homelessness is currently being expanded.

The Human Resource Development Association (HRDA) of Halifax has, since 1978, hired over 1000 welfare recipients in businesses it has developed and operated. Most go on to other jobs and/or more education. It has also provided training to an additional 800 people. Overall sales from HRDA ventures since its founding have been over $22 million. There are currently 164 employees. Through support of the Social Planning Department of the city of Halifax, welfare funds were diverted to capitalize HRDA businesses. This policy innovation appears to be worthy of replication elsewhere.

The Loan/Technical Assistance Model

The Loan/Technical Assistance model focuses on debt financing, the provision of loans and loan guarantees to individual entrepreneurs, and worker cooperatives or other forms of community owned businesses and projects. It often provides advisory and training support to clients.

Aboriginal communities or tribal councils own 33 Aboriginal Capital Corporations (ACCs) in various regions of Canada. About $100 million are currently out in loans and guarantees and another $70 million in additional capital has been committed. Maximum loan limits are usually in the range of $250,000, the average loan size being around $35,000. All ACCs provide advisory services related to accessing credit. Some have pre-venture training and after care programs and some also contract to deliver business development services on behalf of the Federal Aboriginal Business Development Program. There are also 13 native controlled Business Development Centres, a program option under the Community Futures Program. The maximum Federal commitment of capital possible under these BDCs is a little over $20 million. In three cases, these funds are managed in conjunction with an ACC.

Dana Naye Ventures (DNV), a Yukon aboriginal controlled organization that has integrated the resources of the ACC program and the BDC option, is emerging as one of the more innovative examples of how this model is stretching the elastic band of the Loan Technical Assistance model to becoming a comprehensive development institution. They presently have $7.3 million in capital, $600,000 of which is equity created when they bought out the old Indian Economic Development Loan Fund. DNV lends to non-native entrepreneurs outside of Whitehorse as well as aboriginal businesses. Plans are underway to increase the capital base for lending by another $1.5 million and DNV is applying to the Aboriginal Business Development Program for $1 million in equity capital. If successful, DNV will be the first ACC to access this option, which is reserved for self-sufficient ACCs with a solid track record. It has already been successfully involved in two equity investments. In addition, DNV contracts to deliver the Aboriginal Business Development program, has developed the basis for an aftercare program for loan clients, is negotiating a joint venture to deliver CED training and technical assistance to Yukon communities, and is undertaking planning to establish a financial management company to provide audit, bookkeeping, and consulting services. Lastly, the Yukon government, which has a loan program of its own, is entering into discussions with DNV to explore DNV taking over delivery and management of the government loan program. Why? Because DNV is much more cost effective and has a better track record!

In addition to the ACC and BDC programs, Indian Affairs provides flow through dollars to First Nations and Tribal Councils. About $17.3 million was used for business development in 1993. These dollars can be used as either re-payable or non-repayable contributions. They can also be used for direct equity investment in business ventures. The decisions are in the hands of the relevant Community Economic Development Organization (CEDO).

Calmeadow Foundation has established the First Peoples Loan Fund—a micro-enterprise credit program involving 15 communities and 40 loan circles. The major feature of the approach is small scale credit of under $2,000 for self employment. Each member of a loan circle must guarantee each others loan. They are also presently conducting pilots in Vancouver with CCEC credit union and in Shelburne County, Nova Scotia with Royal Bank.

Outside of the aboriginal setting Community Futures sponsored BDCs are prominent; 215 BDCs are serving approximately 2200 municipalities under 60,000, small towns, and villages with a total population of about 6.5 million. The maximum capital available for any one BDC is $1.55 million. Collectively these BDCs have the potential for managing $333 million in loan funds to target various types of small business. Colville Investment Corporation started by the Nanaimo Community Employment Advisory Society (NCEAS) is one of the best known BDCs in Canada. NCEAS was started in 1975 when CEIC was beginning to explore CDCs as a new developmental program. NCEAS was one of four pilots. The first efforts were related to employability training. However, the community was in decline and jobs of any sort were hard to come by. Training was not enough and NCEAS started to lobby for a fund to help create new businesses. CEIC gave a one time grant of $500,000 and Colville was launched. Colville has created 1300 jobs, has maintained commitment to marginalized clients, and has maintained training programs through NCEAS. It now has an asset base of $3 million. A cost benefit analysis done by the Economic Council of Canada determined that the net benefits were clear and demonstrable although NCEAS is not yet self-sufficient.

In the urban setting, examples are sparse. Two credit unions, Bread and Roses ($8.3 million) in Toronto and CCEC in Vancouver ($10+ million) give priority to CED project related lending and services. In Quebec, there are examples of *Caisse Populaires* becoming involved in innovative CED initiatives. A $1.3 million loan fund that has been created in Montreal through the collaboration of three Community Economic Development Corporations, the Quebec Solidarity Fund, and the City of Montreal.

Human Resource and Employment Development Model

The human resource and employment development model places an emphasis on some combination of human resource planning, life skills training, job readiness and skills training, client advocacy, outreach to community businesses and institutions to create opportunities for job experience, job placement, and self employment training and support.

The scope of aboriginal involvement in this model is more difficult to characterize. CEIC, through the Pathways program, spends $200 million annually on aboriginal related training. It covers the entire scope of pre-employment and vocational training. Aboriginal boards make the decisions on community based funding at the sub-regional level; thus, the level of CED related training is dependent on board priorities in particular areas. Tracking is difficult but there are examples of how this model has been the focus of CED attention in aboriginal communities.

The Eskisoni Development Corporation houses a human resource and employment development thrust and an investment thrust. The Eskisoni Enterprise Centre combines life skills training and literacy development with skill training, outreach, and job placement services. The Centre also provides entrepreneur training with start up guidance and an incubator which provides office support and technical services until businesses can graduate into the community.

A particularly promising application of the human resource and employment development model has evolved in several native and non-native communities in Alberta. A network of technical assistance providers and trainers have developed a human resource planning and development model which integrates and tailors motivational and skills training to community and band leadership, staff, and membership. A balance is defined among social needs, economic growth, and leadership development; training is placed in a five year plan and builds partnerships around implementation. Dramatic results are achieved in social, economic, and organizational development terms.

Variations on the human resource development model represent much of the CED work in urban areas. The Learning Enrichment Foundation (LEF) in York started in 1979 with a mandate to promote multicultural arts and offer job training and child care services. The mandate was expanded, after 5 years of slow growth, to include business development assistance and advising both public and private sectors on employee training needs. The Foundation has a business incubator, a business consulting service, a wide range of skills training programs, day care centres which service 500 children, literacy and ESL programs, and various services to immigrants. Only nine staff work for LEF directly; another 150 people work in related programs that are valued at about $9 million annually.

Regroupement pour la Relance Economique et Social du Sud-oeust de Montréal (RESO) has a mandate for the revitalization of the southwest district in Montreal. RESO is controlled by representatives of the community and uses a multi-dimensional approach, centred on consultation and partnership, to meet the needs of the residents and businesses in five

distressed neighbourhoods. The two main services are employability services and services to businesses. The organization is also involved in issues
related to land use, development of infrastructure, promotion of the area,
and the broader spheres of activity of representation, consultation, and
promotion related to CED in the Montreal region. Currently RESO is trying
to find a way of stretching the elastic band still more to become directly
involved in equity investment.

Hundreds of projects take on a much smaller piece of the human resource
development pie. Many could not be readily classified as CED, such as a
literacy project that stands alone or life skills training that is not linked to
the economic dimension in any way. Others, such as A-Way Courier in
Toronto, link the training of people with a history of mental illness with the
provision of a revenue generating courier business. Seven full time and 43
part time employees are involved in different levels of organizational,
operations and decision making. Similar types of experiments in training
enterprises are taking place with street youth and immigrant women. Advent
of the Federal Labour Force Development Boards and various provincial
labour force planning and training boards may lead to a reduction in ad
hoc, project based funding in the employability area. Strategic planning,
including a comprehensive human resource development plan for community based initiatives, will be increasingly required and has the potential for
leading to a more strategic and systematic approach.

Planning and Advisory Model

The planning and advisory services model provides planning and technical assistance to a defined membership or geographic area. Research is
also often a feature of this model. The services are generally rendered to
both individuals and other community institutions and businesses.

Fifty-eight tribal councils that provide services to their constituent communities and individuals are the main examples of this model in the
aboriginal setting. Another 273 First Nations are not affiliated with a tribal
council. In all, about $21.3 million in operational funding and another $5
million in planning was targeted for spending in 1992/93. Additionally, 13
aboriginal only Community Futures Committees (CFCs) undertake general
planning, research, and brokerage functions relevant to CED, particularly as
it relates to labour market development focus.

This model is represented in the non-aboriginal community by a range
of organizations, not all of which would be necessarily included under the
CED rubric. Examples are the 217 Community Futures Committees, and an
unknown number of economic development commissions related to regional districts and municipalities. These often focus on general promotion
and recruitment of business investment. The most interesting examples of
the model from a progressive CED perspective (Brodhead, 1994) is the
Corporation de Developpement Communitaire de Bois Franc in Victo-

riaville, Québec. The corporation is made up of a coalition of over 60 community based organizations and provides a range of services to member organizations including training, technical assistance, representation on other boards and committees, and so forth.

Intermediary Organizations

Technical Assistance to CED Initiatives

CED is a relatively recent strategy in Canada but initiatives have mush-roomed in the last decade; so also has the need for organizations with the capacity to provide competent training and technical assistance to CED organizations. Issues related to the integration of community organizing, business development, and social development are complex and there has been little professional training through mainstream institutions. Organiza-tions have emerged to fill the void and to help meet the needs of those on the front lines who must contend with the pressures and challenges of effectively managing the CED process in underdeveloped and distressed communities. Westcoast Development Group, a subsidiary of the Centre for Community Enterprise, has existed for 15 years. In the last four years Westcoast has concentrated on developing training materials and broader approaches to training practitioners and others involved in CED. About 2,200 people have been involved in Westcoast training since 1989, its materials are used widely in Canada, and have been recently introduced into the U.S. Westcoast also provides technical assistance, research, networking, publica-tion of a quarterly newsletter, and data base services. In Quebec, IFDEC, based in Montreal, is involved in research, training, and networking associated with the evolution of CEDCs in Montreal and, more recently, in other parts of Quebec.

Universities and colleges have become increasingly interested in CED. Some have been heavily involved in entrepreneur training and enterprise development and others have had relationship to cooperative development, community planning, or native management education. Weak linkages with practitioners has been problematic; much of what is available from univer-sities is theoretical as opposed to the practice based training and advice practitioners desire and need. A range of private consultants and freelancers also do some work under the CED banner. The Community Futures program has gone through a process to identify and select accredited trainers for the delivery of strategic planning services to committees across the country. The next two years will provide an indication of the quality of consulting and training services available in the private sector.

Development Finance Intermediaries

Examples of alternative development finance intermediaries are begin-ning to emerge. The Crocus Investment Fund, put together by the Manitoba

Federation of Labour, in conjunction with business, cooperatives and government, has recently organized a development finance vehicle focused on retaining local capital, promotion of employee ownership, and retention and expansion of Manitoba based business and employment. Crocus has equity investment and lending capacity and is different from other labour based investment funds in that it is specifically interested in enhancing economic democracy through worker ownership.

Community loan funds focused on housing and business lending in poor neighbourhoods are starting to take shape, notably in Montreal. These are well developed in the U.S. with over $73 million and 40 different loan funds. The funds seek lenders, usually from individuals, foundations, or churches at zero to near market rate interest, and then broker the capital into projects at an interest rate mark up of 2%. The Montreal Fund (ACEM) had developed a capital base of approximately $232,000 by the end of 1992. In Vancouver, the Women Futures loan guarantee fund has organized a similar vehicle with loan guarantees for women.

The Centre for Community Enterprise, a privately capitalized non-profit corporation, has successfully experimented in both equity investment and various types of loans. Projects have included front end risk capital to purchase land for affordable housing in Edmonton's inner city, working capital for a Cape Breton workers cooperative, and a loan guarantee for micro-enterprise credit program run by the Mennonites to assist refugees in the start up of micro-enterprises. Investments of about $600,000 have leveraged about $8 million in private and public sector investment, which would not otherwise have flowed into the projects.

Concluding Comments

The scope and characteristics of CED in Canada reflect an exciting range of innovations and approaches. Almost twenty years of experimentation has led to a body of proactive approaches and knowledge that, while still thin, could be the basis for a systematic expansion of CED as a strategy. Issues that require elaboration include:

- More effective training of CED practitioners and development managers.
- A much more systematic way of qualifying and then supporting comprehensive initiatives through which community resources are mobilized, integrated, and local capacity strengthened to effectively combat poverty through CED.
- Coordination of Federal and provincial policy and programs to avoid turf wars and duplication of effort and to increase the cumulative, positive impact of investing scarce resources.

- Addressing the equity gap in a manner that increases the ability of community economic development organizations to be effective actors in distressed communities and regions.
- Strengthening the quality and accessibility of technical assistance resources available to CED initiative.

The most glaring gap in Canadian CED is almost total absence of any systematic approach to CED policy and programs in Canada's urban centres. ✓ Community Futures, although not comprehensive in approach, has a budget of $50 million per year and the authority to place up to $350 million in debt capital into the hands of community controlled business development centres where it can work for years to come. The rationale is to combat rural decline in over 2200 communities under 60,000 people. In aboriginal communities, the Canadian Aboriginal Economic Development strategy involving CEIC, IS&T and INAC are spending over $800 million over a five year period to build the institutions and the capacity to build more self-reliant and sustainable aboriginal communities. This level of investment will have to be sustained for many more years if the demonstrable progress made in many parts of the country is to be consolidated and expanded.

On the other hand, there are 18 million people who live in urban areas where, in terms of absolute numbers, poverty is greater. Yet, there is no policy or program context evident to support urban CED in distressed and declining neighbourhoods. This contrasts with the United States where 2,200 CDCs operate, mainly in urban centres. The Canadian experience, although demonstrably promising in individual cases, is episodic, almost accidental. Initiatives to date have come primarily from pilot programs. What is needed is to move urban CED from a pilot status to a significant policy thrust. North Portage Development Corporation in Winnipeg, RESO and the other Montreal Community Economic Development Corporations, HRDA, Westend Community Ventures in Ottawa, Colville Investment Corporation, and a handful of others have shown what can be done and have taught us how to avoid some basic mistakes. It is time to get on with the job.

6

Regional, Local and Community-Based Economic Development

Tim J. O'Neill

Regional economic development has a long history as a concept and as a focus of policy. Community-based economic development is of a more recent vintage although there are examples of a regional development efforts in which the focus has been on specific local communities. Clearly distinguishing regional, local, and community-based economic development is necessary to properly understand the role and functioning of CED and its interaction with social development objectives. The purpose of this paper is to contrast the three approaches. All three relate to economic development in a spatial context and, in all three, there is interaction with social development (even if unintentional). In fact, depending upon the definition of community, regional and local development could be argued to be forms of CED. What features of community-based economic development distinguish it from other types of development? Is it unique with respect to goals and objectives, mechanisms and instruments, processes, results, size and type of locale? Are the dividing lines among regional, local, and community development clear and well defined or blurry and vague? Is the community-based approach a broader form of development, integrating economic and social elements? Are the public sector policies appropriate to each type of development similar or radically different?

Several factors have caused increased interest in CED in recent years. First, economic disparities among Canada's regions persist; the perception that policy attempts of the past have been a failure has led many people to look for alternatives. The community-based approach has attracted attention as a possible mechanism for encouraging change in the economic performance of regions and provinces by improving performance in their communities. Second, this approach has received increased attention from policy-makers from both federal and provincial levels of government in Canada. The Community Futures program of the Canadian Employment and Immigration Commission is an example of the type of federal government involvement in community development. All provinces have some form of

CED programming in place. Third, CED is undergoing important changes. Various forms of community-based development efforts have been attempted over the years. The cooperative movement took root in Canada in the 1930s but the current approach is becoming both more pragmatic and more businesslike. Some recent community development efforts have elements of an unconventional form of entrepreneurship or of community—collective entrepreneurship.

Definitional Issues

The term community can be utilized in a variety of ways: administrative, spatial, cultural, economic, social, religious, and so forth. Municipal boundaries establish administrative units—cities, towns and villages—typically referred to as communities. It is less common to use the term community when referring to groupings of municipalities larger administrative units, such as counties or even provinces. A purely administrative definition of community may not be entirely appropriate since it can include the lapping together of such diverse entities as small rural villages and large cities. Communities are often defined in this way for convenience; statistics are usually gathered for administrative units but not for functional economic or social units. A spatial concept of community includes, but is not restricted to, administrative subdivisions since it refers simply to geographical areas. Parts of municipalities (e.g., east end Montreal, North Vancouver), sub-provincial areas (e.g., north-eastern Nova Scotia, Nova Scotia, southern Ontario, interior British Columbia), and provincial groupings (e.g., Atlantic Provinces, Prairie Provinces) are all eligible to be referred to as communities in a spatial sense. A social or cultural approach would define communities as collections of people with similar ethnic backgrounds, cultural attitudes, racial origins, and so forth. Communities might also be defined in terms of economic activity or function, political or social interests, or religious belief.

All of these concepts of community involve a collection of individuals who share or have something in common—a geographic area, a cultural heritage, a work activity, a political interest, and so forth. The term community must include a spatial dimension. Communities are located in geographic areas. In addition, the people in that area have something in common that gives them (and others) a perception that the geographic area is a community. The community may be linked by a shared employment activity, cultural heritage, social interests and norms, religious beliefs, and the like. However, this leaves the concept too broad for the purposes of delineating among the different concepts of development. A community is a more or less circumscribed geographic locality in which the residents tend to see their destinies as somehow bound together. The residents share a common view of life and share membership in most of the organizations in which they participate. These may both say too much (how can a "common view of life" be reasonably expected in any sizable group of people?), and too little (about what aspects of their life would there be a common view?). However, the notions of linked destinies and shared memberships provide the beginning of a functional definition.

Whether the people in a local community perceive it or not, their lives are linked together by interdependent economic, social, and political activities and institutions. The links are direct and immediate ones. Single industry towns must have businesses other that the dominant one, but virtually all business activity is based on the existence of the dominant firm. Local communities share common public services such as libraries, hospitals, and schools, and infrastructure like roads, power, and sewer systems. Geographic boundaries may encompass part or all of a single municipal administrative unit or several such units. The geographic area is, however, much smaller than a province or state. The shared political institutions are of a small scale variety. In short, a local community is a geographic area in which the residents participate in interdependent economic, social, and political institutions and directly share a variety of public and private services. The term region is used to refer to the larger community—major segments of provinces, provinces, and groupings of provinces. Local or community development refers to communities in the small sense—small spatial areas in which there is a significant economic, social, political interdependence among the area's residents.

Three relevant points can be made about the meaning of economic development. First, economic growth (as measured by a few primary economic indicators such as income, employment, and production) is distinguished from economic development, which includes economic growth but adds to it changes in the structure of the economy (ranging from adjustments in industry mix to adaptation of new technology). Second, economic development is frequently argued to involve more than improvement in economic elements but extends to a variety of social components (infant mortality rates, air and water pollution levels, access to political institutions, and so forth). Merging of economic and social indicators is not straightforward and easy. Thus, establishing criteria for success in development efforts and in assessing impacts of such efforts is difficult. At a minimum, social indicators should complement economic ones, rather than restating them in another form. Third, for many supporters and practitioners of the community-based approach, the process by which economic development is achieved is as important as the end result. That is, the mechanisms by which prospects for economic development are enhanced become ends in themselves (increased autonomy of communities, reduction in power of large externally controlled corporations, empowerment of marginalized groups in the community, and so forth). It is, however, debatable whether these should be seen as ends or as means to achieving ends. Many supporters and practitioners of CED believe that the concept of economic development is far too narrow when applied to community-based efforts.

However, if community-based development efforts are assumed to be fostering economic development, than economic well-being should have a high priority. Wealth and employment creation are among the key objectives of CED efforts. The distribution of gains from such creations, however, may and should be different from that which would occur if the development were being driven by individual or corporate business gain. Success criteria need to include economic indicators such as income and employment growth (or retention), business start-ups, investment spending, and so forth. These are measures of well-being. Social indicators may improve but the emphasis is on economic measures. The role of social development efforts is not trivial but it is a subordinate one. Social investment should complement or underpin a broader array of economic development efforts but should not supplant them.

Community autonomy in economic decision-making and economic and social empowerment of individuals and groups are properly seen as means to an end in community-based economic development. They may be very laudable goals in their own right but they are not the goals of CED. How much autonomy and/or empowerment can be achieved through collective efforts within a community? The impact that autonomy/empowerment may have on the economic and social well-being of a community's inhabitants is also worthy of discussion. But these social goals are, at most, intermediate objectives when focusing on economic development efforts. What is unique about CED is that wealth and employment creation, structural change in the economy, and revitalization of economically declining communities are achieved by collective efforts at entrepreneurship. This is a new twist on a concept normally viewed as applying to individuals with personal gain as the prime motivation. In CED, the perception of opportunity, risk-taking on investment, and innovation and creativity in pursuing opportunities are community efforts.

Separating regional, local, and community-based economic development requires distinguishing among: (1) efforts to foster economic development in communities in the large sense (large sub-provincial areas, provinces, groups of provinces); (2) efforts to foster development for local communities; and (3) efforts to foster development by the local community. In the latter instance, public sector programs may be utilized and individual private investors sought but initiation of development efforts comes from within the community. The history of efforts at regional, local, and community-based economic development will give some concreteness to the distinction. Much of what passes for regional economic development has come from the federal government.

Regional Development Policy

Generally two types of policies were proposed and adopted at the federal level prior to the late 1940s with respect to economically underdeveloped regions. Transportation subsidies were provided to assist particular industries, and second, ad hoc conditional and unconditional grants were provided to the poorer provinces to alleviate the problems of insufficient revenues. The establishment of equalization grants in 1957 represented a systematic approach to reducing inequalities in provincial revenue bases. In the early 1960s, the federal government went beyond industry and income maintenance programs to develop policies designed to generate structural adjustments in underdeveloped regional and provincial economies. The Area Development Agency (ADA), created in 1963, provided capital investment subsidies to attract new manufacturing establishments or to induce expansion of existing plants in areas of acute and persistent unemployment.

The Atlantic Development Board was established in 1962 to deal solely with the economic problems of the Atlantic region. Initially the board served as a research and planning body and recommended development projects to the federal government. The role was expanded in 1963 to include the administration of a regional development fund and the formulation of an economic development plan for the entire region. Most of the actual expenditures were on social overhead capital or infrastructure (i.e., highways, electrical power development, industrial parks, water and sewage lines, and so forth).

The Agricultural Rehabilitation and Development Act was created to deal with problems in that sector. It was soon broadened to the Agricultural and Rural Development Act and focused on rural poverty and underdevelopment. An uncoordinated proliferation of programs and agencies emerged in federal regional policy during the 1960s. Objectives were often dissimilar yet with a tendency to an overlap of responsibility. In 1969 the federal government responded to widespread criticism by creating the Department of Regional Economic Expansion (DREE). A single government department was to take on responsibility for developing and coordinating programs and policies to deal with regional economic disparities. DREE had an initial mandate to focus economic development efforts in Atlantic Canada and the Gaspé region of Quebec. The emphasis on eastern Canada did not last. The Quebec crisis of 1970 raised the spectre of separation and increasing amounts of development money went to that province in an effort to avert the threat. But political pressure from the rest of Canada led to an extension of regional development programs to virtually all provinces.

The most important function of DREE was to establish the Special Areas Agreements and the Regional Development Incentives Act for enhancing growth and development in Canada's under-developed areas. The Special Areas program singled out 23 areas for infrastructure expenditures to enhance their prospects for development and growth. The Special Areas had a demonstrated or apparent potential for successful economic development. Unlike ADA, the Special Areas communities were probable winners rather than historically proven losers in economic terms. The Regional

Development Incentives Act (RDIA) program designated the Atlantic Provinces, most of Quebec, and Northern Ontario as regions in which new firms could settle and be eligible for location incentives grants. The mechanisms were similar to those of ADA but the specific local labour market areas of ADA were replaced by designated regions of RDIA.

Three years after its creation, DREE replaced the Special Areas program with general development agreements (GDAs) which could encompass any number of sub-agreements for specific purposes. Costs of these programs were to be shared between federal and provincial governments. The focus on the most troubled regions was further diluted, however, as agreements were signed with all provinces except Prince Edward Island, already covered by a 15-year Comprehensive Development Plan which had begun in 1969. The RDIA program was retained essentially intact but its share of total DREE expenditures remained relatively small.

Another change in emphasis occurred in 1982 when DREE was combined with the Department of Industry, Trade and Commerce to form the new Department of Regional Industrial Expansion (DRIE). The Ministry of State for Economic and Regional Development had a coordinating role within the new scheme, but the Department was short-lived. The reorganization was largely prompted by severe cyclical problems, which especially afflicted central Canada; money intended to stimulate structural changes in disadvantaged regions was diverted to overcome these cyclical difficulties. The principal tool for delivery of assistance programs became the Industrial and Regional Development Program (IRDP). Companies anywhere in Canada could apply for assistance, although the level of assistance varied according to a development index, calculated to reflect local economic circumstances. The nomenclature of general development agreements was changed to economic and regional development agreements with similar purposes, but requiring more money from the provinces to implement sub-agreements.

The mid–1980s saw further developments aimed at moving emphasis back to needy regions from the national emphasis embodied in DRIE. New programs were set up by DRIE to provide special incentives to Atlantic Canada, particularly Cape Breton. The Atlantic Enterprise Program had interest rate subsidies and other forms of assistance. The Atlantic Opportunities Program was designed to increase the share of federal purchasing going to atlantic Canada. Dissatisfaction with efforts made in regional policy led both administrative and functional revamping of regional policy structures. The general features of this restructuring were that regional agencies and programs would have local administration. Authority, program, and themes would be tailored to unique characteristics of the specific region, there would be more flexibility in mechanisms of business assistance and in the range of programs to be carried out, and there would be more direct interaction with the regional community—business, labour, academics, provincial governments, and non-profit organizations. Three regional agencies were created—the Atlantic Canada Opportunities Agency, the Western Diversification Office, and Federal Economic Development for Northern Ontario. As well, the federal department of Industry, Science and Technology had responsibility for regional development in Ontario and Quebec. The federal approach to regional development maintains the focus on groups of provinces as the object of enhanced economic development.

In summary, several instruments for fostering regional economic development have been utilized by one or more of the three levels of government. Tax rebates, tax incentives (e.g., accelerated depreciation), low-cost loans, non-repayable grants (automatic and discretionary), various input subsidies, and expenditures on infrastructure have all been tried. Capital reallocation programs (moving jobs to people by using investment location inducements) have been more prevalent than labour mobility programs (deliberately encouraging people to move to jobs). Investment subsidies (e.g., grants, low-interest loans, special tax credits) have been extensively used while labour subsidies (underwriting part of the wage bill) have rarely been used. Subsidies for other inputs such as transportation, energy, and land (by individual provinces and municipalities) have also been provided as incentives for potential investors.

Second, regional development policy in Canada has been mainly oriented towards regions which have experienced prolonged decline or stagnation but which have not had a history of industrial development. Canada has not had the more common European experience of industrialized regions going into a prolonged slump. Sudden or gradual decline in this country has been more associated with rural and semi-rural, resource-based economies.

Third, it would be difficult to find another area of economic policy, especially at the federal level, which has been as subject to such frequent adjustments to scope, objectives, administrative structures, and roles of operation as has been regional development policy. This may reflect a variety of considerations including political pressure from all regions to spread the wealth in what is arguably the most decentralized federal system in the industrialized world.

Finally, despite the obvious difficulty of evaluating any policy which is subject to as many changes as regional policy has been, most observers conclude that Canadian efforts have largely been unsuccessful. The objectives of reducing disparities in income and unemployment among regions have not generally been met. Income differences have been reduced but mainly because of personal and inter-governmental transfers. Differences in unemployment have fluctuated over time but there has been no downward trend. There has been some positive adjustment in the structure and performance of the weaker provincial economies. Unfortunately, we cannot readily determine whether this is due to regional policy impacts or to other factors. Strong proponents of regional policy claim things would have been worse and opponents suggest the evidence proves inherent weakness of regional and national policies. What the experience may demonstrate is that the relative influence of other policy measures, such as monetary, fiscal, and trade policy, is more powerful than regional policy measures designed to offset the inimical influences of the national policies.

Local Development Policies

There have also been instances of policy thrusts aimed explicitly and primarily at local communities. The Area Development Agency (ADA) was established in 1963 to provide incentives to industries to locate in 35 areas of acute persistent unemployment and of slow growth. The areas designated were Canada Manpower Centres; the boundaries weren't precisely those of municipalities but the areas covered were small enough to count as local communities by any reasonable definition. ADA reflected the conventional view that economic growth and stabilization was to come mostly through industrialization. Incentives were conditional upon the firms creating new employment in the area. Three indicators were specified in the ADA program—average income, unemployment rates, and employment levels— but the primary emphasis was on income and unemployment rates and especially the latter. Two major criticisms of ADA program were that it was assisting the wrong type of community (slow growth with low potential) and that the exclusive focus on manufacturing took no account of the specific features of the designated areas. Many were not suitable locations for manufacturing activity.

In 1967, the federal government, in conjunction with the government of Nova Scotia, established the Cape Breton Development Corporation (DEVCO), a crown corporation whose mandate was to provide a new economic base for the industrial Cape Breton area of Nova Scotia. The steel and coal industries, that had formed the foundation of the economy of that region, had been marginal operations for decades. Both industries had significantly reduced the size of their operations and eliminated jobs. The continued economic vulnerability of industrial Cape Breton has led to DEVCO to continue employment creation attempts.

The Special Areas program of DREE's early years had a decided orientation towards local communities. Twenty-three areas in Canada were singled out for infrastructure expenditures which were expected to enhance prospects for development and growth. The Special Areas were ones with demonstrated or apparent potential for successful economic development. This approach was based loosely on the growth centre concept—e.g., that these areas had the potential for self-sustained growth. They had characteristics which, given the proper kind of infrastructure development, were expected to make them very attractive locales for new plants or expanding ones.

Three other federal policy thrusts had a local community orientation and warrant brief discussion here. One was a loosely structured, seemingly ad hoc, policy of relocating government offices and departmental branches from Ottawa to other localities to bolster the economies of those communities. The number of such relocations has been small and criteria for the choice of recipient community unstated. The local communities receiving the relocated government activity have benefited from the new employment. A more ambitious development was the creation of the Ministry of State for Urban Affairs (MSUA) in 1976. MSUA grew out of the concern about the implications of rapid urbanization and the evident problem of urban decay. But MSUA was hampered from the beginning by the constitutional constraint that municipal affairs is the responsibility of the provinces. This precluded any direct federal involvement with cities. MSUA had no policy development or implementation authority and no budget except for research activity. Its mandate to coordinate federal programs having an impact on urban areas was never realized because it had no leverage to force other federal departments and agencies to cooperate. The intrusion on provincial territory created hostility and resistance from the provinces and the lack of funding power led to disregard by the municipalities. MSUA was disbanded in 1979 but its demise was predictable from the mid–1970s.

From 1974 to 1979, the federal government operated the Community Employment Strategy through Canada Employment and Immigration Commission. The objective of the program was to open up employment opportunities for persons experiencing difficulty in finding satisfactory employment and who relied on some form of transfer payment. CEIC had, for a number of years, used a variety of short-term, job-creation programs to reduce severe seasonal and structural unemployment problems. The CES program represented an experimental approach to creating more permanent jobs by taking into account the characteristics of different communities. Provincial and community involvement in working out the details of the job creation package in a local area was to be an integral part of the program. The community involvement aspect of the program worked with varying degrees of success. The program ran out in 1979, but it spawned a number of continuing community development corporations. It also generated the Local Economic Development Assistance (LEDA) program of financial assistance to community organizations; the purpose was to develop new business activity and to create additional employment opportunities in local communities. This was a forerunner to the current Community Futures Program.

Community-Based Economic Development Initiatives

The increased interest in and acceptance of locally-based economic development is partly due to the perceived failure of past attempts to deal with the disparities in income and job opportunities in different regions, provinces, and sub-provincial areas. The search for a different approach has led many countries to reduce the commitment to traditional forms of regional policy and put more responsibility on lower levels of government. The premise of any economic development strategy is that there are more business opportunities available than have been realized. This has been the implicit basis for government policy designed to alleviate regional disparities. Governments have focused on identifying the actual opportunities, attempted to create new opportunities, or have tried to change investors' perception of opportunities. Public sector activities have traditionally been direct involvement in regional policy such as framing a development strategy, choosing winning firms or sectors, investing in infrastructure, and so forth. In recent years, more indirect methods of promoting development have been used such as attempting to foster an entrepreneurial culture or creating a climate for business development. This arm's length approach to economic development has renewed interest in locally based efforts.

Deficiencies in the Local Economy

Lack of information is one of the constraints faced by firms in any location. Information on market conditions and information on technologies are likely to be in short supply in smaller more isolated communities. In larger urban centres, part of the task of collecting and assessing information is carried out by financial institutions, by market research and other types of consulting firms, and by colleges and universities; there are informal networks among businesses in which relevant information is disseminated. A CED organization can serve as a partial substitute in smaller communities for the formal and informal structures found in larger centres. It can utilize knowledge of local natural resources, capital stock, technology, human skills and capabilities, and infrastructure to determine what market opportunity and technology information is relevant to local enterprises and to the development prospects of the community.

Some communities face critical gaps in basic services such as housing, health care, education, and training. The public sector usually provides all or most of these services but some communities can benefit from community-based initiatives in the provision of health care, training, and housing. Such activities can not only improve the lives of local citizens but also make the community a more attractive place in which to establish or expand a business. Provision of services can be an important supplement to economic development efforts by the community.

A third deficiency for businesses in smaller communities is inadequate access to capital—both debt and equity financing. Local businesses in many communities with stagnant or declining economies find it difficult to borrow on terms comparable to those offered to firms in larger centres or in rapidly growing communities. Furthermore, the supply of equity capital is small or non-existent in the more remote communities. These conditions adversely affect the rate of new business formation and economic stagnation or decline is perpetuated.

Community-based economic development efforts may have an advantage in dealing with the problems of higher costs in more isolated communities. Local development organizations that operate businesses can operate with a lower rate of return on their business activities than would be feasible for a private firm. This is because the LDO will view its business venture from the perspective of the community's net gain. The community-based operation may generate social benefits (such as reduced unemployment) that would not be the basis for operations of private firms. LDOs also make frequent use of voluntary labour resources. The staff or the board of an LDO may provide labour and management services at little or no charge so that the LDO has lower operating costs than would otherwise be the case. Community-based development initiatives allow communities to create new opportunities by enhancing the knowledge and skills base of their populations and by tapping their store of entrepreneurial potential.

Current Approaches to Community Economic Development

Community initiatives actually undertaken in Canada fall into two main groupings. The first group are those designed to enhance the use or quality of local resources, especially human resources. This constitutes a supply side approach to development. The second set of activities involves a response to market forces or market opportunities—a demand side orientation.

Enhancing local resources—the supply side approach—can involve one or more of three types of activities: employing idle human and physical resources, expanding the community resource base, and increasing the productivity of local resources. Most efforts in CED are directed at increasing employment of the local labour force. But they can also be directed at the use of idle physical capital. The takeover or buy out of an operation which has closed is an obvious example. Alternatively, a community development project might involve restoration of a building which can serve as an attraction for tourists and increase business for local firms. Establishment of programs to provide financial capital to local businesses is another form of local resource base expansion. The supply of financing may be increased by establishing new institutions or by pressing for new public sector programs to provide loan capital for community-based development. CED efforts may also be designed to improve the effectiveness or productivity of the local resource base. Several local development efforts have focused on training and skills development for workers especially for the long-time unemployed. Improvement in the quality of human resources need not be the direct responsibility of a community development organization. Its contribution might simply be to identify skills shortages or needs along with the most effective programs to deal with the shortages.

A focus in local economic development initiatives on demand side activities—responding to market forces—can involve making increased information on new opportunities (especially in external markets) available to existing business or potential investors, promoting the community in external export markets and to indigenous and outside investors, inducing investment by private businesses, fostering entrepreneurship in the community, and directly investing in business ventures for local and external markets.

Community development initiatives can be directed to collecting and evaluating information on market opportunities. The knowledge about new or expanded markets that can be exploited by local firms is fundamental and will be the critical factor dictating the pace of economic development. CED efforts could also be directed at expanding external markets for locally produced goods and services and at encouraging non-local investors to consider the business opportunities in the community. These first two types of initiatives can, by themselves, influence the investment and operating decisions of local firms and potential entrepreneurs. Successful community based business ventures can similarly serve as a spur for local business activity.

Efforts made by community-development organizations in these directions have been very limited and have tended to focus on assessing the strengths and weaknesses of communities faced with economic adversity, promoting the community to itself, and providing leadership for community interest groups. The first stage of activity, when community-based development efforts are spurred by local economic adversity, is to try to mobilize the community behind efforts to revitalize the local economy. This will involve some form of evaluation of the community's long-term economic prospects and establishing realistic expectations about the future. Building the community's awareness of its plight and of its options, promoting cooperation and self-determination, and channelling resources towards goal-setting and planning are also part of the mobilization process. Some of that effort involves analyzing and disseminating information. Some of it involves promoting the community internally—trying to convince groups within the community that survival and revitalization are realistic possibilities.

The final vehicle for demand side involvement of community development efforts is the direct investment in business ventures. Such activities bring employment benefits, provide a role model for private investors, and may induce additional investments. Community Development Corporations (CDCs) are community organizations which engage in direct investment. The CDC carries out functions typical to a privately-owned firm such as planning and implementing investment strategies, managing day-to-day operations, and making decisions about changes in production, employment levels, and introduction of new techniques. Such investment ventures act as a lever for the community to implement its economic development strategy and provide a way for the CDC to become more self-supporting. When community groups go into business they get involved in innovation and risk-taking and, like other business ventures, they have had their share of failures. Community development organizations have become entrepreneurs because they have been able to identify and exploit business opportunities often on the basis of specific knowledge of their locality and region. The risk-taking activity of community groups is the single most influential effort that has been made to promote economic development at the local level. The more successful CDCs seem to have benefited from adopting a strategy of investing in several sectors rather than focusing on one or two. Diversification helps reduce vulnerability when market conditions change in a particular sector or industry.

CDCs face several problems. One is the potential conflict between social and economic objectives within the same development strategy. For example, survival of the enterprise may dictate a reduction in staff size thus making achievement of a community benefit goal more difficult. Another problem is that economic self-sufficiency is difficult to attain, at least in the short run, for most community development organizations. Too heavy a dependence on public sector support may obviate the contributions of a CDC to local control and to innovation in the community's development activities. Finally, the issue of competition with local private sector businesses has arisen in some cases. This can blunt the efforts of a local development organization to ensure widespread community support and to enlist the assistance of those in the community with the business skill required by the CDC.

Current Programs of Support for Community Development

The Community Futures (CF) program, introduced in 1986, is one of six components of Employment and Immigration Canada's job strategy and is specifically designed to address development problems of communities. The program is aimed at non-metropolitan communities hit by mass layoffs and plant closures, communities faced with chronic unemployment, and communities that are struggling with economic decline. By March 1989 more than 200 communities had been selected for assistance; expenditures for 1988–1989 were just under $118 million. The breakdown of spending in the CF program indicates a steady increase in expenditures, from $64 million in 1986–87 to an estimated $143 million in 1989–90. With the reallocation of some unemployment insurance transfers to the program, spending is expected to be about $173 million in 1990–91. The 170 Business Development Centres have been the largest budget item.

Six options are currently available under the Community Futures Program. Community Futures Committees must be set up in each community participating in the program. Each committee must have representatives from both the private and the public sectors and has responsibility for establishing a development strategy for the community. A maximum of $100,000 per year for two years is available. Second, self-employment incentives are provided to recipients of unemployment insurance and welfare benefits who wish to become self-employed; a weekly allowance of $180 is available for up to 52 weeks while they develop and implement a business plan. Third, business development centres (BDCs) can offer services ranging from business counselling to direct financial assistance. The latter may be grants, loans, loan guarantees or equity participation. The centres receive funding for up to five years with an upper limit of $1.5 million. Those offering technical and advisory services may receive an additional $635,000. Fourth, direct purchase of training provides funds for occupational training either through course purchase from local establishments or through training allowance and travel assistance. Fifth, a community initiatives fund supports development initiatives identified by CF committees as part of their development strategy and which cannot be supported by other options or other federal programs. Assistance is on a cost-shared basis and must involve matching funding contributions by the private sector and/or government. There is an assistance ceiling of $50,000 per firm or individual. Sixth, relocation and exploratory assistance assists unemployed persons seeking employment opportunities at a new location. Relocation assistance up to $5000 per worker, $7500 under certain circumstances, is offered.

7

An Integrated Development Model for Building Sustainable Communities in Canada

Marcia L. Nozick

Daily we read about the loss of jobs due to global economic restructuring—downsizing, plant closings, and flight of capital out of Canada. What we do not often read about is the resulting loss of community. Loss of community along with environmental destruction are the most critical issues we face today. Once vibrant farm towns are dying as rural populations dwindle and the local farm economy is replaced by large scale agribusiness; single resource towns are facing total devastation when their only industry shuts down or moves across the border; inner-city neighbourhoods are being ravaged from within by the destructive effects of poverty, homelessness, violence, and alienation.

These are not random occurrences but are the result of complex global forces undermining and dismantling the structures of community and the social relationships which for thousands of years have been a source of genuine support and identity for people. Rootlessness, transitoriness, and dispossession are the by products of an economic system based on free mobility of capital and global competition. People move to find jobs, corporations move to find cheap labour and tax breaks, and the food on our dinner table comes to us from thousands of miles away. In the last decade industries have grown from large scale to become global in size and control of the world market to where 25% of everything produced in the world comes to us from transnational corporations. These corporations continue to expand, accumulate, and concentrate huge amounts of capital into fewer and fewer hands by merging, buying out, and putting large and small competitors out of business. In the process, hundreds of towns, neighbourhoods, cities and entire regions of the country are being marginalized and written off as bad investments.

Focusing economic and political attention on integrating Canada into the global economy loses sight of priorities at home. Resources are diverted away from meeting community needs. Urban and rural communities across Canada are facing social and economic crises as a result of external pressures undermining the foundations of community life. The major pressure points of community breakdown are:

- declining local economies due to de-industrialization and the draining of wealth out of communities by large, outside-owned companies.

- loss of citizen control as decisions affecting the future of communities are made by higher levels of government and corporations who have no personal stake in the community.

- social degradation and neglect of human needs as increasing numbers of people are abandoned to homelessness, joblessness, and unsafe living conditions.

- environmental degradation as local water, air, and soil are poisoned by industrial and consumer waste and auto pollution.

- erosion of local identity and cultural diversity as we conform to the homogeneous values of a mass consumer society.

CED must take into account all of the related areas of community breakdown to revitalize rural and urban communities. A holistic approach which integrates economic, social, ecological, political, and cultural development is needed. The goal of CED must be more than creating jobs in the short term. It must be to strengthen the capacity of communities to withstand the forces of shifting capital and to build vital communities which have the power and means to regenerate and sustain themselves over time. In other words, to build sustainable communities. Five major components or action areas provide a framework for an integrated development strategy. They are: creating local wealth through economic self-reliance; gaining community control over land, capital, industry, and planning; meeting the needs of individuals; becoming ecologically sustainable; and building a community culture.

Creating Local Wealth Through Economic Self-Reliance

Self-reliance starts with the idea of people in communities producing the things they need for themselves rather than getting them through exchange. Each community and region relies on its own physical resources and human capabilities to produce for local needs instead of depending on outside producers. The orientation is inward, rather than outward—the antithesis of a global free trade economy, which is based on importing and exporting mass goods to and from foreign markets. A self-reliant and sustainable economy tries to retain local capital by putting it to productive use creating new industries which are designed to serve local markets. Jane Jacobs (1984, pp.59–71) has pointed out that supply regions, which depend on exporting resources to far-flung centres for processing, and cities, which manufacture goods primarily for export, are building in the conditions for economic stagnation, even if initially they profit from high world prices for their product. A truly vibrant and self-sustaining economy is one that is built upon a complex web of interchange among a multitude of different local producers and consumers. Diversity, ingenuity, and flexible entrepreneur-ship are the cornerstones of economic regeneration. These must be nurtured and made an ongoing part of a living economy.

What is often not recognized is that people have the resources and means within their communities to meet many or most of their needs. Every community in Canada, even the poorest, has income, skills, and physical resources. A community develops these resources by plugging the leakage of dollars out of a community and intensifying the level of local exchange among members of a community; money that is spent back and forth creates wealth. Three tactics that can be employed are: making more with less, making the dollars go around, and building collective self-reliance among a group of communities.

(i) Making More With Less

New wealth is created when an economy can produce more while using the same or less amount of energy and resources. Economic growth is tied to ecological efficiency. The same maxims apply to environmental conser-vation—reduce, reuse, and recycle. Lucrative savings are derived from efficient use of resources. The municipal hydro company in the town of Osaga, Iowa, (pop. 4000) was able to cut local consumption of electricity and gas by making relatively simple technologies available to homeowners. Over a ten year period, the hydro company was able to pay off its debts and accumulate a large interest bearing surplus. It cut hydro rates which in turn attracted two new industries to the town. In addition, it saved $1000 per household per year that would otherwise be leaving the community to go to outside suppliers of energy. The local bank has received a 10% per year increase in its deposits of which 10% is directly attributed to energy savings (Lovins, 1991). David Morris estimates that only 13 cents of every dollar spent on energy remains in a community (1982, p.129). Therefore, it is in a community's economic interest to conserve on energy use. The Sudbury Corporate Plan recognized this fact when it targeted retrofitting 5% of its city's housing stock annually as part of its sustainable development strategy.

Proximity planning is a new land-use planning focus which concentrates the activities of work, recreation, shopping, and living within close distance of each other. It is a tool to reduce local energy consumption and save on the high costs of building roads, bridges, sewer lines, and other infrastruc-tures. A study in Portland, Oregon showed that reviving neighbourhood grocery stores would save 5% of the city's energy consumption spent on driving trips to shopping centres (Morris, 1982, p.139). Vancouver has adopted the principles of proximity planning to guide future urban development and expect both environmental and economic benefits.

Conservation saves money. The cost of building a new aqueduct for the city of Winnipeg is slated at $400 million. The need for this aqueduct is based on projected increases in water consumption by a rate of one percent per year. Current rates of water use by city dwellers are already twice what people in France or Germany use. If every household would simply maintain their current rate of water consumption, the city would not need to build an aqueduct for another fifty years, thus saving $400 million of tax payers money.

Recycling also creates wealth by stretching out the existing resource base of a community. Cities and towns can mine their waste streams for raw materials such as glass, paper, plastics, rubber, and aluminum. Governments can support this growing industry through curbside pick-up programs, bulk purchases of recycled paper, environmental research, and assisting in setting up local reprocessing plants. Governments through guaranteed purchase agreements could help to fill the gap in local markets for recycled materials. The concept of recycling extends to older buildings. Deindustrialization has left behind hundreds of empty warehouses and plants which could be used for social and commercial purposes. Restoring older neighbourhoods has the added benefit of helping to maintain and preserve a community's heritage and identity.

(ii) Making the Dollars Go Around

Every time a dollar changes hands, it becomes a new dollar for somebody else to spend. Dollars that circulate multiply and the economy expands. Money that circulates within a self-contained system generates wealth for that system but when it leaves the multiplier effect stops. A dollar circulates six to eight times in a healthy economy, in a poor community dollars leave almost immediately. Plugging the leakage of capital from a community is a first step toward intensifying the level of exchange among members of a community and keeping dollars in local circulation. Bank savings and imports are two major sources of money leaks out of a community.

Money put into bank savings are taken out of circulation. This would not be detrimental to a local economy if a portion of this capital were reinvested by the banks as loans to small and medium sized local businesses. Instead, however, Canadian banks have chosen to take the money out of the community and the country by investing in foreign loans, international money markets, and government term deposits and mortgages. During the 1989–1992 recession, banks withdrew credit lines to small local businesses and cut back small business lending by more than 11% while increasing lending to big business by 11%, despite the fact that small businesses have provided 98% of all new jobs in Canada since 1989.

The U.S. Community Reinvestment Act requires banks to reinvest 16% of earnings in decaying neighbourhoods as a way to combat the flight of capital from inner-cities. The Canadian government might consider similar legislation. A number of credit unions, such as VanCity in Vancouver and Assiniboine Credit Union in Winnipeg, have set up community investment accounts to provide loans to local businesses which would otherwise be unable to access capital. Public sector union savings amounts to 25%–30% of the pool of money banks lend out and is a major source of capital to be harnessed for community investment purposes. The Manitoba Federation of Labour, with provincial and federal government support, set up the Crocus Investment Fund in 1992 to invest in small and medium sized Manitoba businesses. Investors receive a 20% tax credit from both the Provincial and Federal governments.

Loss through imports is the other source of leakage of wealth from a community. Local dollars are exported to outside suppliers. Further, a large percentage of money spent at national or transnational chain stores and subsidiary branch companies goes to support head offices in other cities. To combat the outflow of local dollars, there needs to be an import replacement strategy whereby communities begin to manufacture products for local consumption. Targeting specific products for import replacement is a first step. Existing resources in a community, people's needs, and local markets should be considered in choosing import substitution products. A local economy should try to extract the greatest amount of work and energy out of a given resource by processing it into finished products. A community gains added value from turning potatoes into French fries, wheat into bread, canning local fish, and making furniture out of lumber. The process of finishing off a product triggers new industries which in turn feed off of each other and supply each other with needed parts and accessories, thus creating spin-off wealth for a community.

People's basic needs provide a ready-made local market for producers. Take the need for housing. In poor inner-city neighbourhoods rent paid to absentee landlords accounts for a major outflow of capital. Government programs and non-profit development groups which assist residents to own, either cooperatively or privately, their own homes, help to stem the outflow of capital from a neighbourhood. Housing is big business. Building and developing local housing is one of the most effective tools for generating wealth and accumulating capital in poorer inner-city neighbourhoods. Import substitution should tie into existing markets. A community needs an inventory of what products are currently produced and purchased in the community and from whom. Local producers must be linked up with businesses which will become purchasers of their products. Matchmaking between producers and consumers is a crucial, yet often ignored, part of the CED process.

There are other tools which can be used to promote local circulation of dollars. Local currency movement is one example. Several rural towns in Saskatchewan and Manitoba issue community cash through their local credit union at Christmas time. This cash allows three months interest free spending and can only be applied to purchases at local stores. Community barter exchange networks, such as the Local Exchange Trading System, build trading relationships among members of a community. Members trade goods and services freely among a collective membership using a central computer system to keep track of individual accounts.

(iii) Building Collective Self-Reliance

Collective self-reliance is a trading strategy which avoids exploitation and domination of one party over another. It is a strategy of exchange among equal partners for the purpose of building collective strength among a block of cooperating communities. This can happen by making trade alliances with communities which are at about the same level of development and by trading primary products for primary products or manufactured products for manufactured products. Trade between rich and poor regions works by creating dependency of one upon the other but trade between equals can build collective strength through interdependence. Examples include native communities buying services and goods from native owned businesses, cooperatives supporting other cooperatives through purchases, and local businesses in a neighbourhood agreeing to purchase goods and services from each other in recognition of the collective benefit for the community economy.

Community Control Over Land, Capital, Industry, and Planning

The social and economic well being of a community depends upon a community's capacity to shape and influence its future. To increase a community's autonomy and decision making powers requires a shift of powers from government bureaucracy to grassroots management and service delivery, from outside ownership and control of capital to local ownership and control, and from hierarchical to non-hierarchical structures. Bottom-up, community power is structurally different from top-down power. Its strength lies not in exerting control of a few over the many but in sharing power among a broad membership, building coalitions, and making horizontal connections between diverse groups. Many types of organizations contribute to community empowerment—self-help groups, neighbourhood associations, umbrella organizations, and community-run services. Community development corporations (CDCs), community land trusts (CLTs), community loan funds, and cooperatives stand out as innovative models for giving communities greater ownership and control over land, capital, industry and planning decisions.

Community Development Corporations

A community development corporation (CDC) is formed to represent a specific community. It can receive and distribute funds from public or private sources for the purpose of community development. CDCs are involved in initiation, coordination, and delivery of a wide array of social, cultural, and economic community programs. A CDC is managed and controlled by residents to deal with a variety of local problems. CDCs may act as intermediaries in the distribution of funding from higher levels of government to the community (many U.S. corporations are designed for this purpose), or may take on the direct role of developer by building needed housing, managing properties, forming partnerships with private developers, starting new businesses, and operating community loan funds. CDC have the capacity to develop broad and comprehensive revitalization strategies which balance economic and social goals.

Neighbourhood associations, through their community organizing and development activities, can play a similar role to CDCs in shaping the course of development in a community. The Downtown Eastside Residents Association (DERA) in Vancouver's core has a membership of 4,500 in a neighbourhood of 12,000. It has succeeded in developing some 500 units of cooperative housing, two popular parks, and Canada's most used library and community centre in a restored heritage building. DERA has improved safety in the community through increased lighting, street programs, and by getting the city to close down the neighbourhood's liquor store and most offensive hotels, resulting in a reduction in the murder and crime rate in the area. One of DERA's major accomplishments was to pressure the city into enforcing its own bylaws, which led to laying some 10,000 charges against owners of residential hotels and forcing them to bring the buildings up to standard.

Community Land Trusts

A community land trust (CLT) is a non-profit corporation with an open community membership and elected board. CLTs are set up to purchase and develop properties and lease land to local homeowners and businesses. Community ownership of land can be a powerful tool for helping to stabilize a community. Land is removed from the cyclical boom and bust pressures of the real estate market and from both speculators and absentee landlords. A CLT acquires and retains ownership of the land but sells the houses which it renovates to responsible families who are active members of the CLT. A CLT is able to balance individual and community interests. In a ninety-nine year lease agreement with the homeowner, the CLT controls the resale value of the home and retains the first option to purchase. Houses revert back to the trust and can be resold to other CLT families at affordable prices. A CLT both provides affordable housing for families in need today, and ensures permanent affordable housing for future generations.

CLTs finance their operations through donations and loans from churches, unions, governments, individuals, and businesses. Many CLTs use the sweat-equity labour of prospective homebuyers to further lower the cost of construction. A collective learning and development process occurs through choosing land sites, strategic neighbourhood planning, construction and renovation, financing, and outreach to the community. The people in the neighbourhood must work together to make it happen. The board of a CLT is usually made up of equal portions of CLT lessees, other members of the neighbourhood, and representatives from the community, such as churches and community organizations. Government is not a participant in the process except in its support through donations of property and block funding. The CLT model is being adapted and used in over 40 American cities. CLTs are just beginning to take root in a few Canadian communities such as Toronto Island and Montreal. The Milton Park neighbourhood in Montreal is an exception; in the 1970s citizens began organizing against a high-rise development project which threatened to destroy several blocks of Victorian houses. Citizens eventually won the fight; Canada Mortgage and Housing Corporation agreed to purchase the twenty-five acre package, renovate the houses, and place them under the management, control, and ownership of fifteen cooperatives and six non-profit corporations.

Community Loan Funds

Community projects and local businesses require capital. Gaining access to loan capital is a major stumbling block for people who are poor, and have few material possessions to use as collateral. Many community-based non-profit groups have set up revolving loan funds to lend to high risk clients for local businesses start up. Loan decisions are based on both social value and economic viability of the business plan. The pool of loan capital may come from a range of sources including foundations, unions, individuals, churches, and governments. Money is either donated or lent to the organization at reduced interest rates for a specified time period. Loans tend to be small (less than $10,000); as they are paid back the money is reinvested in new community ventures. Often there is a requirement for the client to work with a business adviser to ensure ongoing good management and payback of the loan. Tying the loan to receiving technical assistance has proven to be a winning combination. The Women's Economic Development Corporation, St. Paul, Minnesota, has helped start over 1000 businesses in the past ten years; loans of over $900,000 have been made to high risk clients with a loss rate of only 4%, compared to over 20% loan loss of traditional banks.

There are many types of community loan funds. For example, the Women's World Bank, which has affiliate organizations in Canada, uses a pool of capital as loan guarantee to help women borrow money from conventional banks. Revolving loan funds can also be used for purposes other than business ventures. Winnipeg Habitat for Humanity operates a revolving loan fund to construct houses at reduced cost for poor families who then become the new homeowners. The family receives a no-interest mortgage on their home to cover the costs of construction, which are kept to a minimum because of donated labour and materials by thousands of volunteers who join the house-building work camps each summer. The principle paid on the mortgage goes back into the revolving fund to build more houses. The loan fund is topped up by ongoing donations from businesses and individuals and also receives donations from a subsidiary company called Habitat Re-Store, opened in 1991. Habitat Re-Store sells second-hand construction materials which it salvages from demolitions or receives as gifts. The Habitat Re-Store is a business that provides local jobs, contributes to meeting local housing needs, and is an ecological enterprise. Other, more institutional, loan funds are designed to foster local economic development. The Manitoba and Saskatchewan governments have established a program whereby rural communities can issue bonds to raise capital for specific economic projects. The process starts with a company looking for a capital loan and a place to locate. The company applies to the provincial government, which screens the projects internally. Only after the company has passed the provincial test and a location is chosen, does the community get involved. The bond issue is open to anyone in the province to invest, with an individual limit of 10% of the total issue. The government guarantees investors return of their capital after a five year period, but does not guarantee the interest.

Cooperatives

One of the goals of CED is to diversify and decentralize ownership and control of industry within a community. Small scale privately-owned and owner-operated businesses are encouraged. Cooperative models of ownership go a step further by erasing the differences between owner, worker, manager, and consumer. A member of a food cooperative is a consumer and a worker and a manager deciding on what to sell and at what price. A member of a worker cooperative is both a worker and an owner, dually motivated by the need to make a profit and the need to create secure working conditions. Cooperatives can be horizontally integrated into a system to purchase supplies and services from each other—a form of collective self-reliance. The interlocking of producer, service, consumer, and financial cooperatives has proved to be a highly successful model for economic revitalization in Mondragon, Spain, where residents built up an elaborate network of some 200 cooperatives, half of which are industries employing 20,000 people. The model need not be that large. In the Evangeline region of Prince Edward Island, a network of worker, consumer, and service cooperatives has turned a dying economy, that twenty years ago was dependent on fishing, into a vibrant and diversified economy. Today, a variety of cooperatives employ nearly one-quarter of the area's population.

Meeting Basic Needs of Individuals

A community is only as strong as its individual members. If basic needs are not met, if homelessness, hunger, violence and alienation are allowed to fester, a community can have no hope or future to build upon. When children are abused or allowed to go hungry their self-esteem diminishes, their performance in school suffers, and they are blocked from developing their potential as healthy contributing adults in society. The entire community pays the price socially, economically and spiritually. Sustainable development must concern itself, first and foremost, with meeting the basic needs of individuals.

In a healthy community there is an interdependent, reciprocal relationship between the individual and community. Individuals give to a community through work, participation in community life, and caring for others; in exchange the community provides the individual with security, protection, opportunities for meaningful work and self-fulfilment. It is a kind of social contract. Yet, as part of modern development, this social contract has broken down. Increasing numbers of people are not being given protection, security, or opportunities to improve their lives. Throwing money at the problem hasn't worked and we can no longer afford the cost. Expanding the social service bureaucracy does nothing to free people from the cycle of poverty in which they are trapped. Large scale redevelopment projects, while they may bolster a city's image to the outside world, do nothing to empower people to improve their lives.

Over the last fifty years, there has been a steady erosion of community life and community self-reliance. Institutions have replaced community in providing for people's needs. Social relationships have become increasingly contractual in nature as individuals look outside the community to third parties—professionals, governments, and corporations—to meet their needs. The cost to society is enormous, requiring a huge regulatory bureaucracy and legislative system to mediate between competing interests—labour and management, citizens and governments, consumers and producers, corporations and corporations, and industries and environments.

A Manitoba example illustrates this point. The Hutterites, a religious sect living in colonies in rural Manitoba, have survived and thrived as a community through the practice of mutual aid expressed in common ownership of land and the sharing of technology and labour. In 1991 there were complaints by local businesses that a Hutterite-owned demolition business was underbidding other businesses by almost one-half. The

Hutterites were charged with having an unfair advantage over other companies since they were not required to pay workers' compensation premiums or minimum wages to workers. In response, the Hutterites told another side of the story. They said that within their community there was no need to pay minimum wages because every member owned everything equally and every worker was a manager. All capital was collective property. There was no need to pay workers' compensation because the Hutterite community took care of its own sick, injured and elderly (Winnipeg Free Press, July 23, 1991, p.3).

Here are two contrasting models of social organization, one based on adversarial, contractual relationships, the other on moral, cooperative relationships. The Hutterite cooperative community is the more economically efficient. Society pays a high price to legislate and administer the values of caring, sharing, and personal responsibility, which are given of freely in authentic communities where people trust and rely on one another.

A whole new approach to development is called for whereby *community* becomes the focus of production for human needs. In Winnipeg, the Core Area Initiatives, a tri-level government program aimed at revitalizing the inner-city, spent $198 million over ten years. More than half of the money was allocated to bricks and mortar development including two shopping malls in the downtown area. Other money went to pay for consultants' fees, salaries to administrators, and public relations. The remainder went to fund community organizations and employment training programs for a temporary period. In 1991, when the program ended, dozens of community groups running on shoestring budgets with volunteer help were forced to close their doors. These organizations—women's centres, street programs, drop-ins—had become a backbone of support for thousands of needy individuals. The questions from a CED perspective is, how could these much needed community-run services have been kept alive on a sustaining basis? One alternative would have been to establish a Community Trust Fund from the initial $200 million, administered by an elected board of community residents. The annual interest (some $20 million) would have funded community groups and local economic initiatives on a ongoing, permanent basis, keeping intact the original funding. It is this type of permanent funding and self-governance model that is much needed to give a community greater security and control over the allocation and use of community resources.

Self-help groups play an important role in building community self-reliance. Self-help, whether in the form of a local exchange trading club or a personal recovery group, could as easily be called a "help others" movement because it is founded on the principles of reciprocity and mutual aid: in helping others we help ourselves. Society receives a large pay back by supporting community and self-help type of organizations. They are not a drain on the public purse as they tend to squeeze the most value out of every dollar spent. The productivity of volunteers and people helping others in self-help groups is exceptional, yet virtually unaccounted for by the GNP. Economist David Ross figures that Canadian volunteers working for formal organizations gave some $16 billion worth of unpaid labour in 1986–87 (*Perception*, Vol. 14, no. 4, 1990).

CED, as an integrated development strategy, must take into account the full range of people's material *and non-material* needs. Human needs fall under three major categories. There are *personal needs* of the self for wholeness or autonomy including the need for identity, self-worth, creativity, freedom, self-actualization. Second, there are *social needs* for integration including the need for belonging, participation with others, and affection. Finally, there are *physical needs* of survival which includes the need for health (clean air, sexuality, nutrition), security (shelter, safety, protection), permanence (peace, sustainability).

There are many ways that CED initiatives can address the broad spectrum of human needs—social, physical and personal—within a community. Personal development and community development can be integrated into the process of economic revitalization. *How* we organize to meet people's needs for shelter, food, safety, is often more crucial than the end product. In Toronto, a group of homeless people organized to design and build their own shelter in an abandoned warehouse. The project is called Street City. It is a small "town" comprised of seventy-two residents (half women, half men), complete with houses, streets, trees and recreation areas, built inside the shell of a large abandoned Canada Post warehouse building which has had skylights added to its spanning the length of the ceiling. All of the people living at Street City have come from the streets. Security and privacy are primary concerns to residents, who set the rules in their own community and work out conflicts as they arise through a mediation process. They hold regular town hall meetings to decide on issues. (There are two mayors—one male, one female). Residents have started up their own small grocery store, banking service, maintenance service and recycling project. They even reach out to the broader community preparing a weekly dinner banquet open to all street people for a charge of $1.25. With the security of a place to call home and a mutual support network, residents can take the next step toward reintegrating into society. Some have gone back to school, others to a job. Some are working with other homeless people at a new Street City being planned elsewhere. Street City is an example of integrated development in that it not only provides needed shelter, but meets people's needs for belonging, security, income, participation in decision-making, and self-esteem.

Meeting the needs for personal wholeness and self-esteem is an essential ingredient to the economic revitalization of communities. Social change works from the inside-out, beginning with self-healing and self-growth which affects personal relationships and eventually transforms community relationships and the institutions of society. Building self-esteem is a personal development process, yet a community plays a pivotal role by providing opportunities for self-growth through community-based literacy courses, abuse treatment, and various adult education programs. Most of all, changed social attitudes demonstrating respect for those who have been most devalued by society can help to validate the worth of the individual. Employment equity programs and consensus decision-making processes are some of the ways that society can validate the worth of every individual. Economic benefits flow from meeting people's needs for safety and needs for belonging. Crime and violence are the products of social alienation. Safety and protection are best achieved in small communities where people know and trust one another. When people feel ownership of a neighbourhood and bond together as a community, crime and vandalism decreases. The crime rate in the Logan community in Winnipeg's inner-city dropped dramatically since residents set up a community-run, self-sustaining housing project. The project also has an active community centre with an aboriginal school, gymnasium, and local newspaper. Everybody in the small community of 250 people knows each other. The crime rate in the Logan community is one-thirtieth that of the immediate adjacent areas.

Becoming Ecologically Sustainable

A healthy community, like a healthy person, is made up of many different interrelated parts or sub-systems, all working together and mutually reinforcing one another for the well being of the whole. Development needs to be directed toward achieving greater self-reliance and autonomy for a community but is not an isolated activity. Every development impacts on other social and natural systems because all things, from the individual to the community to the region and upward, are interconnected. They are both wholes unto themselves and parts of a greater whole. Sustainable CED calls for an ecological consciousness which views development as fitting harmoniously within the larger social and natural eco-system of which it is a part.

Jane Jacobs (1985) uses the term organized complexity to describe the life and process of a city; every urban issue is a complex of variables, all of which are interconnected. How we deal with the relationship between the various parts is crucial in developing healthy cities and neighbourhoods. The Royal Commission on the Future of the Toronto Waterfront (Crombie, 1992) began as an inquiry into a specific area of the city but soon grew into a study of the entire Greater Toronto bioregion, stretching 40 miles east and west of Toronto and inland 30 miles. This area is fed by 16 rivers whose waters eventually end up in the Toronto harbour. It became impossible to separate the lakefront from the rivers flowing into it or from the human activities which affect the water's quality. The Commission recommended an eco-system approach to planning which would bring together 30 municipalities and 6 regions included in the watershed to work in partnership for the sake of the whole. The hope is to transcend narrow interests in dealing with the issues of environmental stress—water and sewer systems, dispersed settlement patterns, lack of landfill sites, consumer waste, commuter use of automobiles, and pollution by 600 industries. What does all this have to do with the development of particular communities? Everything. Environmental degradation is location specific and directly affects the health and future of people who make up a community. As a problem of organized complexity it must be dealt with at the community level and by direct dealings with other communities, by making horizontal connections between all of the interrelated parts of the problem. Top-down legislation is not enough. Each community must come to share a common understanding of their part in the greater eco-system, a task that requires building ecological consciousness.

The pressing issue in the field of sustainable development is how to create an economy which will meet the needs of people yet not harm the environment. The goal of economic self-reliance for communities and surrounding regions is a sustainable development strategy; by producing what is consumed and consuming what is produced, the distances that goods must travel to market is reduced, eliminating wasted energy and pollution. A self-reliant economy, which tries to extract the maximum amount of work out of existing resources, helps to reduce the amount of material waste and pollution released into the biosphere. Care of the environment has opened up a vast new area for business opportunity. The environmental industry is the fastest growing industry in Western Canada; two hundred new enterprises have started up in the last two years, generating over $200 million a year in new wealth, and employing an average of six persons each. Community-based businesses dealing with recycling, conservation, and environmental technologies help to build a more balanced relationship between the social and the natural world.

Making linkages between city and country, between food producers and food consumers, is another focus for CED initiatives. The food industry, once highly diversified and localized, has become global in size, uniform in content, and is under the control of a few giant transnational companies. Industrial farming has replaced the family farm and has promoted unsustainable agricultural practices including dependence on herbicides, insecticides, chemical preservatives, and monoculture farming.

Community shared agriculture (CSA) is a step toward healing the relationship between people and the land, between farm producers and urban consumers. This is a partnership model whereby urban families collectively purchase shares in a local farm operation. The money pays for farmers to grow organic vegetables which are harvested and divided up among the community membership. CSA enables the small farmer to raise capital early in the season without having to take out a bank loan. The community receives a steady supply of organic vegetables during growing season. Producers and consumers share directly in the real costs and the real risks of food production. In 1992, a group in Winnipeg initiated a CSA project called Shared Farmer. For a payment of $140, urban consumers received a $14 basket of fresh, chemical-free produce once a week for ten weeks delivered to neighbourhood depots in the city. In the first year over two hundred families joined the program. CSA is expanding. More families and farmers joined in 1993. Local farmers are guaranteed a local market for their product and can bypass the food chain intermediaries such as large wholesalers and multinational retailers. One of the CSA farmers donated ten acres of his 1000 acre farm to a group of refugees from El Salvador who have been living in the city on social assistance. The ten men, after learning the skills of market gardening on the prairies, will move out to the farm and participate in the Shared Farming program growing organic food for city dwellers.

Building a Community Culture

Communities are able to sustain themselves over generations on the basis of a common identity, purpose, and culture that binds people together. A community identity is shaped by its local traditions, the way people express themselves in art, a geographic landscape, shared experiences of the past, and people's dreams and hopes for a future. These items cannot be bought or manufactured but they can be nurtured by development. Culture is the spirit and binding force that keeps communities alive even in the face of economic hardship and disaster. The task of building and preserving a community-based culture is a daunting one given the powerful forces of mass culture and globalization which are working to erase local culture from our memories and imaginations. As the Holiday Inn ad states, "You can travel 'round the globe and never leave home." Home has come to mean a place that is both everywhere and nowhere, defined by mass media and mass consumption—shopping malls with chain stores, MacDonald's arches, and amorphous suburbs. The shift from understanding home as a special place of origin where we live, work, belong, and feel a sense of identity and social responsibility, to the perception of home as a world class city is the result of powerful economic forces producing cultural uniformity. A community culture evolves out of the collective memory of social experiences over time. It is a process of unfolding and continuity that grows out of history. Four areas to be considered in building a community culture are a community's social history, natural history, cultural and ethnic groups, and the ways that people interact.

The social history of a community is often embodied in many of the older neighbourhoods of a city or town. Heritage conservation is a development activity which makes the past a living part of a community's identity and is an effective tool to revitalize older inner-city neighbourhoods. The saving of the Milton Park community in Montreal was a heritage restoration project that renovated and upgraded 600 units of housing. The Samuel and Saidye

Bronfman Family Foundation established an Urban Issues Program in 1992 based on the following four principles: supporting revitalized communities; making a living history; uniting heritage and community development; and putting local culture before global uniformity. The program gives grants to community groups for community heritage initiatives which link heritage with environment, governance, economy and community.

Heritage preservation is more than buildings. It can mean preserving a way of life for a community. Toronto's Kensington market covers several city blocks and attracts visitors to its crowded narrow streets filled with stalls and exotic smells. It is a cultural heritage resource for the city, an expression of the multiethnic community which lives in the area. Discovering and developing what is unique and particular about each neighbourhood and town both creates a sense of continuity and meaning to place and creates spaces which are of special interest to outsiders.

Local heritage is a major economic stimulant for a community. Cultural tourism is the largest growth sector of the tourist industry—people are travelling in order to learn about other people and places. The market exchange district in downtown Winnipeg has the best North American collection of turn-of-the-century, terra-cotta, and cut stone buildings. It is a valuable economic and heritage resource for the city. Many of the old buildings stand vacant and deteriorating although they are protected from demolition by legislation. City and provincial governments could, as part of an economic revitalization strategy, fill the buildings with their own offices instead of renting accommodations elsewhere.

One of the keys to building community identity is to discover and celebrate the inherent and historic meaning of special places. Every community has these. Besides the Exchange District, Winnipeg has the Forks, a one hundred acre piece of land in the heart of the city where the Assiniboine River meets the Red River. The site was publicly reclaimed from the CNR in 1989. The Forks is a special place imbued with natural beauty, symbolic meaning, and historic significance. The Forks is the birthplace of Western Canada, the site of five forts, Hudson's Bay Trading post, and meeting place for aboriginal people for over 6000 years. Different parcels are owned by Parks Canada, The Forks Renewal Corporation (FRC), and the City of Winnipeg. But how will it be developed? The FRC has a mandate requiring it to become financially self-supporting from revenues generated on the site, thereby suggesting extensive development. It is promoting commercial, recreational, office, and housing development. A hockey arena on the city-owned parcel is supported by a number of politicians. Citizens of Winnipeg have spoken against overdeveloping the site. The walkway along the river is what people like best about the Forks. The open undeveloped spaces are used to hold a variety of popular local festivals including the Children's Festival, Folklorama, Canada Games, and Festival du Voyageur. These open green spaces are in danger of being lost if the site is filled with new buildings, parking lots, and roads. A Coalition to Preserve the Forks was formed to protect the site for use as a unique cultural and historic park, a development concept which would compliment existing struggling businesses in the downtown rather than compete with them. A sustainable CED strategy must look at the whole economic picture. Winnipeg has a no-growth economy. Pushing businesses from one part of the city to another will not create new wealth, but can create economic instability. On the other hand, the Forks, as a cultural and historic park, provides an opportunity to develop something that is especially unique to its particular location, and would attract people from everywhere.

The natural history of a place is important in shaping a community's identity. People are attached to the natural features of their communities— the particular trees, rivers, birds, landscape and climate. Many of these have been destroyed by developments which block access to lakes and rivers, block out sunlight, and divert streams into underground sewers. CED initiatives can be tied into natural restoration projects, such as cleaning up rivers, restoring old creek beds, or community tree planting. Sudbury, as part of its reclamation project to restore the natural environment damaged from years of pollution, held community picnics where citizens participated in planting greenery. Winnipeg's largest remaining urban elm forest in North America is threatened by encroaching Dutch elm disease. A citizen's Coalition to Save the Elms formed a first-time-ever environmental partnership with the City, Province, and Federal government and was awarded government funding to establish a citizen forester movement. In addition, a program was set up to train and employ 64 welfare recipients to work at preventing the spread of Dutch elm disease.

Local culture is also defined by the diversity of cultural groups in a community. Canada is a pluralistic society; individuals may belong to several cultural groups at once—women's groups, ethnic groups, arts groups. Community life is enriched by cross-cultural diversity at the grassroots level. CED initiatives targeted for specific cultures, such as native or women's cultures, both help that group to develop and benefit the wider community—neighbourhoods improve, people begin to use their skills and knowledge to better themselves and society, and crime decreases. Support of local arts groups is another way to integrate community economic development with enriching a community's cultural life and spirit. The cultural industries have a high return on investment and an immediate financial impact on a community. Employment in the arts over a 20 year period in Canada grew to 346,000 generating a direct yearly return to the federal treasury of $650 million and an annual return to the Canadian economy of $17 billion. In Winnipeg, 75% of grants received by the arts community were returned in various forms of taxation; 900 new jobs were created as well as a spin-off wealth for the economy. Werrier (1993) estimates that 120 jobs are created for every $1 million in grants to the arts.

Sharing common experiences and meaningful human interaction within a community is necessary for a local culture to develop. People need to have reasons to get together, to meet, to work, and to do battle together. Community initiatives bring a focus to a neighbourhood. They can include almost anything—publishing a community newspaper, planting a community garden, writing the history of a neighbourhood, staging a community festival, taking on a community recycling project, organizing to save a park or build housing. People's fear of others decreases as they spend time together. A goal of CED should be to promote and restore community as the primary producer of culture. In the words of Lewis Mumford,

> We must create in every region people who will ... know in detail where they live and how they live: they will be united by a common feeling for their landscape, their literature and language, their local ways, and out of their own self-respect they will have a sympathetic understanding with other regions and different local peculiarities. They will be actively interested in the form and culture of their locality, which means their community and their own personalities. Such people will contribute to our land planning, our industry planning, our community planning, the authority of their own understanding and the pressure of their own desires (1938, p.386).

Conclusion

An underlying framework for CED is based on the five theme areas of self-reliance, community control, individual needs, ecological sustainability, and local culture. Together these provide an integrated development model aimed at revitalizing and building sustainable communities. The themes are interrelated. A self reliant economy relies on local markets, and is responsive to the needs of individuals in a community. Localized production and consumption reduces long distance transport of goods which is more ecological in terms of energy use and reducing pollution. A community culture, grounded in the appreciation of a particular landscape and history of a place, is a protector of local environments. As people come to know and trust each other, they are drawn into more direct dealings; this adds to the safety and security of a neighbourhood and builds community culture.

Despite common components, CED remains pluralistic in its approach due to the particular needs and traditions of different communities. The emphasis in rural areas has tended to be on economic regeneration, with a strong business and commercial orientation with less attention placed on social goals or building community support systems. CED has a more comprehensive social-political-economic focus in urban neighbourhoods where economic deterioration is inseparable from problems of chronic poverty, substandard living conditions, and social decay. Urban CED is seen as a tool for personal and community empowerment with housing often the focus for developing a community economic base.

CED in rural areas tends to be more institutionalized and narrowly defined than in the urban context, perhaps because of its close association with government programs such as Community Futures, Grow Bonds, Local Economic Development Corporations and Community Round Tables. By contrast, CED in the city is more ad hoc, less defined, and there are fewer government programs to support CED activities. What exists in urban areas is a diversity of local projects, most of which are not defined as CED but which, nonetheless, are critical to the social and economic regeneration of poorer neighbourhoods. The project by project orientation of development in urban centres results in splintering among many special interest groups, each competing for the same small amount of dollars. A comprehensive strategy is needed to tie together existing urban community initiatives under a common goal or vision and to develop programs to guide, support, and promote new projects aimed at building viable, healthy, and sustainable communities.

8

Scope and Characteristics of CED: Summary, Policy Implications and Research Needs

Richard Nutter and Michael McKnight

ommunity economic development (CED) is a strategy for dealing with some of the social and economic problems facing Canada today. The foundation of CED is combining social and economic elements. This is often a difficult union. Frequently, supporters of economic development and supporters of social development have viewed each other with suspicion. The explicit combination of economic and social development makes CED an attractive alternative to single focus models of intervention for addressing poverty and powerlessness in communities that are socially and economically underdeveloped.

But the dual focus is also problematic. In Canada, the right wing corporate elite has sought to represent economic interests while social initiatives have been championed by grass roots left wing community organizations. The relationship has become increasing adversarial, not collaborative. The business community does not have a strong record of social responsibility and often follows Milton Friedman's dictum that " ... there is one and only one social responsibility of business—to use its resources and engage in activities designed to increase its profits so long as it stays within the rules of the game, which is to say, engages in open and free competition, without deception or fraud" (1962, p.133). This latter qualification seems more unction than practice.

Canada is experiencing increasing unemployment, homelessness, and poverty. These trends cast doubt on past state attempts to address these issues. Public programs and expenditures over the last 35 years have focused on decreasing individual strategies such as employment training and individual economic assistance on the one hand, and increasing tax, capital, and debt grants to business for projects, both mega and small, on the other. For example, Family Allowance has dwindled from a significant to an insignificant proportion of most families' income. Changes in tax law have resulted in dramatic decreases in the proportions of government revenues paid by business and equally dramatic increases in the proportion of government revenues resulting from individual income taxes and consumer sales taxes. This combination has not been successful. Growing costs and growing dissatisfaction may foreshadow the acceptance of different approaches to these problems. Strategies that encourage economic and social forces to work together towards affordable, effective, sustainable enterprises that encompass the needs and culture of the community seem likely candidates for acceptance.

Themes

The three chapters in this section deal with the scope and characteristics of CED from a Canadian perspective. The range of discussion emphasizes the diversity of debate in attempting to define and describe this model of community vitalization. Tim O'Neill generally focuses on the economic factors of CED, while Mike Lewis includes social factors in describing four models of CED. Marcia Nozick adopts a more holistic view of human social functioning in her discussion of CED. In doing this she views the money economy as one of many social phenomena that may be used to promote individual and collective well-being.

Mike Lewis examines CED through the description of four CED models and the extent to which each or a combination of them are operating in rural, urban, and aboriginal communities. He identifies four ingredients that must be present for CED to succeed: (a) debt money to loan to local business; (b) equity money to invest in local businesses; (c) planning and research including regional economic analysis, strategic planning, and research specific to the mission; and (d) training for human resource development and organizational capacity-building. Equity growth emphasizes building equity that can be used by community organizations for reinvestment. Loan and technical assistance emphasizes loans and loan guarantees to assist community entrepreneurs. Human resource development or employment development focuses on human resource planning and development along with recruitment of community businesses to create new job opportunities. Planning and advisory services place an emphasis on providing planning and technical assistance to a defined membership or geographic area. These approaches all include the community as an important element. However, Lewis' discussion of the community does not extend beyond considerations that he ties to the economy. He emphasizes job creation and other economic indicators as evidence of success. The paper concludes with examples of each model highlighting the economic benefits of each.

Tim O'Neill emphasizes economic over social factors in CED. O'Neill compares local economic development and regional economic development to CED; " ... all relate to economic development in a spatial context and, in all three, there is interaction with social development (even if unintentional).

Communities may be defined by geographic boundaries and are linked by common employment activity, cultural heritage, social interests and norms, and/or religious beliefs."

O'Neill emphasizes three points in defining economic development. First, it is conventional to distinguish between economic growth and economic development that includes economic growth. Second, economic development results in more than "improvement in economic elements" but also results in improvement in quality of life (infant mortality rates decline, air and water pollution levels decrease, access to political institutions increase, and so forth). Therefore, "social indicators should complement economic ones, rather than restating them in another form." Third, the process of building and maintaining CED is as important as the results it achieves.

O'Neill places greater importance on economic principles than social development concepts although he recognizes a social component in his discussion of CED. He views economic development as a cause of social change rather than as a result of social change. Employment creation and wealth are among the key objectives or goals of this type of development, although the distribution of profits or gains from CED is, in principle, different from the distribution of profits and gains from private sector ventures. In both cases, measures of success should focus primarily on economic indicators. O'Neill states that, "Social investment should complement or underpin a broader array of economic efforts but should not supplant them." Community autonomy in economic decision making is not a goal of CED, and the level to which it can be achieved through collective efforts in a community is questionable. The uniqueness and consequently the benefit of community involvement in economic initiatives is found in elements of collective risk-taking on investment, innovation, and creativity in pursuing opportunities.

This contrasts with Marcia Nozick's view of community autonomy as essential to CED. "The starting and end point for CED is to develop vital, regenerative communities which can sustain themselves over time and which have the capacity to meet the needs of their present and future generations—in other words, to build sustainable communities." She lists five major components for an integrated CED strategy: creating local wealth through self-reliance; gaining community control over land, capital, industry, and planning; meeting the needs of individuals; becoming ecologically sustainable; and building a community culture. The economic foundation of Nozick's approach is developing wealth from within communities and ensuring that this wealth is kept in the community, thereby assuring sustainability. Nozick promotes CED as a model of (a) cooperation among individuals and community self-reliance; (b) as diversity of enterprise within a community to produce most of the community's needs; and (c) mutually beneficial, non-exploitative, trade relations between communities. Nozick describes a variety of money and barter based ways to enhance the functioning of communities and consequently the functioning of persons who live in those communities. Most of the methods proposed by Nozick either reduce the need for money capital or restrict the mobility of money capital, both of which should result in more stable communities.

A Definition of CED

These three chapters illustrate that a range of perspectives on CED exist within the Canadian context. From one perspective, the challenge facing supporters of CED is to bridge the historic separation of social and economic interests. But O'Neill implies that this may be a false dichotomy when he cautions that social indicators should complement economic indicators, not merely restate them. None-the-less, the economy has been reified to such an extent that many practitioners, researchers, policy analysts, and decision makers view the economy as separate from other social phenomena. Among these three authors, Nozick places the least emphasis upon the formal economy.

There is a confounding of conceptual and social class distinctions. The economy is for the affluent. Social development, clearly second best, is for the poor. Notions that social development may be good for the affluent and that the poor may be key stakeholders and decision makers in the economy are not standard private radio fare, not even mainstream CBC. These confusions may contribute to the difficulty in defining CED. We offer this definition of CED:

> a strategy for dealing with the problems of poor people, powerless people, and underdeveloped communities. As an intervention strategy in an under-developed community, CED does not seek to make the existing conditions in the community more bearable. Instead, CED seeks to change the structure of the community and build permanent institutions within a community. As a result, the community begins to play a more active role vis-à-vis the institutions outside the community, and the residents of the community become more active in the control of the community's resources.

This definition recognizes the use of economic tools to develop sustainable community resources that address problems of poverty and impoverishment. This is a statement of targets and of goals, not a statement of method. It is like a primitive definition of counselling—helping people solve their problems and in the process helping them learn how to solve similar problems in the future. This definition of CED reflects a social class bias and raises the question of whether CED is relevant once a community becomes affluent? Does economic cooperation within communities lead to prosperity, to be replaced by economic competitiveness, which in turn will produce groups of disadvantaged and marginalized persons who will then cooperate to attain prosperity, which will precipitate another cycle of competition and decline? In general, CED is done in Canada by creating and supporting institutions that are owned and controlled by the community itself, but usually started and initially supported with external, government, funding.

Ten characteristics should be present in community economic development. CED should:

1. pursue economic development in ways that increase community self-reliance;

2. pursue economic development in ways that empower people;

3. pursue economic development that is sustainable;

4. pursue economic development that is diversified;

5. seek to enhance local capacity to plan, design, control, manage, and evaluate initiatives aimed at vitalizing the community;

6. include economic, social, ecological, and cultural development as part of a comprehensive holistic development strategy for the community;

7. organize inclusively, not exclusively, to enable disadvantaged and disempowered groups in the community to create partnerships, coalitions, alliances, and joint ventures with others interested in a sustainable future for the community;

8. ensure that benefits accrue directly to the community at large rather than to individuals within the community;

9. arise from underdevelopment and marginalization; and

10. favour medium and longer-term approaches over short-term quick fixes typical of job creation schemes in Canada.

The first five of these characteristics tend to define goals more than process. Characteristics six through eight contain more process direction but also include goals. Characteristics nine and ten describe conditions or process for CED.

Research Agenda

The lack of systematic, well documented information regarding CED is a major obstacle to documenting the success of CED. This lack of systematic evidence is not surprising given the absence of a clear consensual definition and the conceptual immaturity this absence reflects. None-the-less five research priorities can be identified.

1. *Identification and systematic review of CED practice models and goals.* Goals and practice must be clearly and separately specified. Different CED initiates may pursue the same goals using different practices. In other instances, the same practices may be used to pursue different goals. It is almost certain that the nature of the community, the practice, and the goal will interact. Therefore it is

unlikely that one best practice should be used in all communities to achieve a particular goal. Similarly, because CED seeks to respect the diversity of cultures in different communities, there is not likely to be one set of best goals.

The group comparison approaches to social science research are unlikely to be very fruitful. Instead, it will be important to develop a more sophisticated level of conceptualization regarding the resources, activities, and results that characterize CED, and the hypotheses that link these elements together.

The expert opinions of CED practitioners will be invaluable starting points for these "small theories" (Lipsey, 1993). More rigorous theoretical descriptions of CED will be required before systematic data gathering efforts can progress beyond individual case descriptions. This is not to say that individual case descriptions are not a necessary first step. It is to say that their primary value is to suggest relationships that may be important, not to test the importance of the relationships suggested. The confirmation or disconfirmation of the importance of relationships between resources, activities, and results will await systematic replications based on the hypotheses generated from case studies. Basing replications on clearly articulated theory should ensure that data appropriate to testing the theory is gathered. It should also ensure that data will be gathered to support appropriate decision-making by those involved in the CED initiatives.

One goal of this research will be to increase CED's credibility and legitimacy among those sectors of society whose support will facilitate the appropriate use of CED (e.g., financial communities, policy makers, funders, etc.). Research should include specific studies of the distinct nature of urban and rural examples of CED. The information should be stored in a database that is readily available to all regions of Canada and internationally.

2. *Identification of public policies and practices supporting successful CED.* As levels of government reduce grant spending and strive to eliminate overlapping services and responsibilities, supporters and practitioners of CED need to identify those public policies and support that have affected CED project success. Research should initially target examples of cooperative government support that reflect a commitment of effective and efficient support of CED. Studies should include inter-departmental organizational issues as well as the identification of gaps or weaknesses in current social and economic policy at all levels of government. Research should

include studying policies of financial institutions as they relate to funding CED projects.

3. *Evaluation of community economic development.* One continuing criticism of community economic development by mainstream social and economic stakeholders is the lack of a comprehensive and systematic evaluation of CED models. The development of strong conceptual frameworks has not kept pace with the growth of practice. Conceptual frameworks and the gathering of systematic data that support them are crucial for the adoption of CED in mainstream policy agendas. Good conceptual frameworks must be developed to provide the bases for developing evaluation tools and indicators specifically designed to measure the resources, activities, and results of CED practices.

The results of high quality evaluation may be particularly important to garner support for CED. Basic to all CED is the long-term retention of capital in communities. This is most often done through broad-based local ownership and diversification, often through local substitution for formerly imported goods and services. These directions will not be greeted warmly by policy analyst advocates of multi-national corporate world competitiveness.

4. *The training of community economic practitioners.* The need to train new practitioners follows the development of a strong knowledge base and methods of evaluation. The ultimate success of CED will to some extent depend on increasing the number and skill of those involved in policy, program development, and practice. There are a number of research questions related to training: What, is the best practice content? How should CED practice be taught? Who should deliver CED practice training and education?

5. *Development of promotional strategies, networks, and information.* Information must be disseminated more extensively to expand the knowledge, acceptance, support, and utilization of CED. Descriptions, models, and success stories must be designed for different audiences (practitioners, policy and decision-makers, educators, researchers, general public, and so forth). CED information must be marketed extensively to make the strategy more visible and part of the public agenda. This information must be current, relevant, and understandable. Research is required to learn the most effective methods for promoting CED.

PART 3

ENVIRONMENTS CONDUCIVE TO EFFECTIVE COMMUNITY DEVELOPMENT

9

Community Economic Development Revisited: The Preconditions for Success

Mario Polèse

> *... the snake oil vendors in the development crowd are selling illusions, which is a cruel game* (Marcel Côté, 1992, p.198).

In February 1981, William J. Coffey and I hosted a two day brainstorming session (Coffey & Polèse, 1982) bringing together experts from across Canada, on the subject of local or community economic development. The designations local and community economic development are used as synonyms throughout this chapter. The concept sparked much hope, as it still does. What was this beast, we were asked. Could community economic development provide an alternative to the tried and tired regional development policies of the day? Is the answer to the question any clearer now than it was twelve years ago? Have we really discovered a new set of policy tools for the economic development of communities? Or, have we simply succeeded in putting new tags and justifications on old development strategies and ventures?

Within the larger question are three sub-questions. First, what is the role of the community in local economic development? Second, what precisely makes CED initiatives different from more conventional economic development policies or business ventures? Third, are the pre-conditions for CED success different from those of more conventional business ventures? I shall attempt to answer these questions by drawing on the literature and experience. In the latter part of this essay, I shall posit a hypothetical economic development initiative, analyze the factors underlying its success (or failure), and compare it with more conventional ventures.

Community as an Asset

The Economic Value of Community

The economic case for community is nicely summarized by Bolton (1992), "sense of place and local identity ... (are) an important form of intangible capital that have positive externalities" (p.185). The emphasis on community as an intangible factor of production is a supply-side approach, analogous to the emphasis on agglomeration economies or entrepreneurship; the intangible factor is no easier to define. Some economists would say we are chasing a heffalump (Kilby, 1971), the mythical animal originally conjured up by A.A. Milne. Martin observes that "the concept of the...entrepreneur ... corresponds to an unidentifiable residual ... it is tautological ..." (1987, p.64) and he is not entirely wrong. If you succeed, you have it by definition, that magic sense of entrepreneurship, or of community. We are continually searching for that secret ingredient, that special something, which makes some societies work, while others fail.

Various French-speaking European authors have stressed the economic value of *milieu* (most notably Maillat 1990, 1992). The French word *communauté* does not have the utopian ring of community. Its use is often utilitarian as in *Commauté urbaine de Montréal* (the Montreal Urban Community), while the adjective *communautaire* has a social-activist cum social-welfare connotation not generally associated with the English equivalent. Lemelin and Morin (1991) analyze the Montreal experience and use the term *local et communaitaire*, but refer equally to the concepts of intangible assets and factors of production. Why this foray into translation? Quite simply to stress that we are prisoners of language, and should be aware of it when using a culture-laden term such as community, which for many of its users reflects an ideal as much a concept.

Returning to the economic value of community or *milieu* as an intangible asset, Maillat (1992) suggests a definition not far removed from that of Bolton, "In so far as localities (*places*) offer logistical support essential to their development (in the form of externalities, proximity effects, etc. ...) it is in their (*private firm's*) every interest to invest in the integration and the betterment of their *milieu*" (p.3, *our translation*). Both Bolton and Maillat define the value of community in terms of greater security and the reduction of uncertainty. The *milieu* is seen as a collective vehicle, via a myriad of contacts (both formal and informal) and shared values and interests, for reducing information costs and transaction costs. This is economics short-hand for the cost of making deals and negotiating cooperative arrangements. Or, as Bolton (1992, p.194) puts it, the returns to this valuable intangible asset are security, stable expectations, trust, familiarity of surroundings, and so forth; the opposite being malevolence, mistrust, crime, tension, etc. Both individuals and firms have an interest in fostering a viable and cooperative community, whether by investing in schooling, mutual business relationships, vocational training, network-building, or socially oriented initiatives. A functioning and healthy community is good for business. Long-term economic development, meaning innovation and the capacity to cope with change,* is impossible without some sense of community.

The question then becomes why do businesses and individuals not invest more in this intangible collective asset called community if it is so valuable? The first part of the answer is that they generally invest more than may be apparent. The number of community-based organizations in most places is striking—chambers of commerce, tourist promotion boards, the Red Feather, the Lions, local political party organizations, school boards, and so forth. Taxes paid to both local and higher levels of government are the most concrete sign of the value placed on collective security and welfare. The second part of the answer lies in the nature of the asset, community, which is, as economists say, a public good. It is difficult to privatize the benefits derived from it (you cannot exclude others from sharing in it) and the temptation to be a free rider is always there (Lemelin and Morin, 1991). Why should you do it if others will do it in any case? This is one of the reasons why taxation is coercive and not voluntary.

Unless the pay-off to the donor is clear, attempts to fund community-building initiatives can only take one of two paths: appealing to the (private) donor's civic-spirit and sense of duty, or convincing those in public service (elected or appointed) that this is a worthwhile cause. In more abstract economic language, the case for subsidizing community-building initiatives with public funds is that the marginal private benefits (to the individual or firm, of contributing) fall below the marginal benefits for society as a whole. Which is one of the reasons why taxation exists. The problem is that the social benefits are difficult to measure unless tied to clear objectives such as health, education, cleanliness, public safety or transportation. The public will generally not long support public expenditures whose objectives are too broad with little visible output.

Community Economic Development Initiatives

What distinguishes CED initiatives from more conventional ventures or public programs aimed at furthering the economic welfare of a given target group or place? Some authors (both English and French) use the term *local* development as a synonym. Both terms are generally used to designate strategies of economic development based on local initiatives, drawing their strength from the community rather than from the outside (Coffey, 1991;

---

* The emphasis on change and innovation is important. Economic development, defined as a sustained rise in real *per capita* income and welfare, requires both the local population and the local business community to constantly readapt to changing demand conditions and to new technologies. A sustained rise in productivity (and thus incomes) is impossible without innovation, both in the workplace and other social institutions. Maillat's emphasis on *milieu* grew out of his study of small Swiss watch-making towns which managed to survive (and prosper) despite a radical change in technology and tastes. The initial impact of the digital (Japanese) watch on the Swiss watch-making industry was devastating.

Coffey & Polèse, 1984, 1985; Pecqueur, 1989). Other terms such as grass-roots, boot-strap, endogenous or bottom-up development equally evoke a similar philosophy of how economic development can (or should) be promoted. The basic idea is always the same. The impetus for economic growth should come from inside the community, not from far-away bureaucrats or from outside firms. Local development, in its ideal form, means that the community stands on its own feet, beholden to no outside force for charity or economic assistance. In principle, it means fostering local initiative and helping local businesses rather than chasing foreign investments.

But how does one go about fostering local initiative and harnessing the collective resources and strengths of the community to further economic development? Clearly no single recipe exists. Perry (1987), a passionate advocate of community development corporations (CDCs), suggests an eclectic mix of social activism, proselytism, civic boosterism, new-age optimism, organizational acumen and sound business advice, plus guidelines on how to lobby funding agencies, big business and various levels of government. Pecqueur (1989), who also provides a how to guide to CED, takes a more sober view. After paying homage to the more utopian aspects of the local development ideal, but recognizing the economic value of a sense of community (in French, words such as *partenariat, synergie* and *concertation* all convey a sense of cohesion and economic purpose), Pecqueur clearly has doubts as to the wisdom of higher levels of government  subsidizing CDCs or other comnunity-based economic initiatives. Why should the financial risks taken by a CDC (lending to a young entrepreneur at below market rates, for example) be transferred to the rest of society? Does this not go against the very essence of the ideal of local responsibility and grass-roots development?

Activities falling under the heading of community economic development will differ greatly from nation to nation (and from case to case) because perceived needs will differ and public programs will be differently defined from place to place. Francophone European authors appear to be less attracted by the idea of nationally financed CDCs, or local development organizations (LDOs) as the Economic Council of Canada prefers to call them (1990). The institutional culture in some European nations is more conducive to cooperative ventures initiated by the private sector, which tells us something about the functioning of North American economies. Business-labour and business-banker relations are very different in different countries, as well as worker training and worker apprenticeship programs, all which will affect the manner in which community development initiatives will be defined. Wolman and Stoker (1992), referring to the U.K. experience, note that the traditions of local government finance provide few fiscal incentives for local authorities to engage in economic development activity; senior government aid programs define what initiatives can or cannot be financed and, thus, define in large part what community organizations do. Put differently, national programs are being delivered through different local vehicles, with varying degrees of local flexibility. The U.S. Urban Development Action Grant Program (UDAG) is another good example (Rich, 1992).

The performance of Canadian LDOs is difficult to evaluate because they are so diverse in terms of organization, setting, and goals. Native bands, rural cooperatives, anti-poverty groups, and neighbourhood self-help associations have all been considered LDOs. The difficulty in evaluating local development efforts has been a major factor underlying the reluctance of government agencies to provide financial support (Coffey, 1991). Wiewel and Hall (1992), in their review of U.K. and U.S. local development literature, deplore the absence of strong quantitative studies. The gamut of activities (especially in the U.S.) engaged in by LDOs or similar groups goes far beyond simply fostering local entrepreneurship and includes funding of convention centers, hotels, office developments, and industrial parks, not to mention a host of financial perks, advice, and incentives for prospective investors, including outside investors (Pagano & Bowman, 1992; Rich, 1992). Many U.S. local development organizations (often tied to the municipality) appear to devote considerable effort to attracting large outside investors, especially when faced with the hard reality of major plant closures and massive layoffs. And who can fault them? But, this is far from the ideal of grass-roots self-reliance and fostering local entrepreneurship.

Other groups specialize in education, training, and job search for their target population (Ranney & Betancur, 1992). The objectives of many urban LDOs are almost the opposite of local job creation and local entrepreneurship; their primary aim is to get people to the jobs, rather than jobs to the people. Some groups are into property development or housing; others such as the two Quebec examples cited by Julien (1991), specialize in enterprise zones, incubators, and technological parks in the hope of setting off a virtual cycle of information, innovation, and local entrepreneurship. In Montreal, CREESOM (Comité de relance économique de l'Est de Montréal) and RESO (Regroupement pour la relance économique et sociale de sud-ouest de Montréal), two well-publicized local examples of active CED organizations during the early 1990s, were engaged in a broad spectrum of initiatives, ranging from business counselling, small-business promotion, networking, lobbying, and negotiating with local employers and unions to working together with other levels of government to deliver programs such as the management of business parks, preparing fiscal incentive packages, attracting venture capital, and structuring worker retraining and placement schemes (Boisvert, 1993).

In short, CED initiatives cover the total spectrum of economic development programs. The actual programs are, in general, not all that different from what has been tried before, but with perhaps somewhat more emphasis on promoting local small business and less on attracting large outside firms. Bennington and Geddes (1992), although ideologically close to the community-building ideal and what may be called alternative left-wing thinking, sum up the situation best when they conclude that "retrospective evaluation of some of the new ... economic development strategies has sometimes suggested that their distinctiveness lay more in their rhetoric than in their actual practice" (p.454).

How to Measure Success: Avoiding the Map Trap

CED has today achieved motherhood status. If the idea was ever rooted in anti-establishmentism, such is no longer the case. More cynical souls would say the ideal has been co-opted. The Mulroney government's appointed *Steering Group on Prosperity*, (1992), probably as good a reflection as any of current orthodoxy, identifies one of the challenges facing Canada as "to recognize the important role played by local economic development groups in promoting prosperity at the community level" and goes on to recommend that Canada "ensure appropriate tools are available to community economic development groups ..." (p.60).

We may accept the premise that locally sponsored development is desirable and that local entrepreneurship is a good thing. The very foundation of our economic system depends on local initiative. The left and the right have found common ground here, even though more ideologically inspired observers would undoubtedly be loath to admit it. Differences are often a matter of packaging. The left inclined person will often couch an initiative in references to alternative development models and community solidarity, with perhaps a few arrows aimed at big business and multinationals. The more right inclined person will most probably welcome the same initiative with references to the importance of self-reliance and entrepreneurship, with perhaps a few negative remarks directed at unproductive welfare programs and big government.

Positing a Community Economic Development Initiative

Let us assume CED initiative, to be called the CCAP, is to be a locally launched computer components assembly plant which will employ two hundred recently laid-off workers (victims of a plant closure) and will be managed by two young local entrepreneurs beholden to a community-based board of directors. Ownership and risks are shared among various members of the community. The majority of financing is provided by a locally developed package, including contributions from local labour unions and credit unions. The local credit union will provide a substantial commercial loan, slightly below the market rate. The credit union judges this to be a sound business decision since many of its mortgage loans are held by the workers to be re-employed by the plant. The labour union representing the employees of the recently closed plant promises to purchase a substantial portion of voting shares via its accumulated pension fund, plus promising to respect a three year wage freeze. The centrepiece of the community effort is a locally subscribed corporate stock issue, making members of the community stake holders in the plant. The municipality has equally done its part by promising the new plant a ten year holiday on real estate taxes. Finally, let us assume that the local LDO, with strong representation on the CCAP board of directors, was a major actor in the process through lobbying, bringing people together, advising and encouraging the two young entrepreneurs, and promoting the community stock issue.

Such a venture would most certainly be hailed as an example of a CED at work. Some might prefer to applaud it as an example of business-community partnership, partnership having equally attained a place of honour in the current pantheon of development buzz-words. The temptation to equate success with intentions, or with the nature of the initiative itself, is very great in the CED game. This is what we call the MAP trap (MAP, of course, refers to Motherhood and Apple Pie). Simply put, one must beware of assuming that there is a necessary relationship between the desirability of an outcome, its political and social acceptance, and its chances of success, although the former attributes may help. No one can be against partnership, community, and local development, but they do not, in and of themselves, guarantee success.

CED risks going the way of previous development prescriptions, such as the Department of Regional Economic Expansion growth poles and trickle-down effects if it does not go one step further in defining goals. The demise of these other efforts was largely attributed to their failure to live up the high expectations they called forth. There is little evidence that regional income disparities in Canada have significantly declined over the last three decades, nor that peripheral communities are doing all that much better. How will CED fare if the same diagnosis still holds in the year 2010?

The conditions for success must be defined in terms which go beyond good intentions and motherhood objectives such as community capacity-building, socio-economic improvement, entrepreneurship and job creation or partnership. This does not mean that such goals are not laudable. Put bluntly, the success of a community economic development initiative must ultimately be judged by its capacity to bring more money into the community than goes out. Any other project will eventually fail, unless continually subsidized by outside taxpayers. Any jobs created will be temporary, unless this criterion is met. In this respect, CED initiatives are subject to the same economic truths as conventional business ventures. It matters little whether business decisions (to hire, fire, invest, innovate, produce, and so forth) are motivated by the desire to help the community or to make a personal profit; payrolls must still be met, debts paid, and investors compensated. At this juncture the great ideological divide between those committed to community inspired ventures and those inclined to more individualistic conventional business ventures reappears. More cynical observers might say that the difference is entirely one of make-believe, rooted in puritanical distaste for ventures or persons whose publicly stated goal is to make money and turn a profit. Even businessmen will often invoke other goals in public, except when addressing stockholders or partners. Idealism, dictates that society be guided by motives other than profit; and so it should be. This is why governments, taxes, and laws exist, to regulate and civilize the market. The question remains nonetheless—what guidelines should a business venture (however labelled) follow if it is to succeed?

Workers will not be paid, loans not repaid, and invested savings lost, if the venture does not bring in more money than was put into it. Barring gifts and transfers from family members living elsewhere, money can only flow into the community from three sources: (a) outside taxpayers via (non-local) government expenditures in the community; (b) outside consumers who purchase the goods and services produced by the community or (c) outside investors and lenders. In general, c will only occur if b shows a good potential. We shall concentrate on b, the capacity of the community to initiate ventures which bring (consumer or investment) money into the area.

The Preconditions for Success

Pagano and Bowman (1992) identified two broad attributes which contributed to the success of local economic development initiatives—the economic health (or strength) of the community and the (low) level of political risk of the initiative. Chances of success are improved if the basic economic structure of the community is sound and if local governments are willing and able to support the project over the long haul. Lemelin and Morin (1991) make a similar point in their analysis of three Montreal LDOs. Without wishing to belittle the findings of these authors (among the few systematic studies of the issue) their conclusions are almost self-evident. Yet, they are illuminating in that they also suggest, if somewhat indirectly, that CED initiatives are subject to the same constraints as other ventures which rely on public support. What factors underlie the success of a business venture, staying with the hypothetical computer components assembly plant (CCAP initiative) as the point of reference? The classical factors of production, which are part of any economic activity, are land, labour, and capital. Less traditional factors of entrepreneurship, location, know how and technology, and community, are added to the classical factor.

Land. Land is generally not a significant variable in business decisions or costs with the exception of agriculture or location choices within urban areas. The real estate tax break given the CCAP initiative will give it additional, although marginal, financial breathing space. But would the community refuse a similar tax holiday to a wholly private local venture, or to a worthy outside venture, both equally bringing in jobs? Probably not.

Labour. The venture, whatever the origin or status, would have access to the same local labour pool. A wise manager, local or not, will seek to negotiate labour force arrangements which are to their mutual benefit and which maximize productivity, including worker training programs. The Japanese experience in the U.S. suggests that local managers are not necessarily any wiser than imported ones. In the CCAP initiative, we can only hope that the two local managers, the local LDO, and the workers involved have the necessary wisdom, organizational capacity, and knowledge to bring labour productivity up to necessary international standards.

Capital. Capital is not a major factor in predicting business success or failure. This now widely accepted judgement (see Côté, 1991) still continues to raise eyebrows. Neither LDOs nor businesspeople have any interest in saying that this is so, since both are always searching for more funds. The main challenge is not raising capital, but knowing what to do with it once you have it, and putting it to good use. Fortunes can be lost; bankers are not infallible. The cost of capital has been reduced for the CCAP initiative, thanks to the generosity of the local credit union and the local citizenry who subscribed to the stock issue. This will give the CCAP initiative an initial edge over competitors. But will this initial edge be sufficient to ensure CCAP profitability over the longer run? And would an alternative initiative (wholly private or outside initiated) have been able to raise capital at an equally favourable rate? The answer to both questions remains open. The CCAP venture, however, would not have taken-off without community support, which is an achievement in itself.

Entrepreneurship. This intangible factor is the presence of persons with the drive, personality, ambition, sense of mission, and willingness to take risks to make business ventures happen. They are the driving force behind the venture. Little will happen without local entrepreneurs. Local entrepreneurship is the bedrock upon which CED rests. If it occurs spontaneously little else need be said or done. The debate continues as to whether entrepreneurs can be created artificially through policy intervention, including LDOs, or whether such personality traits are randomly distributed among all populations. Entrepreneurship can only be deemed a success if the ventures upon which entrepreneurs embark are also a success. If not, the field will be strewn with failed would-be-entrepreneurs, not a very encouraging sight, and not one that will entice others to become entrepreneurs. The young will become entrepreneurs if successful role models exist, which gets back to the core question. In the case of the CCAP initiative, only time will tell if the two local entrepreneurs are successful, and if not, whether they will try again a second time. Nor do we know whether the two locals had the entrepreneurial drive in their blood, so to speak, whether they would have launched something else anyway, or whether it took the CCAP initiative to bring out their entrepreneurial talents. In any case, the CCAP initiative, like any venture, needs entrepreneurs to succeed. Much CED work, especially in the communities that most need it, is founded on the premise that entrepreneurs can and must be created. However, what if few entrepreneurs appear spontaneously; what if the problem is as much social and educational as economic? But entrepreneurs will not come forth as the chances of success appear meagre because entrepreneurship does not appear to offer a plausible alternative to other income-generating options, including emigration. The problem is especially acute in the most isolated and peripheral communities. There is no easy path out of this dilemma.

Location. This is perhaps the cruellest constraint of all. Location is not strictly speaking a factor of production, although no production can take place without it. Location is geographical location, measuring the distance (and associated costs) from markets, resources, information sources, labour pools, capital markets, services, and so forth. More theoretical economists or geographers will talk of spatial interaction costs, which can be viewed as a factor of production in that they imply an input, like labour or capital. We say the cruellest constraint because communities can do little to alter their location; road or communication links with the rest of the world are not generally a community responsibility. There is not much a town in Northern Manitoba or Eastern Quebec can do to change the fact that it is poorly located for most industrial ventures.

It is difficult to argue that community initiated ventures have an advantage in terms of this factor. On the contrary, this is the one point on which non-community initiated ventures hold a clear advantage. First, non-community initiated ventures (i.e., a multi-establishment firm choosing a site for its next investment) have the leeway to choose the best location, while community-committed funds must be spent in the community. This constraint turned out to be the main factor undermining the profitability of Quebec's C experiment in the 1970s and early 1980s. Secondly, and perhaps more importantly, inhabitants of a community are not necessarily the best judges of locational characteristics. What industrial commissioner does not think that his community is a prime business location? Even the most peripherally located communities manage to produce promotional maps showing them to be located at the centre of the universe. Such boosterism is entirely understandable, and community pride is laudable, but they are not necessarily the best foundations on which to build sound business decisions. We can only hope that an overdose community optimism does not lead to bad business decisions for the CCAP initiative.

Know-How and Technology. These are essential preconditions for success. Once a project is decided upon there is little reason to believe that the type of know-how required, including mastery of appropriate technologies, would differ significantly according to the status of the venture. Know-how, depending on the circumstances, covers everything from a solid knowledge of the market and subcontracting networks to knowing where to find the most recent trade information, keeping abreast of the latest gossip about competitors around the world, knowing who the top financial analysts in the field are, and knowing how to draw the greatest profit from the various fiscal and tax incentives available. Do locally-initiated ventures start with an advantage on this factor? Outsiders probably have the advantage. On the

CCAP initiative, it is unlikely that locals, however motivated, match the knowledge-base of large experienced outside firms. This does not mean that failure is inevitable; it simply means that those who believe in the CCAP initiative have to work twice or three times as hard as others to succeed and to overcome the initial advantage of outsiders. CCAP simply has to be better than others.

Outsiders hold an advantage over locals in terms of out-sourcing and subcontracting including the purchase of technology (patents, production licences). A community-based venture will be under pressure to purchase locally (such a constraint might even be written into its mandate), meaning that the non community-based firm will have a freer hand, and thus wider choice, in deciding where to purchase its inputs. The short-term multiplier effect on the local economy of locally-tied purchases will probably be positive but may endanger the long-term profitability of the community-based venture. In sum, the CCAP initiative may be subject to constraints not imposed on others.

The Role of Community. Success cannot be reduced to a mathematical equation. Much of what underlies the economic success of communities (nations, regions, peoples, etc) continues to defy easy explanations. Some of it probably has to do with the equally illusive anthropological concept called culture, the set of rules and traditions which govern cooperative behaviour among individuals, and which by definition must include a sense of community (and some would say exclusiveness). We have come full circle back to the economic value of community. Yet, much of what we have learned about the economic value of community is almost self-evident. Cooperation is better than conflict. Intelligent entrepreneurs are aware of this; no venture succeeds in isolation. Most ventures, irrespective of their status, will depend for their success on a network of friends and relations, and on some kind of group support, however defined. Conventional ventures also draw part of their strength from that complex set of relations called community. The chances of success of all ventures, including those not officially tagged as community-based initiatives, are much better in a cooperative socially cohesive environment.

Let us posit a second more conventional venture in the same community. Mrs Z, a native of the community, launches a venture together with an outside partner with funding provided by a loan from an outside bank. Mrs Z imports specialty fruits and vegetables, and starts up a small distribution and wholesaling operation, equipping a warehouse with the appropriate technologies, to service the community as well as adjacent localities. Thanks to her network of friends and business acquaintances within the community (and her reputation for honesty and efficiency) Mrs Z succeeds rapidly in getting her products on the shelves of most grocery stores. Coming back to the role of community as a business input, may we not say that this more conventional venture also draws on the community for its success? Where is the dividing line?

Let us draw the simulation to a close by proposing two possible scenarios. In the first scenario, which we might call the happy ending, the CCAP initiative has succeeded by the third year in turning a profit, with profits improving over time, and with a growing work force and market share, proof that CED works. In the second case, a less happy ending, CCAP continues to lose money despite efforts by the community to keep it afloat, with bankruptcy becoming an ever-increasing possibility. CCAP will eventually be bought-out and revived by a Korean multinational, much to the relief of community stake-holders, an example of another CED project that failed, only to be saved by outsiders. However, this ending should not be judged a total failure, since CCAP would not have taken off without community involvement.

We can also make the ending to the second scenario happier by adding that Mrs Z's venture eventually matures into the largest food wholesaling firm in the province, with branches in the U.S. and Mexico. Mrs Z is later being heralded as a model of local entrepreneurship. Eventually, Mrs Z's heirs will buy the CCAP plant from its Korean owners, bringing it back under local ownership. But what was the role of community in each case, and how were the preconditions for success different?

Conclusion

Can we say that the chances of success for the hypothetical community-based CCAP initiative were better than those for a more conventional business venture? Organized community involvement constitutes an advantage on some aspects, but not on others. Community-based initiatives may be at a disadvantage with respect to access to outside technology, freedom of procurement, and locational flexibility of direct investment decisions. These disadvantages may be offset by (initial) lower capital costs and community commitment, an intangible asset whose economic value is difficult to assess *a priori*. The trade-off between the two will vary from case to case. Community-based initiatives will hold an advantage for those ventures where the role of community is most important, compared to other factors of production. This will generally, but not always, mean smaller scale activities oriented to internal markets or activities with largely standardized technologies and informational needs. Community-based initiatives will probably be at a disadvantage for ventures directed at changing international markets and dependent on a diversified web of international suppliers and information networks as well as mobile capital and labour. However, the distinction between community-based and non community-based initiatives may often be largely artificial. In the end, the pre-conditions for success are largely the same for community-based and conventional business ventures.

10

Socio-Economic Policy: The Challenge of Global Trends

R. A. (Sandy) Lockhart

In so-called Western industrial culture there can be few subjects that so command public attention as much as economic development policy. The premonitions of financial institutions, the expectations of citizens, and the fate of those who seek public office are predicated to a singular degree upon the established lexicon of development indicators. But economic indicators, no less than the more complex real world environment that they purport to reveal, are as much conceptual as empirical artifacts. The development measured by rates of growth in the quantity of production and consumption assumes a very different kind of socio-economic environment than one that seeks to measure quality of life indicators, such as long-term economic security, social equity, cultural continuity, and environmental sustainability. As a consequence, factors chosen for measurement in the esoteric world of objective economic modelling have a tendency to conceal from the purview of policy makers those realities which do not, perhaps can not, find such concise expression. The established conceptual paradigm through which past performance is selectively measured and then projected thus becomes as much the engine which drives our economic future as the mirror that reflects our past economic performance.

It is now apparent, however, that policies extrapolated from the established indicators have, in recent times, consistently failed to achieve their anticipated goals. Given this, it is not surprising that the current economic policy environment is one in which we appear to have abandoned middleground incrementalism in favour of two rather polar opposite experiments. At the high profile end is an extraordinarily bullish commitment to a rapid restructuring of the national economy into conformity with the vision of those who explain the failure of established cures in terms of radical new environments. The advent of a new world economic order has allegedly rendered a parochial national economy hopelessly obsolescent and hence incapable of grasping the new opportunities which globalization offers. At the opposite, and lower profile policy pole, is a small but growing dalliance with the diametrically opposed CED perspective. The CED perspective does not argue against international trade as such, but is particularly sensitive to the dangers associated with the high stakes, high risk international market place. Thus CED emphasizes localized, participatory economic planning as the most effective alternative to the insecurity, dependency, and vulnerability typically inflicted by large-scale, remote, socially detached, and politically non-accountable economic organization (Clamp, 1987; Lockhart, 1982, 1985, 1987, 1989, 1990, 1991).

How are we to understand such a confusing policy environment given the conceptual gulf separating these two approaches to economic development? Is it but the latest manifestation of the ongoing ideological contest between a left wing David and right wing Goliath? If so, then the policy odds-makers are betting on Goliath. Is the CED rump only a cynical hedge against the possibility that the odds-makers are wrong? If so, then policy support for CED is the equivalent of putting ten percent of your investment portfolio in gold. Or is CED the nascent stage of a popular movement? If so, then it represents some sensitivity in policy circles to the gross contradiction which the globalization initiative represents with respect to the new social awareness of quality of life, limits to growth, and sustainable development issues. If you scratch the surface of the policy establishment, all three perspectives are likely to be found alive and well, though clearly not in equal portions. We are at something of a critical historic juncture, since the policy environment will very much affect the future role of CED, either as sponsor or suppressor.

Should the dominant globalization policy initiative bear early fruit, CED will likely be assigned a band-aid function—a kind of latter day missionary role applicable to those primitives who are left out of, or choose not to join in, the brave new world economic order. In the absence of adequate public funds to support safety net programs, it is both cheaper and more effective to try to contain the economic marginalization with localized self-help initiatives. In this scenario, CED would help re-establish a pre-industrial subsistence economy, which would interact hardly at all with the new post-industrial high tech economy. Welcome to the third-world dual economy syndrome!

Should the globalization shibboleth fail to deliver us into the promised land of milk and honey, or become a disastrous excursion into a mine-field from which none escape unscathed, then we are bound to see the reinvention of the national policy along with a return to regionally specific development initiatives. In this scenario, both the evolving concepts and the now well established practices of CED are likely to play a more central role. Unfortunately, neither the established practitioner base, nor the existing academic or other training capacity is anywhere near a level from which critical CED process facilitation and local capacity building could be rapidly multiplied (Lockhart & McCaskill, 1986). Only the independent Westcoast Development Group has an established capacity for delivering CED facilitation training, complete with an impressive inventory of original curriculum material as well as a practitioner supporting Newsletter. However, Canada Employment and Immigration's recent sponsoring of the development of a comprehensive CED trainers guide and establishment of a nascent trainer network may well be a harbinger of better things.

The key question for the future of CED is very strongly tied to a better understanding of what is really happening in the economic world. No one is omniscient, and fewer still unbiased, but the assumptions that underlie the so-called new world economic order have yet to be subjected to anything like the critical analysis the concept and its real world manifestations deserve. I confess to being a hostile witness, but, nonetheless, offer the following perspective on the challenge of global trends as a starting point for what may become a more insightful debate.

The Globalization Shibboleth

For those accustomed to resolving all of industrial society's socio-economic problems by moving to every higher levels of organizational aggregation and specialization, the new buzz word is globalization. If economies of scale, relative advantage, and access to undefended mass markets are the means by which big business triumph over small, then it is assumed that a similar breaking down of the State's own parochial tendencies will resolve the economic and political crisis that is today so endemic to governments everywhere. But this kind of simplistic sophistry ignores both economic history and the new realities which have unquestionably placed limits on the old economic cure-all of growth through merger and integration.

Thus, the theoretical rationales deployed today in support of globalization parallel the two-stage logic deployed during the industrial revolution. The new worldly philosophers of that era first argued that freeing economic decision-making from the traditional, community imposed moral order (meaning socially determined reciprocities) would, in the end, benefit everyone. Their assumption was that the unfettered new productive forces would quickly overcome chronic scarcity, thus allowing all to prosper. However, the market's hidden hand had a darker side. With no restraints on competition and no inclination to support even the most basic public sector infrastructures, the social obligations that any economy must first meet if it is to survive were no longer being enforced.

Thus, the extreme *laissez-faire* advocacy of the early free market apostles eventually gave way to a more moderate recognition that if the traditional community locus of social control over the redistributive side of the economic equation was no longer viable, then the nation state needed to be so empowered in order to assure the level of public benefit required to sustain the social fabric.

Today, the advocates of globalization have succeeded in resurrecting the notion that socially motivated economic decision-making represents a cancer within the body economic. Like the once socio-economically integrative community structures of the past, the nation state is now seen to be placing unacceptable social demands upon a market system in which the major corporate players have chosen to operate trans-nationally. In accordance with their long beloved "convergence" development theory (e.g., W.W. Rostow, 1960 and Kerr et al. 1964), these trans-national corporate interests consider the vestiges of cultural diversity to be found within national identity formations, no less than the tendency of nation states to reasonably protect their domestic economies, as creating unacceptable barriers to corporate mobility.

It is instructive to note that these very same "convergence" development theories have been rigorously applied (through the world bank and other foreign aid instruments) in the third world for at least four decades. The results have been alarmingly consistent. The experience of most third-world countries which followed this formula has been akin to the experience of most once self-sufficient communities during the industrial revolution. For those not strategically located, or already in possession of leading edge technology, the theory of relative advantage became the reality of unequal exchange. The concept of individual opportunity is transformed into the reality of collective poverty; the corporate advantages of mass production and mass marketing produces economic stagnation, cultural deprivation, and social dislocation for the host region (Matthews, 1983).

Today, like the communities of the earlier industrial revolution, the nation state is running out of options. Even the largest and most powerful states are finding it impossible to maintain their economic infrastructures, let alone their redistributive social programs, in the face of chronic fiscal crisis. Much is made of the alleged inefficiency of the public sector in explaining this fiscal crisis. But it is also self-evident that there will be an inevitable imbalance between public and private wealth distribution in a world that so systematically constrains the visible politics of public interest but places no such limits on the opaque exercise of private power. Thus, if one jurisdiction gives a corporate tax break, or a subsidy, or more favourable labour standards, then the level playing field rules of the international marketplace demand that all jurisdictions make similar concessions or face the consequences of out-migrating industry.

The Nation State in Crisis

With large corporate taxation largely beyond reach, the nation state has no option but to increase personal income and consumption taxes in order to meet ongoing social obligations. There are political limits to these unpopular taxes; approaching these limits produces a depressing effect on the domestic economy. National governments are thus caught between a rock and a hard place and have been forced to choose between increasing indebtedness to, and hence dependency on, international money markets (themselves an artifact of transnational corporatism) or allowing domestic economic infrastructures to decay, social programs to atrophy, and political credibility to erode.

This seemingly hopeless situation has caused many national governments to reverse their historic preoccupation with national sovereignty. These nations look toward integration into the international marketplace in the hope that they may benefit from the promise of market-driven economic rationalization such as the North American Free Trade Agreement. More socially conscious governments (predominantly in western Europe), that remain sceptical of the capacity of the uncontrolled market to improve the human condition, are seeking political as well as economic integration in the hope of regaining collectively the capacity to impose some regulatory and taxation powers over multi-national corporations (e.g., European Community Market).

Society in Crisis

For a decade or so, Western political-economic soothsayers have been declaring that, in order to survive in this brave new world of international competition, fewer and fewer persons are going to have to work harder and harder. Neither motivation nor educational preparation will be sufficient criteria for job security. To survive, we all must be prepared, on a regular basis, to put social relations at risk, to relearn living, to rethink cultural values, and to reinvest in consumer and production technologies—in short, to accept the ever increasing turbulence of an economy that is literally out of control. It is out of control because there is no longer any effective source of social accountability to act as a governor on market forces. The globalized market is threatening rather than serving its social base when those who interpret market signals on behalf of giant, over extended corporations focus only on the labour-saving side of competition, become fixated upon market share, are judged only in terms of smoke and mirror methods of ensuring a bloated quarterly dividend, and continue to pursue the Holy Grail of growth through predatory mergers and hyper-risk speculation in a time when inadequate social security ensures that aggregate demand will continue to fall.

Yet the shibboleth of globalization remains the goal lest we be damned to an even worse fate. This is to extend the icon of the hidden hand to the same level of destructive absurdity as the sorcerer's apprentice wielding of his master's magic broom. The internationalized marketplace is in the process of rendering the nation state impotent and unable to facilitate a humanly serviceable economy just as the earlier apostles of socially and politically non-accountable economics did to the community. But, unlike the earlier situation, there is no higher level of established governance available to reimpose the required balance between the productive and redistributive requisites of any workable economy.

Public reaction to the crisis is in the opposite direction to that of governments. There is a turning back toward regionalism and communitarianism rather than seeing hope in the direction of ever larger and more remote political-economic orders. This reaction is being acted out most dramatically in the former Eastern Bloc countries which, having seen their own variant of mass economy and mass society fall apart have not been notably anxious to follow their leadership's blind leap into a mass market for which they are even less prepared to cope. On the contrary, people are seeking a return, violently if necessary, to the security of community and ethnic ties. Historians will not be surprised. The popular reaction has always been to retreat back into the safety of community ties, whenever centralized forces have failed to legitimize their call to some universal allegiance. Two centuries of modernism can hardly be expected to obliterate the survival logic and genetic imprints of hundreds of millennia of human evolution (Polanyi, 1957, 1968).

The West is experiencing similar tensions as the capacity of nation states to facilitate reasonably equitable economic opportunities, and to provide needed social redistribution programs, rapidly diminishes. To continue to treat these problems as if they were cynical manifestations amenable to the old cures is to ignore such fundamental new realities as:

- The consolidation of wealth and power to a level that now exceeds any single state's capacity to enforce reasonable corporate contribution to host communities, regions, or nations.

- The systematic reduction in occupationally-based distribution of economic benefits as technologically-based productivity increases faster than economic expansion can re-absorb displaced workers. This has not been dealt with in terms of innovative programs through which both the diminished employment opportunities and the expanded benefit potentials could be equitably shared, but rather by systematic discrimination against younger, older, and more market exposed workers at all levels. The distribution of wealth among individuals, regions, and nations has become increasingly concentrated and mobile. The resulting increased demand on social programs, in combination with a decreased capacity to tax concentrated wealth, has produced a fiscal crisis which is now endemic to all nation states.

- This redistributive crisis has precipitated a dramatic change in social structures beginning with family formation. Just as the industrial revolution transformed the extended family into the nuclear family, the current economic climate is transforming the nuclear family into the sub-nuclear. The current family formation trend is to fewer, later, less stable, less fertile, and less economically manageable, less self-sufficient families. In Canada, over 60% of the growing number of single parents and their children are below the poverty line.

- A deepening public cynicism over the failure of the political process to provide relevant and accessible forums through which the common voice may find expression on critical communal issues. This systemic failure leads to proliferation of single issue political organizations that undercut community-based organizations and action on fundamental equity issues. Ironically, the self-imposed isolation tends only to reinforce the sense of individual disempowerment as it precludes common front organization around more fundamental political issues.

- A massive failure to develop human potentials and to match these to the tasks required to maintain both the social and economic foundations of a functioning society.

- A parallel failure to replace the lost icon of economically driven progress with a viable new vision of a future worthy of either economic or social investment.

- A morbid sense that the more priority is given to meeting the demands of the so-called new world economic order, the more imperiled all local, regional and national economies become. This misanthropy now afflicts those in the world's mercantile centres as well as those confined to the economic periphery.

Trends, Choices, and Solutions

The great virtue of trend analysis is that it points directions; the great danger is that it can be mindlessly extrapolated to unlikely end points. The pendulum is already embarking upon its reverse swing. Canada is not on the brink of economic annihilation, though the potential is apparent. Nor does Canada need to embark upon a crusade aimed at purging all aspects of modern industry and international exchange in order to return to some romantic notion of past simplicity and purity. Most Canadians have become too addicted to the comforts of mass produced consumerism to reject out of hand the kind of economy that produces such goodies. But if the above trend analysis reveals anything, it is the sad irony that our dominant economic policy, if taken to far, will only assure that fewer and fewer Canadians are going to be able to participate in the positive benefits that modern industrial economies have the potential of bestowing, provided they remain socially and politically connected. What is needed now, as never before, is a recognition of limitations and of a need for balance. The assumption that workers displaced by productivity enhancing innovation will be reabsorbed through economic growth is no longer tenable in a world that has reached, perhaps even surpassed, social and ecological growth limits. Canada must anticipate a full-blown dual economy—and the social and political unrest that such polarized socio-economies inevitably spawn—to the extent that we pursue economic policies that envision a future of high capital intensity without some of the economic benefits being reinvested in more labour intensive and socially responsive activities.

The rational policy choice is a middle road one. That, at least, is very Canadian. There is nothing to prevent Canada from following regionally articulated and sectorally specific trade agreements with a wider range of partners if our mega-trade agreements prove unmanageable. The State's fiscal crisis needs to be addressed, not in terms of endless cut-backs, but as part of an agenda that seeks to revitalize the local civic sector (Wolfe, 1989). A strategy is needed to reverse the erosion of social, economic, and political accountability by ensuring a sense of community affiliation and obligation that allows individuals to identify their long-term economic interests as fully consistent with their neighbours social well-being.

CED has proven that many local communities possess the human and physical resource potential to survive and prosper economically, socially, and psychologically (Cottrell, 1987). But is there a political will to support the necessary institutional changes and capacity building as part of a national economic strategy that seeks a balance between the international market driven competitive options and the more socially responsive, self-reliant, communities based cooperation options? Such a strategy would most certainly free us from our current, all-the-eggs-in-one-basket, policy gamble and would begin the process to lower current levels of dependency upon domestically uncontrollable external factors in attempting to plan a viable economic, social, and political future.

11

Making Communities Work: Women and Community Economic Development

Lucy Alderson, Melanie Conn, Janet Donald and Leslie Kemp

Since 1985, WomenFutures has been involved in facilitating workshops and discussions about women and community economic development (CED). In the workshops women are always invited to describe their vision for the future of their communities. The descriptions vary but share the concept of a holistic, inclusive and integrated system that values all the work that contributes to long-term community health. Women recognize that they are talking about fundamental social, economic, cultural, and ecological change that must take place at the interpersonal, community, and global level. This paper provides information about the features of women's CED in Canada and the implications of the work for public policy.

Many organizations and communities across Canada have adopted CED as a strategy and are creating their own blend of theory and practice. Much CED activity focuses on policy and planning, supporting local resource maximization, and reduction of dollar leakage from the community. The creation of stable jobs in regions and in population sectors with high unemployment has been another focus. CED has also evolved in various communities of interest where specific projects have been developed to support activities that reflect the unique strengths and priorities of the community.

Women's CED has emerged from the experience of women dealing with the implications of conventional economic development and discriminatory policies that have left them and their communities without adequate resources or choices. It is a dynamic process that evolves as women analyze and respond to the needs and strengths of their communities. There are many dimensions of women's participation in CED. Some groups have documented the social impact of economic development on women and their families, and have used the research as a basis for advocacy work. Women have become self-employed through small business initiation, have started employment cooperatives, and have joined economic development committees to broaden the definition of community economic health. Others organize and attend women's workshops to de-mystify economics and share ideas for economic development strategies that empower women. Informal provincial and national links are evolving as are innovative intermediary structures.

The Features of Women's Community Economic Development

Women bring a particular perspective to CED based on their participation in home and community life and as those who have paid the biggest price for conventional economic development. Each project has its own characteristics but four main features of women's CED work emerge as a common framework: redefining productivity, establishing a multiple bottom-line, developing collective resources, and ensuring inclusivity.

Redefining the Meaning of Productivity

In conventional terms, productivity is defined as the profit created by labour through the efficient production of goods and services. The drive for productivity and profit dominates the agendas of government programs and policies, business practices and procedures, and in turn affects the lives of everyone in the community. Women who look at the economy from the perspective of women's experience have long recognized that productive activity is not confined to the marketplace. Unpaid work in the home and in the community, done primarily by women and often in addition to paid work, is an essential part of the economy. Without this work the formal or cash economy would not be able to operate. Various studies have estimated domestic and other unpaid economic activity as 40% to 80% of the gross national product of Canada (Ross and Usher, 1986; Giarino, 1980). In women's CED, productivity is redefined to include all the work performed by women.

Recognizing the reality of reproduction in women's lives has been a primary goal of women's CED projects. Defining reproduction as productive work does not mean paying women for bearing children. But, rather, the potential for pregnancy should not keep women out of jobs or training programs, prevent promotions, or make women vulnerable in the workplace. The complexity and importance of the issue is illustrated by the efforts of a Vancouver women's video production collective. They have sought to design a structure that would anticipate individual partners' financial needs while on parenting leave and also provide continuity for the business. In addition, the members wanted to ensure that each one of them would share the opportunities and responsibilities involved in a shared parenting leave plan. Such a structure could only be built on mutual trust, long-term commitment to the group, and a recognition of the reality of women's lives.

Women working in CED are also determined to acknowledge unpaid domestic work. Caring for children and elders, providing the nutritional and emotional support to enable family members to go to school and work, and carrying out household chores are key aspects of domestic production involving hours of daily work for most women. In addition, the number of women struggling with the double day is growing. In 1991, 68% of all women with children living at home were in the paid labour force, an increase from 61% in 1986 (*Vancouver Sun*, March 3, 1993). A non-profit housing society in Vancouver is a good example of how domestic production can be supported. The society was started by single mothers who wanted secure housing for themselves and their children. Family preparation time (for making lunches and for dropping off children at daycare or school) is incorporated into the work day. Another example of accommodating domestic responsibilities is a decision by a worker co-op to install a washer and dryer on site to allow members to do laundry during the work day. Other worker co-ops provide hot meals for staff at lunch to decrease members' food preparation time and to ensure a nutritious mid-day meal.

Child care is a priority for women's CED. The history of labelling child care as a private issue has meant that women have taken responsibility for locating, scheduling, paying for, and even creating available child care services. Women's CED projects have adopted a number of strategies to ensure children are cared for when their parents are unavailable. These include providing child care on the work site or covering child care costs when members attend meetings or participate in other work-related activities. A common policy of many women's organizations is to pay child care costs for women who are invited to conferences or workshops. Sometimes sharing child care is the reason for a group coming together in the first place. Five women weavers on a B.C. gulf island organized their collective so that each woman cares for all the group's children one day a week, leaving four days for members to work on their craft. Another aspect of women's CED involves working on child care issues within the community and lobbying all levels of government. Some groups have participated in advocacy work for affordable child care services and others campaigned against the amendments to the Canadian constitution that posed a threat to a universal child care program.

One more area of redefinition relates to unpaid community work. Counselling, tutoring, administrative work, health care support, community kitchens and other informal and formal structures for providing services to the community are all examples of unpaid community work which has no value in conventional economic terms. Redefining the work as productive means recognizing that it maintains communities as networks with lives apart from, and sometimes in spite of, the industries that control the primary cash flow. David Ross (1985) calculated that such activity reflected $16 billion annually in the Canadian economy. Women's centres and organizations which rely on unpaid work to provide services to the community are common sites for CED activity. Women's CED honours the role of the unpaid worker in such organizations as complementary to the labour of the paid employees. The history of a Vancouver Island thrift store provides an illustration of how unpaid community work directly contributes to the economy. It was started in the early 1940s at the kitchen tables of women who were upset because the only social service available in the community was a Christmas basket program. The thrift store has grown into the largest organization in the community contributing funds for new social programs. Such organizations are important components of the community and need to be adequately supported.

Establishing a Multiple Bottom Line

Conventional economic development elevates the financial bottom line above all other concerns in the community; a healthy social, cultural, ecological, and spiritual environment is secondary to making a financial profit. Women's CED does not pretend that economic activity happens in a vacuum, isolated from community life. Instead, initiatives are designed to integrate several objectives—a multiple bottom line. First Nations women from northern B.C. describe the work they are doing in their communities as part of a long-term vision. The development process is guided by their strong linkages with the past and with the future. Their ability to bring the essential components of traditional culture and community organization into the CED process is the essence of the multiple bottom line approach.

A Vancouver-based women's loan guarantee fund is an example of integrating community and business development. The group's criteria for guarantees take into account more than the profitability of women's CED initiatives. Eligible businesses are women-controlled, economically feasible, provide stable employment, take into account the affordability of the product or service, and will enhance the quality of life of women in the community. Another Vancouver group, a women's printing collective, has an twenty-three year history of making business decisions that reflect the social and political objectives of the company. The collective seeks business viability but also insists that any work undertaken must not perpetuate racist, sexist, or homophobic stereotypes or attitudes. The multiple bottom line for the company means that work will be turned down if it violates the principles of the workers.

Women working on CED at a global level have a similar perspective when they consider the implications of national and global strategies that elevate the commercial bottom line and enshrine it in free trade policies. Through the National Action Committee (NAC), women are campaigning against the North American Free Trade Agreement (NAFTA) because of its perceived destructive impact on community health in all three countries. Strong links were developed with women's groups in Mexico where the operation of free trade zones has created intolerable conditions for women and their families. This established the basis for Canadian women's conviction that the NAFTA will impede, if not eliminate, the potential for strategies such as CED to stimulate and support healthy communities.

Developing Collective Resources

Conventional economic development programs and policies are permeated with rhetoric extolling personal and corporate competitiveness as the key to economic success. In contrast, the most progressive definitions of CED propose cooperative relationships within and between communities for mutual benefit. Collective activities have offered the best way for women to achieve control over critical aspects of their lives. Women bring a wealth of experience in working collectively and have demonstrated considerable success at it. Women's expertise is based on their personal and community relationships and activities, as well as in their considerable skills in organizing and working in groups.

In communities across Canada women have pooled their financial resources and their expertise to start or expand cooperative businesses. In addition to sharing the profits and the risks of the enterprise, members have created an opportunity to control their working conditions and to support one another in developing skills and achieving personal objectives. The success of women's lending circles is another good example of women developing resources together. Lending circles, or peer-group lending, refers to a financing model where each member receives a small business loan and the group provides mutual support. The process is halted if one member of the group fails to make a repayment instalment. These lending programs are often the only source of small amounts of capital for business start-up or expansion. In some programs, members of the group are also responsible for repaying the loans of other members in the case of a default. Therefore, group support is an essential component of the programs. The Vancouver-based loan guarantee fund provides another example of women collectivizing their resources in response to the lack of access to credit for women. A small group devised the fund as an innovative financial structure centred on the concept of pooling investments and risk to guarantee loans. The fund has appealed to a broad base of individuals and groups and has raised $50,000 in investments and donations in its first year of operation.

Enthusiasm for working collectively to meet a common objective is illustrated by the high level of participation by women in establishing and operating housing cooperatives. Cooperatively-owned property represents an invaluable contribution to the community infrastructure as a precious source of permanent, affordable housing. Co-ops rely on their members who contribute time and energy to maintain a healthy physical and social environment. Some co-ops have focused specifically on creating safe environments for women, such as co-ops that were established by women for women and their children. A co-op in Ontario has declared itself a domestic violence free zone.

The process of building women's control over their lives through collective action is easy to observe at many women's centres across the country where a number of cooperative CED activities have emerged. The work starts with the personal issues women bring when they walk through the door—low self-esteem, domestic violence, sexual abuse, and unavailability of child care, financing, or housing. Women's centres have responded to these issues and established a number of collective activities and structures through community development and organizing. An organization formed to address the needs of Filipino domestic workers in Vancouver illustrates the powerful role a women's organization can take in facilitating women's CED. With virtually no external assistance, the centre collectively rents a house to provide permanent and part-time accommodation for Filipino women who are live-in domestic workers. The centre also organizes fund-raising events, operates a catering business, and supports its members in overcoming various oppressive immigration policies and regulations. The centre maintains a prominent role in the campaign to change immigration policy to recognize the value of the work carried out in Canadian homes by its members. The campaign seeks to reverse immigration regulations that make it very difficult for domestic workers from the Philippines and other developing countries to reside in Canada on a permanent basis.

Ensuring Inclusivity

The exclusion of women as active participants and decision-makers in conventional economic development has been well-documented (Waring, 1989, Women for Economic Survival, 1984, Women's Unemployment Study Group, 1983, Project Mayday, 1985 and Women's Research Centre, 1979). Neither the strengths nor the concerns of women have been well represented in economic programs and policies adopted by governments and communities. The objective of inclusivity is an important feature of women's CED and is reflected in efforts to ensure that women are included in CED planning and activity within local community, provincial, and national networks.

Cooperative structures are a framework for equalizing power through democratic decision-making. Many groups are skilled in group process and value the structures they have created to encourage members to participate, to resolve contentious issues, and to accommodate diversity. Members are willing to participate in lengthy discussions and to take responsibility for learning about a variety of technical and operational issues in order to come to decisions based on consensus. Women involved in collective activity acknowledge the challenges of working in a structure committed to including a diverse membership. Some women's CED businesses have adopted policies of affirmative action hiring to ensure that women of colour and First Nations women will join their collectives. Groups have also worked to increase their sensitivity about diversity in other areas such as class, age, ability, and sexual preference. Careful attention and planning is required to ensure that meetings, workshops and conferences represent the communities they serve. The timing of meetings and their setting, the pace of the agenda and the language used are all important factors in encouraging participation.

Policies that Enhance or Restrict Women's CED

When women discuss the conditions that help or hinder their CED work, they describe factors from all the contexts that relate to their lives and to their work: personal, group, community, regional, and global. Although CED represents an alternative to conventional economic development, systemic discrimination around race, gender and ability are still major forces that impede women in planning and implementing their CED activity.

At the same time, opportunities exist at all levels to support and enhance women's CED. There are specific opportunities for politicians, policy makers, senior level bureaucrats, and program deliverers. Unfortunately, when barriers to women's CED exist at many of these levels, the work becomes overwhelming and the activity is marginalized. Although women's CED proceeds, progress is slow and resources are stretched to transparency.

This section provides examples of macro policy decisions in governmental and non-governmental resources that have assisted or blocked women's CED activity.

Policies Affecting the Re-Definition of Productivity

National policies do not recognize the value of women's unpaid work as productive. Despite persistent and well-organized lobbying, there is still no universal, affordable child care policy to meet current community needs in Canada. The current immigration policy on domestic workers does not acknowledge the rights of the workers nor the value of domestic work in supporting the economy. The live-in requirement of the policy exposes women to exploitation and harassment and the contract of employment leaves the domestic worker in a vulnerable position with immigration authorities if she wishes to change employers.

On the positive side, Statistics Canada has announced it will be inquiring about household and volunteer work in the 1996 census. Further, the United Nations has acknowledged the value and volume of women's work throughout the world even if it is not registered in the gross national product. Most development organizations recognize women as the catalysts for community development; many, such as Canada International Development Agency (CIDA), insist on the participation of women in projects and require demonstration of a positive impact on women as a criterion of success. Strategies initiated by unions to create family friendly workplaces acknowledge the home and family responsibilities of workers. They provide examples of policies and initiatives that assist people, especially women, to carry out their dual responsibilities.

Policies Affecting the Establishment of a Multiple Bottom Line

There are a number of federal policies that impede an integrated approach to economic development. The North American Free Trade Agreement is a major threat to women workers in the three countries involved. It inhibits women's ability to establish adequate working conditions, fair wages, and control over local resources—essential components of the multiple bottom line in women's CED. Revenue Canada's slow progress towards permitting tax credits for non-profit organizations and foundations to support CED work is another restrictive policy. The department's adherence to a narrow definition of charitable activity that excludes other forms of community support limits the scope of many CED resource organizations. The Western Economic Diversification Fund was established to assist regional development, but has done little to assist women's CED. The criteria and scale of the Fund exclude most strategies put forward by women. On the other hand, the Atlantic Canada Opportunities Agency (ACOA) has funded organizations that assist women's CED, including cooperative and micro enterprise that consider social as well as commercial objectives.

There are also policies that have supported a multiple bottom line framework. Health and Welfare has established exploratory funding for CED research under its National Welfare Grants program, an initiative that developed from the department's expanded definition of welfare to include both economic and social concerns. The Secretary of State Women's Program has funded projects that combine social and economic objectives. Unfortunately, the department has undermined women's CED with its recent policy to eliminate or reduce core funding to women's centres.

Many non-governmental resources have stepped in to fill some of the gaps in government programming. OXFAM–Canada has developed a clear understanding of CED based on its overseas work and has provided no-strings-attached funding to women's CED projects. Foundations such as the Canadian Women's Foundation and the VanCity Community Foundation have provided funding or have helped leverage additional funding for new or innovative projects.

Developing Collective Resources

National policies have failed to encourage cooperative collective activity or have impeded it. The co-op housing program of Canada Mortgage and Housing (CMHC) played a critical role in the establishment of affordable housing in Canada. The Federal government's decision in 1992 to eliminate the co-op program makes it almost impossible for communities to build housing outside the commercial agenda of the real estate market. The decision flies in the face of the growing need for new co-op units and the knowledge that women are the major consumers of cooperative and non-profit housing.

The Self-Employment Assistance Program has always been available for collectively-structured business but the program has failed to make this information available across Canada. In many regions, technical assistance and other information for developing a worker co-op cannot be found in the local Business Development Centre, funded by Canada Employment and Immigration (CEIC). In regions (such as Cape Breton) where there is a history of working collectively, CEIC programs have been used to develop the potential of cooperative enterprises.

Policies that Affect Inclusivity

Ensuring the inclusion of women continues to be a difficult struggle. The experience of bringing equity group representation to the Canadian Labour Force Development Board (CLFDB) and subsequent provincial/territorial and local boards has been a major advocacy initiative for equity groups. Initially, the CLFDB included only business and labour representatives. Equity groups successfully fought for a place at the national level and are now lobbying for seats at all other levels, region by region. Some provinces and territories have been open to participation by equity groups, but many have not.

There are also examples of more inclusive policies. To receive second-generation funding in the Community Futures Program, local committees must reflect their community's diversity on the board, in committees, and in program participation. The Canadian Co-operative Association (CCA) established a Women in Co-ops Task Force to examine and highlight the role of women in co-ops. The CCA has also made a commitment to reflect the multi-cultural base of their membership.

Conclusion

The focus of this paper has been a detailed description of the scope and features of women's CED. It is clear that the education and advocacy components of this work are critical if women's CED is to access appropriate resources and guide macro policy development.

Understanding the features of women's CED clarifies the policy changes required to strengthen women's participation in CED. Embracing the assumptions and objectives of women's CED represents a major step in changing the way CED is practised.

12

Environments Conducive to Effective Community Economic Development: Themes, Policy Implications and Research Needs

France Asselin and François Dumaine

Gathering all the factors essential to the success of a CED project is a daring undertaking and it is even more rash to attempt to establish a hierarchy among these factors. Environment, however, is one factor that cannot be sidestepped when analyzing a CED project. The term environment for CED must refer to a "community." But, as Mario Polèse states, community is a term that is difficult to define as it refers to elements that are often intangible. Nevertheless, a community could be defined as being made up of three main components. First, there must be a certain number of individuals having common interests as they face situations that are relatively similar. Second, these various individuals must live in proximity to one another. Third, these individuals must share a certain number of values on which to base possible intervention strategies.

Once these parameters have been set, the nature and scope of the environment must be specified. Environment can be analyzed from two different angles. First, as Sandy Lockhart remarks, the external environment surrounding a community directly affects the CED process. For instance, the breaking down of commercial boundaries between nations has forced the various economic sectors to become more competitive and aggressive. As a result, an approach centred less on trade wars and more on the quality of life along with sustainable development has taken hold. This is precisely the context in which CED can take place. Moreover, free trade has weakened the sovereignty of various national governments already hit hard by tax crises stemming from enormous deficits. This type of environment can also force state leaders to rely more heavily on communities' assuming direct responsibility for themselves through CED. Finally, other factors such as legal and financial structures as well as public policies complete this economic environment.

On the other hand, environment can be viewed as being a series of preconditions vital to a CED project's success. Mario Polèse defines these as an adequate territory or locality, access to skilled labour, capital, entrepreneurship within the community, and a suitable location for access to various markets. Lucy Alderson, Melanie Conn, Janet Donald, and Leslie Kemp also refer to environment as being a series of factors defining a particular approach to economic development. They believe that productivity must be redefined to include unpaid work, an area heavily dominated by women. When analyzing an economic project, one must make certain that the essential factors include not only a commitment to profit but also a commitment to the community's social and cultural development. Lastly, CED projects must enable individuals to develop resources collectively and the process of defining CED projects must be an open one that includes the community's various groups.

Implications for Public Policy

The various factors in an environment favouring CED obviously stem from a series of public policies defined within laws, regulations, and administrative policies that have an impact on a CED project's efficiency, soundness, and ability to get off the ground (Brodhead, 1994). The process used to define these policies must be taken into account in our analysis of CED. It is in and of itself part of an environment that may or may not benefit CED. Thus the attitude of local governments and of provincial resource centres are factors that directly affect CED (Lewis, 1994). The role of public policies and programs is determinant if CED is to develop its potential as a social and economic development tool in a complex and unsettled environment. Lucy Alderson and her colleagues stress that several current policies directly affect women's ability to initiate viable projects. Day-care programs, access to basic data making it possible to identify target groups, overall economic policies maintained by various governments, and mandates given to economic development organizations all significantly affect the community's ability to develop effective CED projects (O'Neill, 1994).

Research Needs

CED offers a context in which dynamic, participatory, and action methods of research can readily be used. CED implies involving a number of community members in the various stages of development including evaluation. The methodology used in action research contributes by involving the members of the community in defining the various stages of research and by providing specific and useful information on the needs and problems based on community members' views of them. This research approach assists in developing awareness and mobilizing the community to look for solutions and take action. The research needs to be directed to develop tools used to measure the effects of CED policies and programs as well as to better understand the impact of existing policies and programs (with a view to suggesting improvements, if need be). It is difficult to identify clearly the extent of the social and economic impact of CED. Research could fill this gap by conducting cost-benefit analyses to demonstrate CED's level of efficiency in a given community. It is vital, however, that this type of analysis take into account social as well as economic benefits and costs.

Research is needed to develop guidelines that may be used by all levels of government at CED development stages. These guidelines should serve to identify the possible social and economic effects of policies and programs being considered. In this regard, it would be helpful to make an inventory of a few models and guidelines already existing and to assess their relevance and usefulness for a broader application. The community could be given a head start with access to the tools that would enable it to conduct a careful analysis of the area's social and economic situation as well as environmental conditions. This would facilitate the planning and implementation process.

A better understanding is needed of the problems relating to access to funding for CED projects including identifying and assessing provincial and federal funding regulations for CED. There is a need to assess the steps that could be taken to ensure that the transfer system includes funding for CED projects without impeding its role of assisting those who are in need. An evaluative study of the applicability and effectiveness of job-readiness programs on CED would be helpful. Some provincial departments with responsibility for development and employment have recently undergone restructuring. Comparative research on these various organizational models and the importance within these models of programs funding CED would be useful.

PART 4

EVALUATION OF COMMUNITY
ECONOMIC DEVELOPMENT

13

A Review of Four Evaluations of CED Programs: What Have We Learned in Two Decades?

Ken Watson

Canada Employment and Immigration (CEI) has funded several CED initiatives in the past twenty years. The earliest of these programs was the Local Initiatives Program which began in 1969, the first year of the Trudeau administration. It was followed, in 1973, by the Local Employment Assistance Program (LEAP). At the same time, the federal and provincial governments undertook a social security review which resulted in the Community Employment Strategy (CES, 1975). This program funded experimental community employment projects on the assumption that "members of the target group and those with access to and control of community resources should play the major role in identifying the employment needs of the target group and proposing ways to meet those needs" (Canada Employment and Immigration, 1981). An evaluation study of the CES was completed in 1980.

In October 1980, based on the CES experience, CEI launched the Local Economic Development Assistance Program (LEDA) with the assistance of the Department of Regional Economic Expansion. A little over two years later, LEDA was amalgamated with the infrastructure component of the Canada Community Development Program, and parts of the Local Employment Assistance Program, to form the Local Employment Assistance and Development Program (LEAD). This program intended to produce permanent employment in economically troubled communities by funding community development corporations to initiate infrastructure and enterprise projects. In 1985, the Neilsen Task Force reviewed the program and raised a number of questions about the effectiveness of LEAD (Canada, 1985). In the following year, Canada Employment and Immigration undertook an evaluation study of the program (1986). This led, in 1986, to the Community Futures Program which was announced as part of the Canadian Jobs Strategy. This program operates in about 200 communities, selected because they were slow growing non-metropolitan areas with chronic high unemployment and a limited economic base, and about 30 communities which, although they did not meet the Community Futures criteria, had been established under the predecessor program LEAD and were continued. In 1990, there were two evaluation studies of the Community Futures program (Canada Employment and Immigration, 1990a, and Employment and Immigration 1990b).

From 1981 to 1990 three versions of community economic development funding were evaluated: the Community Employment Strategy (Canada Employment and Immigration, 1980), the Local Employment Assistance and Development (Task Force on Program Review 1985; Canada Employment and Immigration 1986), and the Community Futures program (Canada Employment and Immigration, 1990). This chapter reviews the evaluation studies of these programs, the lessons learned from each study, and how subsequent programs reflected those lessons.

Evaluation of the Community Employment Strategy

The Community Employment Strategy included projects in twenty communities across Canada. These projects were designated as experimental "for the purpose of testing the effectiveness of the CES concept and developing policy with respect to the possible implementation of a permanent and broad-based program" (Canada Employment and Immigration, 1981, p.6). Therefore, evaluation of their effectiveness was very important. The federal government was feeling its way towards a new approach to community economic development. The evaluation study undertaken in 1980, however, had some features that limited its value as a guide to future policy. Separate studies of the CES projects were carried out by consultants in each province and a synthesis of the findings of these studies was written at EIC national headquarters. This descriptive and qualitative approach to the research meant that heavy reliance was placed on subjective judgement about the outcomes of the projects.

> The principal limitations to the evaluation of the CES arose from the short period available for the implementation of projects and the absence of a test design. The time constraint precluded a realistic assessment of labour market outcomes and limited the evaluators to qualitative judgements based on process recording. From a national perspective the evaluation was also constrained by the fact that too few communities were available to establish replicability. The approach adopted therefore relied on a synthesis of qualitative regional data and the subjective assessments of regional evaluation consultants and Ottawa-based evaluation staff (Canada Employment and Immigration, 1981, p.7).

Nevertheless, an attempt was made to structure the evaluation research by focusing on five criteria of CED effectiveness.

1. Concrete evidence that in any given community significant numbers of the target population were able to find "decent continuing employment" which relieved them from or substantially reduced their dependence on transfer payments. Research found that the time required for communities to develop employment strategies had been underestimated and that "little could be said that was not highly speculative" about the permanence of the jobs associated with the CEF. The researchers were skeptical about the attribution to the CEF of jobs and long-term impacts, as claimed by local associations and public officials. What was observed was the creation of short-term employment opportunities that had the effect of substituting unemployment insurance payments for provincial welfare payments (Canada Employment and Immigration, 1981, p.8).

2. Concrete evidence of a community's enhanced capacity to assess the employment-related problems of the target population and, with such assistance from government officials as may be appropriate, to develop relevant community-based solutions to such problems. The evaluation research found that, by and large, the communities lacked the requisite skills needed to tackle the type of economic planning exercise that the early designers of the CES envisaged. As well, there was a tendency to by-pass existing organizations that "was clearly demonstrated in the failure of most associations to involve local business elements in the planning process" (Canada Employment and Immigration, 1981, p.15).

3. Existence of sound community-based evaluations of current programs and services which (insofar as the federal government is concerned) may be effectively used to propose improvements in the existing array of programs, especially those of CEI. Although some critiques of government services emerged piece-meal, there was little local innovation observable. "Local innovation became entangled in administrative and funding guidelines ..." (Canada Employment and Immigration, 1981, p.18).

4. Concrete evidence and perception by the community of improvement in the efficiency with which existing programs and services are used to open up employment opportunities for the target population. The researchers reported that the CES did not generally increase the efficiency with which existing programs were used and had limited success in enhancing local access to existing programs (Canada Employment and Immigration, 1981, p.22).

5. Substantial improvement in federal-provincial, and interdepartmental, cooperation in the implementation of employment-related

programs and services for the target population. The researchers spoke of a "widespread failure by CES to coordinate government programs at a local level." The lead provincial departments tended to be in social welfare fields, not labour, and had little to offer to a program that stressed employment through economic development. As well, "the ambivalent support received by CES can, in part, also be explained by provincial wariness over creating new demands. The provinces felt, on the basis of past experience, that when federal programs, such as the Local Initiatives Program, were terminated, additional pressure was placed on them to take up the slack in services" (Edwin Reid and Associates, 1982, pp.xx-xxii). In addition, the researchers state that "paralleling the widespread regional failure to develop effective coordinating mechanisms, the national CES office never fully articulated its policy role. Policy development remained largely discretionary and depended on informal mechanisms" (Canada Employment and Immigration, 1981, p.27). Overall, the researchers found a "need to relax the capital expenditure constraints ... if these programs are to be anything more than short-term palliatives. Current modes of assistance do not meet the needs of communities suffering a shortage of investment capital and having limited entrepreneurial skills." As well, organizational and administrative failures were cited:

The delineation of roles and responsibilities was not clear ... Organizational structures were not closely matched to operational requirements ... The analysis of community readiness was inadequate ... the planning horizons were too short ... government officials lacked community development skills ... and, more emphasis should have been placed on involving local business interests and securing the participation of existing public and private agencies (Canada Employment and Immigration, 1981, p.28).

Evaluation of the Local Employment Assistance and Development Program (LEAD)

Neilsen Task Force on Program Review

The Local Employment Assistance and Development Program (LEAD) had been operating for only two years when the Neilsen Task Force review was done in 1985. Its predecessor, the Local Economic Development Assistance program (LEDA), had been in place since October 1980. The organizational design of LEDA had drawn upon the evaluation of the CES, especially in setting criteria for community selection, emphasis on technical and managerial assistance, and provision of training for LEDA staff. LEAD had four components: (1) funding community development corporations to identify economic opportunities, provide technical assistance to entrepreneurs, and manage an employment development fund to provide loans or investments to local businesses to a maximum of $25,000 per company per year; (2) funding commercially viable enterprise projects by community-based organizations; (3) funding infrastructure projects to enhance a community's capacity for economic growth; and (4) funding planning projects. LEAD spent about $100 million and was administered by approximately 170 federal government staff in 1985–86.

The Neilsen Task Force was not a research-based evaluation. It was a short review of all federal government programs, based on interviews, file reviews, and reading secondary research. The report stated that LEAD duplicated other federal programs, especially those of Regional Industrial Expansion and the Native Economic Development Agreement Fund. Questions were raised by business persons concerning the qualifications of EIC personnel to assess small business projects. The reviewers found the practice of providing money without some meaningful financial involvement on the part of the applicant questionable. In conclusion, the study team said:

> (We) recommend that the government consider the termination of this program: no new activities would be funded under LEAD and the existing program would be phased out as present commitments to communities terminate ... in light of ... long lead times to pay-off, high risk factors, and apparent duplication ... However, there would likely be opposition to terminating the program from potential program beneficiaries, especially in the Atlantic provinces and Quebec. (Task Force on Program Review, 1987, p.68).

CEI Evaluation of LEAD

After the Neilsen Task Force Report, the Evaluation and Audit Committee of Canada Employment and Immigration commissioned a study of four broad questions that they considered unanswered: the incrementality of the jobs created, the viability of the businesses supported by LEAD, the cost per job created, and alternative solutions. This study undertook interviews of the LEAD corporations, as had the earlier CES study, but in addition it attempted to gather information directly from the businesses that had been assisted by the corporation. However, the study team experienced difficulty in obtaining complete lists of the LEAD assisted clients. Some corporations declined to supply the information. CEI was able to obtain names and addresses for fewer than 700 of approximately 900 recipients of assistance. The study team decided to base the analysis solely on the corporations that provided complete lists. Therefore the analysis was based on 284 cases. This may have introduced significant bias into the results. "It is reasonable to suppose that certain negative aspects of the program were concealed from the evaluation team by the elimination of some clients from the original lists" (Canada Employment and Immigration, 1986, p.18).

The problem of non-response bias was made worse by the fact that some clients who were among the unbiased sample of 284 did not answer all the questions asked. For example, only 130 (out of an original total of 900) answered the question "Would you have hired all these workers without the corporation's assistance?" For what it is worth, 21.5% answered that they would have hired all the same workers, and another 25% would have hired some of the workers at that time or later. There was no objective verification of these responses and no comparison group with which to validate them. Therefore their reliability as estimates of hiring behaviour in the absence of LEAD is dubious. Clients of the LEAD corporations received funding from other sources in the ratio of about $3.8 for every $1.0 dollar of LEAD funding (Canada Employment and Immigration, 1986, p.77). The researchers did not allow this to lessen the estimates of the incremental effect of LEAD; rather they made the assumption that the $3.8 was in some sense caused or leveraged by the $1 of LEAD loan or investment. This assumption is highly favourable to the program.

The question of job displacement was addressed in a qualitative way. For example, LEAD was intended to deal with corporations not eligible for or that had been refused funding by the Federal Business Development Bank. The researchers note "the fact that LEAD's directives regarding a preliminary approach to the FBDB are not being followed is serious, and should be looked at more closely to make sure that there is no overlapping of client groups. This is all the more important in that, if such displacement is occurring, the program's positive incremental effects would be illusory" (Canada Employment and Immigration, 1986, p.78).

The researchers dismissed the possibility of displacement of jobs from firms in competition with the recipients on the dubious grounds that "only a minority of employers, about a third, mentioned the existence of other firms in the community operating in the same line of business as themselves" (Canada Employment and Immigration, 1986, p.78). Displacement arising from competition with employers in other communities was dismissed as compatible with the objectives of LEAD. "This type of displacement is entirely compatible with the objectives of the program, the goal of which is first and foremost to assist specific communities" (Canada Employment and Immigration, 1986, p.79). This is a doubtful proposition since it is unlikely that the federal government meant LEAD to aid some communities at the expense of others. The cost-per-job calculations will not be described because the underlying calculation of the number of incremental jobs created is not credible.

The inter-community job displacement problem was addressed under the successor program Community Futures, by defining an eligible community as a geographic area covering a self-contained labour market, normally outside metropolitan areas. However, this leaves the intra-community displacement problem unaddressed. The LEAD evaluation study recommended that

> (after) the five years of contributions and grants that CEI provides ... CEI
> should gradually withdraw ... the corporations need solid encouragement to
> seek out other economic partners. (However) to ensure that the corporations
> will continue to concentrate their efforts on job creation ... once they are
> forced to become self-sufficient [the federal government should] include a
> clause on this subject in the agreement to be signed by both parties.
> Corporations should be required to continue submitting reports on job
> creation. In addition, CEI should ensure it will have the right to check on
> corporation activities on a yearly basis for three to five years after its financial
> support has stopped (Canada Employment and Immigration, 1986, p.97).

This suggestion was not adopted by the Community Futures program on
grounds of impracticality. The LEAD corporations became the Business
Development Centres under Community Futures but they were not required
to become self-sufficient, although they were encouraged to seek other
funding that would prolong their life as investment sources.

Evaluation of the Community Futures Program

Community Futures began operations in 1986 and was evaluated in 1990.
At the time of the evaluation study, Community Futures was active in more
than 200 communities and had expenditures of approximately $150 million
per year. Communities were selected because they were slow growing,
non-metropolitan areas with chronic high unemployment, and had a limited
economic base. An additional 30 communities were selected, although they
did not meet the Community Futures criteria, because they contained
Business Development Centres that had been established under the predecessor LEAD program.

Telephone interviews were attempted with a sample 8392 past participants in LEAD, Community Futures, BDC clients, and a comparison group.
Interviews were completed with 2993, and 4113 persons could not be
contacted (Gallup, 1990, p.17). The likelihood of the respondents being
unrepresentative of the client or comparison group population is high,
despite statistical adjustments meant to minimize bias. The two main
adjustments were for presumed self-selection bias on program entry, and
refusal-to-interview bias. Neither is capable of verification.

The Community Futures evaluation took a different tack on the analysis
of incremental job creation. The study team compared the Community
Futures communities, before and after the program, with regional averages,
instead of gathering unsupported claims of jobs created from companies
that had received assistance. The initial intention to make comparisons with
matched communities was frustrated by two things. First, there were few
comparable communities that were not taking advantage of the program;
and, second, the boundaries of the Community Futures communities did
not match with those for which various types of data had been gathered

over the years by various levels of government (Price Waterhouse, 1990). The Community Futures communities, except for communities in Ontario, achieved above-average improvement in their local economic status, as measured by reductions in unemployment insurance beneficiaries. "However, it was not possible to determine whether this relative performance is due to the impacts and effects of the program, to the selection process identifying winners, the particular program options, or a third set of influences" (Canada Employment and Immigration, 1990a, pp.15–16).

About one-third of the companies that LEAD had assisted in 1986–87 were still in business in 1990. However, many of these businesses were still receiving government financial help to survive. Training assistance under Community Futures for those who were not employed at the time of training was found to have no long-term impact on employability. For those who were employed at the time of training, some increase in earnings after training was observed. Community Futures offered both adjustment (relocation) and development interventions, resulting in lack of clarity about the program's intentions. "The program does not make a distinction between economic development and adjustment assistance" (Canada Employment and Immigration, 1990, p.vi). The evaluators and the program managers found it difficult to agree how serious this confusion of objectives was. The evaluators reported that the relative lack of use of the adjustment (mobility) aspects of the program was troubling in regard to communities whose long-term prospects for prosperity were not good.

Community selection was a problem, as it had been under LEAD. The new definition of community allowed some communities such as native reserves and adjacent towns to "join together for the sole purpose of becoming eligible for Community Futures program funding ... more than half the CF communities included native reserves ... Some specific functioning difficulties were noted for expanded communities because in some instances the area was too large, cumbersome or distant ...." (Canada Employment and Immigration, 1990a, p.v). As well, the participation of native Canadians was very low even where a reserve had been included within the defined community. In fact, some communities contained more than 100,000 people, far too large for the CED as envisaged by Community Futures. The researchers recommended that the appropriate size of community for this type of program is probably more than 5000 but not more than 50,000 people.

> Attribution of effects to CF was difficult because the program was broad and shallow, giving a little assistance to a lot of communities and consequently diluting the program's effects. The question arises as to whether the program could be more effective if it were to refocus its efforts narrow and deep by offering intensive assistance to fewer target communities, either to the most disadvantaged or to those most likely to benefit or whatever criteria are specified .... In relation to client benefits, the most successful option (excluding the Business Development Centres established under LEAD which also

proved effective) was the Self-employment assistance (SEI), which was found to improve both short and long-term employability as well as yearly earnings ... In terms of moving people off income support, only SEI was found to have a positive and significant influence. (Canada Employment and Immigration, 1990a, pp.viii).

The Community Futures study team also found that the information needed to undertake any analysis of the effectiveness of the program was not available.

> With respect to accountability, the study indicated a need for improvements to the present monitoring system. Reporting mechanisms are not yet uniform nor streamlined, and there are data integrity problems in the program, with critical data gaps in the area of performance measurement. On the other hand, from the community's perspective, there is already too much paperwork and approved funds are not transferred to them on a timely basis" (Canada Employment and Immigration, 1990a, p.ix).

The comfortable assumption that programs would show benefits in the long term was challenged by the study team. Organizations that had been continued from LEAD, and even earlier from LEDA, did not show any better performance than those newly funded under Community Futures (Canada Employment and Immigration, 1990, pp.iv-v). Finally, as with predecessor programs, many administrative problems were noted by the evaluation study team. Questions were raised about the expertise of program staff and about high turnover of the volunteers who filled the local committees. "More than half the respondents note that when CF committees were first formed, the level of organizational skills of its members is low ... it was difficult to recruit volunteers and political appointments to the Board caused some difficulties. Community Futures committees and Business Development Centre boards initially lacked direction and purpose, due in part to a shortage of guidelines and models" (Canada Employment and Immigration, 1990a, p.22).

Conclusion

The federal government, over a period of twenty years, has spent large sums under a series of programs to support community economic development programs of various types. Several evaluation studies and reviews of the effectiveness of these programs have been commissioned. What has been learned that was not known twenty years ago? There has been a lot of churning of programs, with names and components changing every few years, and, in general, each new program has been larger and more complex that its predecessors. On the whole, the programs could reasonably be described as troubled. To some extent, lessons from previous programs have been incorporated into the design of the newer programs, but whether they are valid lessons is still not determined.

Programs and evaluation designs must meet three requirements if reliable lessons are to be learned from evaluation research. First, the program being evaluated must be a replicable treatment of some problem. If the program is not a replicable treatment then nothing general can be learned from it. So far, CEI has not been successful in developing replicable treatments in community economic development. "Communities have had the right to find their own path and to make mistakes. Control and prescribed activities have been minimal ... The content (of the programs) has largely been for communities to decide. In this first phase of program delivery, we have been in a joint learning mode and this has been appreciated by our community partners. It will not be acceptable to continue at this level of amateurism" (Canada Employment and Immigration, 1990b, p.55).

Second, the outcome of the treatment must be measurable. Sometimes measures of the desired outcome do not exist. More often the scale of likely effect is so small as to be undetectable under any plausible circumstances. For example, giving \$10 to charity might be a worthwhile thing to do, but it does not make sense to try to measure its impact. Third, there must be a valid and reliable basis of comparison between those who receive the treatment and those who do not, so that the incremental effect can be estimated.

These conditions were not met in the programs and evaluations so the key policy questions are still unanswered. What sort of local economic development programs create incremental economic activity (jobs), if any? If some do, then at what cost to the federal and provincial governments, and to other communities? Who should be the target beneficiary—the community or people in the community? The latter might be better off moving to another community where the demand for labour is higher. What is the effect on labour mobility? Are there more effective or cheaper alternative approaches to economic development or adjustment? The evaluation studies have not answered these questions. They have tried various approaches such as gathering information from the funded organizations, from companies benefiting from funding, and from Statistics Canada. However, three key failures have precluded reliable and systematic learning about effectiveness—there has been no replicable treatment, the effects of intervention have not been measurable, and there has been no valid basis of comparison built in. These are flaws of program design rather than evaluation design, and the failure says much about the failure of theory underlying the CED approach.

14

Employability Approaches in CED Practice: Case Studies and Issues

Jean-Marc Fontan and Eric Shragge

Problems are raised when CED confronts the issue of unemployment and puts in place programs that attempt to reduce unemployment by integrating the unemployed into the labour market. There has been little in the way of systematic evaluation and the role of CED in employability has not been adequately defined. Four case studies will illustrate differing approaches to employability taken by CED organizations and issues related to the evaluation of employability programs and CED.

The tension between the social and economic aspects of CED underlies discussion of the links between CED and employability. Creation, protection, and preparation for jobs in low income communities is one, if not the major objective of CED. There is tension, however, between CED as business development and CED as a wider strategy of social intervention and social change. Business development is limited as an employability strategy and cannot address the massive unemployment and related social problems created during the last fifteen years. These problems are not related to cyclical swings in the economy, but are part of a major economic restructuring, the consequences of which is permanent high levels of unemployment and exclusion from the labour market for a growing number of people. Therefore, relying solely on an employability strategy is insufficient; CED practitioners need to develop other strategies to address the issue of unemployment.

Employability Strategies and the Labour Market

One of the central goals of CED is to generate employment in communities that face chronic employment. Current unemployment, however, reflects wide stratification of the labour market. CED strategies that address unemployment need to take into account differences among the unemployed themselves and their communities. Three descriptive categories can be used that situate individuals in relation to the labour market. First, are those who were employed on a regular basis in a stable job. The many layoffs among blue collar workers are examples of this group. They have a strong attachment to the labour market and are often skilled. Their integration back into work implies strategies such as retraining as well as the redevelopment and investment in working class communities. As well, this group is threatened by the wider economic conditions such as international competition and free trade. These pressures have pushed many from this group into the second.

The second group includes those who have worked irregularly; finding work in this period of unemployment is a difficult challenge. They are faced with precarious and unstable jobs that require little skill. Their needs will not be sufficiently addressed by new investment or establishing programs offering new skills; approaches that can link these individuals to particular training and jobs are required. A third group are those who have been excluded from the labour market because of personal attributes, the inflexibility of employers, and the lack of jobs. This third group includes those with various disabilities as well as populations, such as single mothers, who have been excluded from work because of inadequate support services. The second and third groups make up the traditional population that has fallen well below the poverty line and find themselves on social assistance.

The approach of CED organizations working with the first group will be different from those working with the other two groups. The second group of more marginal populations are likely to experience poverty and economic hardship because of the nature of the jobs that are available to them. Job creation and limited training may offer little for this group, unless major changes in labour market occur and opportunities are expanded. The third group has had little opportunity to participate in regular employment. CED will require strategies that include other anti-poverty approaches such as the demand for a better system of income guarantees as well as developing training and employment innovations that can address needs of the group.

Case Studies

Four case studies will illustrate different approaches to employability. The results reported by these projects are more quantitative than qualitative. Boulot Vers, a training industry, is an example of projects designed to address the training needs of particular populations and to survive as a productive industry. The second approach to employability is one taken by a CED agency supported by the city of Montreal. It uses an individualized approach, but links this approach to a process of consultation and partnership with both public institutions and the private sector. The third case study is the Human Resources Development Association (HRDA) of Halifax, which has integrated training, particularly for welfare recipients, with business development as a means of addressing the issue of employability. The last case study is of an organization called A-Way Express located in Toronto. This organization works with an ex-psychiatric population, a group that have been traditionally excluded from the labour market. These case studies present a variety of examples of community-based employability and will allow for a critical discussion.

Boulot Vers

This organization was developed in 1983 in the east end of Montreal by two workers concerned about youth unemployment. One of the workers had a woodworking and furniture workshop that produced products for day-care centres. The idea of the project was to produce socially useful products and at the same time integrate young people into the labour market. The target population are youth between 16 and 25 who are marginal in terms of employment. Chronic elevated levels of unemployment in the east end of the city and large numbers of drop-outs from secondary schools mean that many young people face unemployment and total exclusion from the labour market. A training industry provides both specific industrial skills needed and personal skills required in the labour market. The training provides an immediate salary, changes the status of the participant to that of a worker, and breaks the exclusion from the labour market. The trainees produce useful products, such as strollers and furniture for day-care centres and furniture for city rooming houses, and develop a greater sense of belonging to the community.

The program accepts between 40 and 45 new trainees each year. A paid training job is offered for six months. Education is provided in economics and civics. There is support in finding specialized services that might be required, as well as help in job search and placement. Follow up occurs one year after the training is completed. In 1992, the program had five full time and two part-time employees. The operating budget was $700,000, 25% derived from the sale of products. The board of directors, in addition to some representatives from the community, has a large number of high profile business people who are active in promoting the organization.

Government job entry programs have a success rate of about 50%; Boulot Vers has achieved a 70% success rate. By the end of 1992, 400 young people will have completed the training course. Fifty-five percent of trainees enter the labour market, 20% return to school, 15% are referred to specialized agencies, and 10% drop out between signing a training contract and completion of the course. An outside accounting firm recently confirmed that governments recover their investment from Boulot Vers by the end of the first year (Rodriguez, 1991; Levesque and Fontan, 1992). There are several strengths to this approach. The program reaches a group who are difficult to train and integrate into the labour market and has a high success rate. The program is linked with other community services through the manufacturing of socially useful products, has a high profile, and has achieved strong support from both government and the business community.

Guichet Multi-Services pour l'emploi et La Formation

CED agencies of the City of Montreal are located in most of the administrative districts of the city. Their priorities are development of training and employment, promotion of the local economy, and collaboration of community, unions, institutions, and private business. In 1987 a committee to redevelop the east end of Montreal expressed concern about the level of training of the 38,000 unemployed in the district. The CED agency, CDEST or Corporation de développement économique de l'Est, set up a committee made up of all levels of government, public educational institutions, unions, and community organizations to develop an approach to employability. A three-year job placement and referral centre was among its recommendations. This project was put in place in 1989.

The goal of the service is to reestablish the unemployed in the labour market by providing access to employers, information and referral services of existing employment and educational resources, and job recruitment and placement services for the unemployed. Staff were selected from several existing institutions including provincial and federal manpower training offices, municipal social assistance office, and employment and business consultants from the local CED agency. Employment services are comprehensive for both the employer and the unemployed. Services for the unemployed begin with a meeting of clients to describe the services that are offered, to register those interested, and to evaluate services needs including registering with the job bank, referral to another organization, setting up an appointment with a job counsellor for further evaluation, or providing an appointment for personal counselling. The job bank is made up of a list of jobs sought by clients who are able to return to the labour market. These are then communicated to specific employers. Clients may be referred to specific training programs. Counselling is provided for those with particular needs. There are a range of services designed to help clients find jobs. These include assistance in preparation of resumés and job interview, a drop-in centre with a variety of information, and lists of employers. There are corresponding services to employers. The business counsellor receives employer calls concerning manpower and training needs and obtaining grants. Outreach to employers is also carried out and the available jobs are classified and posted. The Guichet works on both sides of the employability equation—both preparing workers in a systematic way for the available labour market and coordinating the process with employers.

In 1991–92 the Guichet expanded its services and opened another point of service. More businesses are approaching the agency to meet their employment needs. An evaluation of client satisfaction was carried out with positive results. Training courses were launched on an experimental basis.

The annual report for 1991–1992 indicated that 513 jobs were offered, 715 were referred to jobs, 126 jobs were directly filled by referrals, and 1437 unemployed individuals sought service of whom 553 participated in workshops and 140 attended courses (CDEST, 1992).

There are several strengths offered by this approach. The employment services offered are comprehensive; the one-stop service brings together many government services that are designed to enhance employment opportunities. It provides easy access to programs that are otherwise restricted by red-tape and bureaucratic definitions of eligibility. Systematic contact with employers provides congruence between services offered and the demand for labour in the local community. The success of this program is its ability to serve individuals on a on-to-one basis. But this is also a limitation as the program does not address the issue of unemployment more collectively. The Guichet, however, is located in a CED agency which is able to do this through the promotion of private business and other projects. Individualized programs, regardless of how effective they may be, cannot really address the larger issue of massive unemployment.

Human Resources Development Association (HRDA)

HRDA in Halifax was established in 1978 to serve persons on social assistance and other disadvantaged persons by providing jobs or training. The project grew out of the complaints by a few welfare recipients assigned to jobs in the Social Planning Department of the City of Halifax who argued that, despite the fact that they were working, they had to submit a welfare check to the bank thus undermining their dignity. The Planning Council, along with individuals from the business community, formed HRDA to create businesses that would provide training and employ recipients of social assistance. This initiative was recognized by the city of Halifax as a means of reducing the social assistance budget. Training is directed at one of three goals: to provide HRDA divisions with sufficiently skilled staff from the target group, to assist trainees to get into other training programs, or to provide an entry into the job market outside of HRDA. There is close integration between the training and the business operations. Of the approximately 125 enroled each year, 60% go on to further training or directly into a job. The major innovation of HRDA is the establishment of businesses along side the training programs. Finding both experienced business people and adequate capital had to be faced. The former was addressed by recruiting individuals with skills and abilities for the board of directors. The second problem was addressed through the welfare budget itself. The city allowed $275,000 to be allocated to this project with the assumption that this money would be saved in the longer term. Later, businesses that hired a welfare recipient for a year were allocated the money that would normally be paid to the recipient.

HRDA has established 13 businesses. Four have failed, three were sold to their employees, and six have been retained. Businesses are selected that can easily employ welfare recipients, but the enterprises draw employees from other groups. For example, Magna Industrial Services provides commercial janitorial and labour activities such as snow removal. Recently, Magna was able to employ 90 individuals, 70% of whom were from the target group. Magna contributes a modest profit to HRDA. Since 1978, Magna has been able to hire 1100 from its target group, most of whom have left for other jobs. The wages paid in the businesses are competitive for those industries. The city has saved money from its welfare budget. HRDA has been able to establish successful enterprises and to link these to training programs. It has established a track record that will allow it to continue to find capital and to maintain support from the city of Halifax. In addition, worker cooperatives have been established, thus acting to further empower the clients of the program (Perry, 1993).

A-Way Courier Express

A-Way Express is a courier business that employs psychiatric patients in Toronto. This project had addressed the employability needs of a group often assumed to be unable to work and almost automatically excluded from discussions on employability. The idea for A-Way was developed by members of Progress Place, a voluntary sector agency that works with the population, and Houselink, an agency that addresses their housing needs. The idea was not only to provide jobs but to create ownership for those in the project. The project began in June 1987 with 10 couriers and 25 customers. By 1992, it had expanded to 50 couriers and office staff and a customer base of 500. Of the 50 employees, 43 work part-time (less than 28 hours a week) and 7 are full time (more than 28 hours a week). Start-up and continuing support has come from the Mental Health Services Branch of the Ministry of Health of Ontario. Revenue has continued to grow from $65,000 in 1989, to $96,000 in 1990, and $135,000 in 1991.

Training for employment is offered through various activities of the organization including accounting, use of computers, publicity, and other activities linked to the functioning of the business. Employees are involved in decision making through the Board of Directors composed of 14 members, half of whom are employees. The management team meets twice a month with representatives of all the activities of A-Way and a general meeting of all employees is held once a month. A-Way has been able to link both social and economic values. It provides a socially useful service to clients and couriers use and support public transportation. The program, however, cannot exist without support from government sources. The linking of their approach of empowerment with economic development is a significant innovation that has contributed to the longer-term strength of this population (Fontan, 1993).

Issues Facing CED Intervention and Employability

These case studies represent different approaches to employability. All are community-based and are run by agencies that are, at least to some extent, rooted in the local community or in the lives of the population served. All are controlled by independent boards that, to varying degrees, represent the clients served. The interventions are innovative and present new approaches to employability. The focus is on individual change and development but each brings another dimension. Boulot Vers, HRDA, and A-Way Express introduce the concept of linking training to a new economic venture with an emphasis on training as well as control and participation in the productive process. Thus there is a link between specific training or employability with wider social objectives. Guichet attempts to overcome the fragmentation of existing government programs by presenting a comprehensive and coordinated service in a local community; local representatives have a voice in the program. All four community level organizations have been able to take on a function that was usually considered the function of government and have produced good results within the constraints of the current economic situation. Comparative research is required to complete a comparison between the community and governmental employability practices, but these cases suggest that the dimensions of solidarity, empowerment, and local control are aspects to be considered in future evaluation.

The role of government in developing and sustaining employment is central and complex. It can act to create or limit employment through macro-economic policies, through expanding or contracting its own programs and expenditures, or through a wide range of support to the private sector. What is the role of CED in relation to these larger players? There is a danger that CED may become the means to deliver and manage state programs as a decentralized extension of government services. This might be positive because CED organizations are locally based and close to the target population. But if CED organizations become extensions of government programs with less power and resources, then their ability to be democratic, community-based and innovative is diminished. What, then, is the appropriate role for CED in relation to both generating employment strategies and in relation to government.

The case studies illustrate that CED organizations have put in place many independent initiatives that act to address the question of employability. These are small scale and provide employment to a relatively limited population. New institutions are created and controlled by members of the local community. Thus employability strategies and interventions are linked to a form of community control. However, given the relatively small scale of their operation, these approaches cannot possibly make up for the massive level of unemployment. The local programs must be seen in a light other than large-scale job creation programs. They may be understood more in terms of a process of community and local empowerment that can create local democratic institutions, but not necessarily as programs that can make a dent in the issue of unemployment.

CED needs to represent the local community to the different levels of government and other funders. CED must become a political voice for disenfranchised communities. This process of representation is built on the education and mobilization of the local population as people try to speak for their own needs. In Montreal, a city sponsored and funded CED organization, RESO (le Regroupement pour la relance économique et sociale dans le sud-ouest de Montréal), has raised demands for jobs and local investment with organizations locating in their community—such as a dormitory of McGill University (Gareau, 1990). Political intervention enables groups to be more than a direct service provider or an extension of government training programs. Political activity is a means of avoiding becoming only a place to which governments can shift responsibilities for programs without the resources to carry them out.

Evaluation of employability programs and CED approaches to them need to be situated in a wider context. The results of intervention in the community can also be assessed in relation to wider economic and social forces. There has been a major breakdown in the labour market as a result of the impact of free trade, internationalization of capital, deindustrialization, and the introduction of new technology. Unemployment is not cyclical but is linked to the wholesale disappearance of traditional blue collar jobs. New jobs have more clearly polarized the labour market between jobs linked to high technology and those in the service sector. The former require advanced training and pay better wages, while, in contrast, the latter are precarious, low-waged, and require little specialized training. The number of technology jobs are relatively small compared to those in the services sector.

Both provincial and federal governments have cutback and redefined programs. Ideology has shifted towards greater individual responsibility for addressing the wider changes in the society and toward the family for caring for its own members in difficulty. Local community organizations have been redefined as an important vehicle for provision. Contradictory results emerge for CED organizations. There is greater recognition for CED because this approach speaks the same language as government by putting emphasis on a redefined market, business development, and individual training as means of addressing social problems associated with unemployment. Increased recognition has lead to greater support; some CED organizations have used the support to develop innovations and programs that help empower community residents.

CED organizations face two types of approaches for developing employability programs. The first is based on individualized training and assumes that through training the individual can find a place in the labour market.

The individual will be integrated into the labour market by developing the supply side of the equation or investing in human capital. Given the difficulties of that market, and the large number of people chasing after the scarce number of jobs, training has the effect of pushing a few to the front of the line and not really addressing the underlying scarcity of jobs. Though Guichet Multi-Service were able to provide a variety of employment related services, they cannot meet the huge demand for jobs in their community.

The second approach is to create the jobs themselves. This can occur through private business development, or through putting in place innovative initiatives such as training businesses, or cooperatives, or community controlled institutions such as loan funds. The program of HRDA, Boulot Vers, and A-Way Express are initiatives of this type. The consequences for job creation may not be significant but the process can help contribute to development of community-based institutions that can build a political and social voice.

The choices of direction for employability are complex. There is a new balance being struck between the private sector, including new private employment finding and training institutes, state programs and services, and both traditional and new community organizations. Income support programs have introduced work and training which embody policies that are punitive to recipients and lead to dead-ended training schemes that do not produce labour market integration or a stable job with adequate wages. They have used training as a means to mobilize cheap labour for businesses, community organizations, and government services. Within this context both policy and practice decisions and orientations become crucial. What should be advocated? A restructured income support system is a policy pre-requisite to develop employability programs and to encourage individuals to initiate projects that link training and socially useful jobs. An adequate income floor must be the first issue debated in an employability strategy, given the very weak and vulnerable position of most people in today's labour market. Only then can innovative and empowering forms of practice can become a reality in the community. The building of community autonomy to create these approaches will be possible if the basic question of income for the poor is clearly separated from employability strategies.

15

The Innovative Profile of Community Economic Development in Quebec

Louis Favreau and William A. Ninacs

Quebec's endeavours in the field of local and regional development[*] are numerous and varied; these include the regional development cooperatives (coopératives de développement régional), the regional development roundtables for concerted action and development which have recently been converted into regional development councils (conseils régionaux de développement), the Community Futures Committees (CFCs), the Manpower Adjustment Committees (MACs), etc. Although the mission of each of these bodies is to improve a community's collective well-being through the economic development of a specific geographic area, they have not, however, been the primary subjects of our research since very few of them have adopted community economic development as an intervention strategy. We in fact subscribe to a progressive definition of community economic development (CED), such as the one recently put forward by the Institut de formation en développement économique communautaire *(community economic development training institute)* (IFDEC):

> ...a comprehensive strategy for the socioeconomic revitalization of marginalized communities in which, by developing local resources and new partnerships, organizations and institutions democratically controlled by community representatives are created, making it easier for the community to have a voice in external institutions that affect the management of local resources (Fontan, 1993, p.16) *(Our translation).*

This choice has enabled us to establish that community economic development arose out of Quebec's social movements, somewhat on the fringes of government programs, and to confirm that it is interrelated with

---

[*] The concept of regional development has been given a meaning which necessarily includes a concern with economic development that involves a socioeconomic transformation leading to a sustainable improvement of the population's standard of living. Regional boards for purely social or cultural development, for instance, are thus not part of this discussion.

the development of a social economy* in Quebec. Although our work remains to be completed, we can state that the current version of CED in Quebec holds out hope for social renewal and change.

The Emergence of Community Economic Development in Quebec

The economic crisis of the early 1980s and the levelling of traditional job creators partly explains the emergence of community economic development in Quebec. Over the past few decades, the workplace in almost all of the industrialized countries has been split into two sectors: a "primary" sector, characterized by decent pay and a steady job, and a "secondary" one where to the contrary, poorly paid, precarious employment prevails. On the fringes of this active work force are totally disillusioned people who have left this way of life for a world of crime, drugs, or transience. More and more people are sliding from the relative stability of the first sector to the insecurity of the second, moving into the "temporary-job-unemployment-welfare" cycle. This vicious circle evolves into a descending spiral when nothing is done to counter this trend of the market economy.

This duality, caused by the fragmentation of the job market (Blakely, 1989, pp.28–32) and exacerbated by the wiping out of traditional job sources brought on by the globalization of markets, has institutionalized a permanent poverty of sorts, resulting in economic polarization and the exclusion of entire communities from production activities. Poverty levels are fluctuating and may even be decreasing slightly in terms of percentage points but there is a rise in absolute numbers (Provost & Deniger, 1991), varying according to age group (youth are hardest hit, whether they be single or heads of families), type of family (single-parent families suffered most from the 1982 recession and have still not made up lost ground), and certain specific classes of marginalized populations (poverty is more prevalent among native populations, immigrants, and disabled persons) (Langlois, 1990, pp.12–41). Impoverishment also affects both urban and rural local communities, hitting metropolitain working class neighbourhoods headlong as well as a number of cities and towns in resource and intermediate regions (Conseil des affaires sociales du Quebec [Québec welfare council], 1989, 1991, 1992).**

---

* "For cooperative, labour and community leaders, the expression 'social economy' refers to three elements of Quebec society: (1) local and regional development strategies whereby attempts are made to set up ventures incorporating economic and social objectives, (2) new types of partnerships that encourage capitalist ventures to take responsibility for social concerns in the realms of the environment, of worker participation and of contribution to the community, (3) the legal expression for a cooperative which, by definition, seeks to combine economic and social values." (Lévesque and Malo, 1992, p.391) *(Our translation).*

** Typology proposed by Tremblay et Van Schendel (1991, pp.365–6) of the three main categories of Quebec's regions.

But the economic situation does not explain everything and it must be noted that social policies in Quebec and the rest of Canada have changed over the last decade with the aim of countering the increasing impoverishment of the jobless and the decline of regions and local communities. This has brought about changes that may provide another explanation for the emergence of community economic development in Quebec: in this case, a political one. On one hand, the focus of job-creation programs has been shifted towards protecting existing jobs through upgrading and developing the employability of highly disadvantaged target groups (Employment and Immigration Canada, 1988). On another level, the shift from adult education to vocational training also took place during those years (Paquet, 1992). In regional development, the federal government went from an ad hoc strategy (Brodhead, 1990, p.42) to programs based on local partnerships via Community Futures Committees and Manpower Adjustment Committees. The Quebec government also opted for similar axes by formalizing regional socioeconomic conferences (Tremblay & Van Schendel, 1991, pp.418-419) and, recently, the new regional development councils.

The explanation of the phenomenon by means of a political variable is nonetheless unsatisfactory in the light of how local communities have shifted as well. The combination of progressively diminishing public services (due to deficits) and soaring job losses in traditional sectors (because of the globalization of markets) forced local communities to change direction in order to survive. The dynamic interaction among local authorities gave way to a new trend towards assuming social and economic responsibility through a variety of local development strategies, all aimed at using a comprehensive approach — i.e., simultaneously economic, cultural, social and political — based on an endogenous development framework (ANDLP & IFDEC, 1989, p.8).

Indeed, in Quebec, an empowerment of communities which had traditionally excluded from the spheres of economic development, took place when they also began to take responsibility for themselves, joining the struggle against poverty, with a determination to deal with the problems of the social and economic disintegration of their environment. Thus, some local geographical communities with a strong sense of belonging (Favreau, 1989; Ninacs, 1991) have been resisting transformations imposed from the outside when the aims did not correspond to their interests. At the same time, young people and women began to regroup on the basis of their identities, which served as a driving force for community action. These two trends provide yet another explanation for the emergence of community economic development in Quebec, one with a prevailing sociocultural perspective, which highlights the capacity for social change of marginalized social groups and local geographical communities, as well as their ability to renew traditional grassroots and labour strategies too often narrowly focused on advocacy and the development of state or community services.

A qualitative shift in community organizing in fact occurred in the 1980s when a significant part of Quebec's communitarian movement plunged into the development process by following the route of partnerships and concerted efforts (Bélanger & Lévesque, 1992, pp.724–736). This incursion into local and regional development was expressed mainly by the setting up of its own structures for pooled effort and action — community economic development corporations (CEDC), community development corporations (CDC) —, its own enterprises (Bhérer & Joyal, 1987), and by adopting this new direction, that of community economic development (Favreau & Ninacs, 1992).

Although, some CED initiatives in Quebec date back to a quarter of a century ago or more (Fontan, 1992, pp.195–222), most were to be found in certain resource areas, far from cities or large urban centres, as is happening in the rest of Canada, with little direct links with the then burgeoning communitarian movement, staying within the confines of the cooperative movement and alternative milieu. It can be argued that CED in Quebec was really launched in 1984 with the emergence of the first CEDC in Quebec at Pointe-Saint-Charles (in an urban centre) and the first CDC in Victoriaville (in a mid-sized city).

At first glance, CED practices would seem to have more of a social connotation in Quebec than in the rest of Canada or the United States. The Quebec model is both affected by its origins in the communitarian movement and influenced by the concerns of the community organizations that set it up — often thus reflecting health and welfare priorities. It was also inspired by outside experiences such as training businesses, community loan funds, and micro-enterprise development, and is being challenged by Quebec's new regional development and vocational training strategies as well as by federal programs for local and work force development.

A portion of Quebec's communitarian movement is thus at the hub of all these models and is seeking to deal with the overall situation with the twofold aim of economic and social development. There are today at least twenty community development corporations and community economic development corporations in Quebec, key organizations for linking and developing businesses and grassroots organizations. Moreover, in many localities, innovative social integration ventures are springing up. These initiatives represent an important watershed: an increasing number of labour and grassroots organizations are no longer relying solely on advocacy strategies coupled with a concept of government dominated social change, but are more and more resolutely involved in organizing local and regional economic development. But these structures, as well as the initiatives closely or remotely related to them, remain little known and are still at the experimental stage. The purpose of our research is hence to obtain a clearer picture of these.

The Research Project

The research is being carried out jointly by the Corporation de développement communautaire des Bois-Francs [Bois-Francs community development corporation] and the Université du Québec à Hull's Groupe d'étude et de recherche en intervention sociale *[Study and Research Group for Social Planning]*. The general aim of our project is to identify the factors conducive to setting up community economic development projects. This is done by studying the conditions, means, and instruments that have allowed this type of development to emerge and strengthen in Quebec, especially over the last decade. Five objectives have been targeted:

- Identifying the conditions which, in the 1980s, allowed community development corporations (CDCs) and community economic development corporations (CEDCs) to emerge, along with the community businesses and organizations that they support, as well as the problems they have encountered.

- Determining the specific contributions of these organizations to local communities: main sectors in which they intervene, types of economic and social actions, clienteles being served, and impact on the community.

- Assessing the internal dynamics of the CDCs and CEDCs: services offered (in the areas of training, financial assistance, management, etc.), democratic operations, human and material resources.

- Assessing the internal dynamics of community ventures from a business viewpoint (employees, markets, funding, infrastructure, etc.) as well as from an associative outlook (membership, internal democratic practices, etc.).

- Characterizing the type of relationship CED initiatives have with the state and its institutions (municipalities, government departments, paragovernmental agencies, etc.).

In this work, we have endeavoured to go beyond previous studies (Fontan, 1992; Favreau, 1989; Bhérer & Joyal, 1987; Lévesque et al., 1989) by comparing CED practices in different environments (urban and rural, near large cities or far from them) and analyzing the conditions, means and instruments used. The study is comparative, cross-sectorial, and interregional and focused on four regions: the Bois-Francs area that gave birth to the CDC model, the Montreal region from which the CEDC model emerged, and the Outaouais and Bas-Richelieu regions that have a dynamic of their very own. Two kinds of CED organizations in Quebec have been taken into account. First are structures for support and concerted action, mainly CDCs and CEDCs, and second, a few cooperative and grassroots ventures or organizations, programs or projects supported by CDCs and CEDCs and through which social and economic objectives are being simultaneously implemented.

Our data-gathering strategy was both quantitative and qualitative and was first aimed at building an overall profile of the CDCs and CEDCs — a core of over 20 corporations. Second, data was sought to determine, from within, the dynamics of these corporations and enterprises. Key information sources were interviewed to better understand the motivations of those who manage and run these corporations, to better understand the strategies that are specific to this sector (as opposed to the public or private sectors), to assess their organizational framework, to appraise their contribution to local (or regional) communities, and to better pinpoint the factors contributing to their success (length of time, local influence, institutional recognition, etc.). These interviews were carried out among people involved at the managerial levels of the CDCs and CEDCs. Moreover, active leaders in some twenty enterprises were also interviewed. These interviews afforded a better understanding of the motivations of those who start up, run and manage a community or cooperative enterprise and provided data to assess the way these enterprises are organized as associations and as businesses, to appraise their contribution to local (or regional) communities, and to better identify the factors contributing to their success.

Some Findings

The weakness in cohesion of the communitarian movement, despite a common culture shared by its members, must serve as a backdrop for the presentation of CEDCs and CDCs. There are striking differences among many of these organizations in terms of structure, activities, and even directions. Moreover, our analysis of available data is just beginning. In spite of these hurdles, many common points enable us to establish some parallels and to deduce similarities between these organizations.

Community Economic Development Corporations (CEDCs)

There are seven community economic development corporations (CEDCs) on Montreal Island and four others may soon be set up in other areas.* The first, the Programme économique de Pointe-Saint-Charles *[Pointe-St-Charles Economic Program]*, was established in 1984 and became, in 1990, the Regroupement pour la relance économique et sociale du sud-ouest de Montréal [*Group for economic and social recovery in*

---

* The CEDCs in the Montreal area are: CDEC Ahunstic/Cartierville (in the process of being set up), CDEC Centre-Nord, CDEC Centre-Sud et du Plateau Mont Royal, CDEC Rosemont et Petite-Patrie, Côte-des-Neiges-Snowdon Community Council, Corporation de développement de l'EST (CDEST), and Regroupement pour la relance économique et sociale du sud-ouest de Montréal (RESO). Three community economic development corporations are being developed in the Outaouais region and one in Quebec City.

southwest Montreal. It took its inspiration from American and Canadian experiences. The history of its early days is similar to that of any new community organization (Corporation de développement communautaire des Bois-Francs, 1987, p.92; Gareau, 1990) and its evolution served as a model for others that followed in Montreal (Favreau, 1989). Despite differences as to the means used, all CEDCs adopt a similar CED model, attempting to:

- attract capital to the community, under terms it finds acceptable;
- improve the immediate physical environment by using local or outside resources;
- increase job and business creation opportunities for community residents by providing training and directly setting up collective enterprises; and
- encourage entrepreneurs or decision makers to offer services or make them available to the local population (Fontan, 1991, p.32).

CEDCs funded by the city of Montreal share other characteristics because of municipal requirements for dialogue building among leaders from public, private, labour, and community organizations (City of Montreal, 1990, p.29) and because of the financial and human resources available to them. The sources of these funds as well as the amounts involved are without precedent in the history of Quebec's communitarian movement. There are nevertheless huge gaps between the budgets and number of employees of first generation CEDCs (the three that were set up in Montreal in 1984–85 have annual budgets allowing for 15 to 25 employees), second generation ones (the two that began operations in 1990 each have ten or so permanent employees), and the last two that are at the implementation stage.

A primary facet of CEDCs, whether they be in Montreal or elsewhere, is that their action seems to be directed mainly outside its structures rather than at the organizations that constitute their membership. In other words, the main goal of a CEDC is not to meet the needs of its members or the community organizations that initiated it, but rather those of the community as a whole.

Another significant fact is that the presumed predominance of the economic aspect of development conceals an important social practice. Here, CEDCs adopt different strategies centring around two main poles. First is employability taken in a collective sense, mainly by means of economic initiatives for social integration, training activities, some of which are carried out in the workplace (training businesses, in-plant training courses). Second is the creation of conventional businesses, mainly through assistance to entrepreneurs, which demonstrates an attempt to make a breakthrough on the economic plain. Additionally some CEDCs are active in the fields of urban planning land use while others assist in the setting up community or alternative businesses.

Community Development Corporations (CDCS)

The situation of community development corporations is less clear and even the name can be misleading. Though Quebec's community development corporations are unquestionably agents of local development, they must not be confused with CEDCs nor with other Canadian (Brodhead, Lamontagne & Pierce, 1989, pp.12–13) or American (Zdenek, 1987, pp.115–117) namesakes which are closely related to CEDCs in almost every respect. Quebec's version of CDCs differs from CEDCs and other development agencies in the following ways:

- they are set up (at the outset, at least) as groupings of community based organizations in a given territory and organized as structures for technical assistance, consultation, and service by and for community based organizations;

- the membership is made up mainly of community based organizations; and

- they implement a process by which the community based organizations first try to get to know and recognize each other and then seek to be recognized by their respective communities and various levels of government.

CDCs differ from other grassroots groupings in Quebec by the composition of their membership, which stems from various sectors of activity (e.g., health and welfare, child care, housing, consumerism, domestic violence, etc.) and represents many kinds of organizations (i.e., service groups, grassroots training groups, lobby groups and, in some cases, cooperatives). Because they often operate within the territory of a Regional County Municipality (RCM), they are often called regional or interregional, cross-sectorial groupings of community based organizations.

There are presently twelve CDCs in Quebec, all but one of which are outside of large urban centres.* In most cases, an informal assembly of community organizations existed beforehand and the CDC filled an obvious need for concerted effort. One CDC describes itself as being simultaneously both a permanent coalition and a natural instrument for concerted action.

The resources available to CDCs vary tremendously and the wide discrepancies render generalizations impractical: the number of employees ranges from none to 20; some have been loaned quarters while others own entire buildings; some have an annual income of $650 while for another, it is $225,000 or more. On this last point, currently all but one of the CDCs

---

* They are the following: CDC Beauharnois-Salaberry (Valleyfield), CDC Brome-Missisquoi (Farnham), CDC d'Amos (Amos), CDC de Longueuil (Longueuil), CDC des Bois-Francs (Victoriaville), CDC des Deux-Rives (Jonquière), CDC Drummond (Drummondville), CDC du Bas-Richelieu (Sorel), CDC du Granit (Lac Mégantic), CDC Région de l'Amiante (Thetford Mines), CDC Rond-Point (Buckingham), and Regroupement des organismes communautaires du KRTB (Rivière-du-Loup).

have no recurring funding whatsoever and the older ones are struggling to survive. They have received no formal recognition from the provincial and federal government that would result in a funding program like the Montreal CEDCs. On the other hand, regional and local structures of the same governments are increasingly acknowledging CDCs by, for instance, inviting them to take part in various committees, asking them to develop new services, etc.

CDCs are set up in economically depressed regions with a goal of combatting poverty and a common desire to deal with the problems of economic and social disintegration. To varying degrees, depending on each CDC's development, this translates into a plan of action directed towards simultaneously strengthening members' operations and developing their communities economically and socially. To this end, CDCs adopt practices from the communitarian movement's other forums, services based on proven experience, such as sharing information and work tools and pooling secretarial or training services (Corporation de développement communautaire des Bois-Francs, 1987, p.158).

CDCs involved in the economic field (Bas-Richelieu, Bois-Francs, Rond-Point, etc.) are more likely than other decision-makers on this level to direct their efforts towards developing a social economy. Their incursions into the economic field take two main forms. The first is direct assistance in setting up new ventures of a more collective nature than conventional private enterprise, and thus CDCs are likely to promote the cooperative model and not-for-profit structures. The second is involvement in the various local and regional development boards. For instance, several CDCs sit in on Community Futures Committees, on Manpower Adjustment Committees, regional development councils, etc. In this way, the community concurs that they reflect a vital social and political contribution to their area, which is something new, and simply their presence within these bodies undoubtedly brings a new dimension to the debates and discussions.

Lastly, CDCs do not merely represent the communitarian movement; they organize and structure its public forays and its strategies for involvement in other official bodies. For example, in the recent process to regionalize Quebec's public health and welfare sector, CDCs served as a springboard for developing concerted actions among the community organizations within their territories, between community organizations and government bodies, and even among community organizations from other territories.

Similarities and Differences

Both CEDCs and CDCs are involved in common struggles (the fight against poverty, the disintegration of the social fabric, etc.) and do so from within structures that are democratically controlled by the members of the community. Moreover, when implicated on the economic front, they both opt for community economic development strategies. Finally, in almost every case, a local community service centre was present at their start-ups, although the degree of involvement varies depending on the neighbourhood and region (Favreau & Hurtubise, 1993, pp.48–49).

CEDCs differ from CDCs in adopting intervention plans centred around the economic pole while CDCs, because of the concerns of the groups that make up their membership, are more likely to be centred around the social one. Another difference is that, since CEDCs favour joint action by agencies representing different communities of interest, they must rely on the help of leaders and entrepreneurs to reach the target populations; on the other hand, CDCs, which favour joint action by organizations already made up of target populations, must seek to further strengthen member organizations.

Other Community Economic Development Projects and Ventures in Quebec

Objectively, most CED initiatives in Quebec differ qualitatively from private sector enterprises and public sector institutions in the following ways:

- by their origins: they are groupings of people having a common social problem that needs resolving (e.g., getting off welfare or ending unemployment);
- by their objectives: these enterprises seek to combine economic concerns with social ones;
- by their type of management: these enterprises generally give some degree of importance to the collective dimension of management;
- by the way they allocate surpluses: they are most often reinjected into the local economy through new goods and services.

Community economic development initiatives have evolved in highly diversified sectors such as housing and land use (housing cooperatives); health and welfare (community home-care ventures and services, child care services, used clothing counters); domestic economy (food cooperatives, community kitchens); recovery, recycling, and re-use; culture; education and vocational training; job-readiness development; and, more recently, management and maintenance of community buildings.

Initiatives aimed at communities in the process of being excluded from the economic mainstream have simultaneous economic and social aims that are interrelated and interdependent. For all practical purposes, CED initiatives are outside of the boundaries of current federal and provincial social policies, although they operate in the same fields: job creation, employability development, vocational training, business development, etc. Therefore, a situation frequently exists where two different approaches — a "top-down" one driven by government programs, the other being "bottom-up" via innovative grassroots initiatives — are concurrently put forward to address some of the issues relating to impoverishment.

Although many of these initiatives are related to CEDCs or CDCs, our research has uncovered a considerable number where neither support structure exists. Some of these CED initiatives may have benefited from the support of other structures in their communities, particularly local community service centres, or government programs such as job-finding clubs funded by Employment and Immigration Canada and the external labour services funded by the Ministère de la Main dœuvre, de la Sécurité du revenu et de la Formation professionnelle *[Quebec department of labour, income security and vocational training]*. Still, many CED initiatives operate on a shoestring. An inventory and an appraisal of such initiatives which are flourishing independently of CEDCs and CDCs would be essential to better understand them.

Unlike government policies which are widely known, CED interventions have had very little study. Their wide range — training businesses, micro-enterprises, youth cooperatives — as well as their straddling fundamentally opposite fields, where for instance, psychosocial intervention borders on production requirements on the factory floors of social integration ventures, make it difficult to adequately classify these interventions and conduct comparative studies. However, convincing data emanating from initiatives in France (Fontan, 1992), Denmark, and Italy (Institute for Cooperative Community Development, 1992) and elsewhere suggests that exploratory and evaluative research work should be undertaken to determine the impact of analogous innovative ventures among underprivileged populations here.

Factors Conducive to the Emergence and Strengthening of CED Initiatives: Certain Elements

The burgeoning of CED initiatives suggests a vitality and synergy within often underestimated social movements. It reflects the communitarian and labour movements' capacity for renewal and change without a loss of their values. The interviews reveal a sustained activist commitment within initiatives that remain against the current, as well as an objective of simultaneous social and economic efficiency based on full participation, democratization of knowledge and of institutional control — in short, the empowerment of communities that are marginalized or being excluded. In a post-Keynesian setting of state disengagement from social policies, empowerment may become a pillar on which to build an endogenous planning strategy based on the maximum use of local resources, supported by government development policies, and following new paths to counter poverty, such as those put forward by the United Nations in recent years (United Nations, 1989).

What factors were conducive to setting up CED initiatives in Quebec? Although our analysis is not yet finished, we nevertheless have some observations stemming from our work so far:

- Women and young people are the main players in CED, on the front lines of many of the initiatives studied (community kitchens, building management, cooperatives, etc.).

- People who ensure that new support structures are set up or who change the focus of existing ventures are often former community leaders using uncommon strategies combining economic and social issues. As to new community leaders, their motivation has often been spurred during intensive training activities. These people stand out by their willingness to take risks in trying to break into the economic field and by a pragmatism that does not reject market imperatives.

- Results seem to indicate that community leaders rather than business persons or social advocates are needed to launch economic development initiatives. This would corroborate findings of non-Quebec authors (Fairbairn, Bold, Fulton, Ketilson & Ish, 1991). One thing is certain: the presence of pre-existing community resources — a more or less formal network of community organizations, a community action program and staff from a local community service centre — favours the emergence of CEDCs or CDCs as most of their leaders emanate from the communitarian movement and its vitality.

- The organizational culture put forward in CED initiatives relates to a form of collective entrepreneurship aimed at social goals such as democratic participation and community control. The economic needs of the enterprise are however not be overlooked as development at this level is vital, much as it is for all other enterprises operating within the present economic system, with financial viability being the cornerstone on which all other objectives depend (MacLeod, 1992).

- The dearth of specific CED training projects and activities is hampering the movement's progress. It isn't "natural" for community activists, volunteers, and militants on the social front to proceed to the economic one. CED demands a qualitative leap requiring a mind open to new strategies and the acquisition of specific technical expertise, such as marketing and strategic planning. Tools that have already been developed are inadequate to deal with the complexity of concurrent interventions on multiple fronts. Business administration training often leaves out social goals pursued by CED initiatives while grassroots educational activities of the communitarian movement often don't speak to economic concerns. Agencies working specifically in the field of CED training, such as Institut de formation en développement économique communautaire (IFDEC) for instance, become indispensable and must be supported and encouraged.

- Organizational support such as lodging, staff and equipment, especially during the implementation phase, as well as the recognition by socially significant institutions rooted in the community, contribute to a public acceptance of CED projects, which in turn helps them to break into the economic and political spheres.

- Launching and reinforcing CED initiatives requires the existence of support structures adapted to the community, such as CEDCs and CDCs, to break down isolation and to ensure the continued presence of economic and social goals.

- CED is intrinsically local and initiatives that follow this path must focus their efforts primarily on local development. Strategies complementary to local development become meaningful in a context of empowering local communities. These include import substitution, locally controlled financial institutions, and community land trusts (Nozick, 1992, pp.41–61; Swack & Mason, 1989). Regional planning deals more with political representation and it is therefore through partnerships with others (the private sector, the parapublic sector, etc.) that the "third sector" can exert some influence.

- A government funding program that is adequate and spread over a sufficiently long period of time to give a real boost (five years, for instance, in the case of Montreal CEDCs) is imperative. CED in Quebec needs specific and consistent support policies from central governments; the lack of their financial support where municipalities have committed themselves could compromise the new CED profile that CDCs represent.

16

Evaluation of Community Economic Development: Summary and Research Agenda

Joe Hudson and Dennis MacDonald

Program evaluation in CED may take various forms; the common ingredients found in these chapters are those of systematically collecting, analyzing, reporting and using information about a CED program or project to assist in making decisions. The chapters in this section address the evaluation of CED from different perspectives using a variety of cases to illustrate key points. Jean-Marc Fontan and Eric Shragge refer to a focus on assessing program outcomes as compared to addressing program process. Four case studies are used to illustrate differing approaches to the evaluation of employability in CED organizations and their implications.

Kenneth Watson reviews three versions of CED programming subjected to evaluation by the federal department of Employment and Immigration—the Community Employment Strategy, the Local Employment Assistance and Development Program, and the Community Futures Program. Watson reviews the questions addressed in the evaluations and the major findings. Emphasis was placed on assessing the relative extent to which the programs achieved their identified objectives, with relatively little attention given to the assessment of program processes and implementation. Watson concludes by emphasizing the importance of clear program definition and the use of rigorous experimental methods. The third chapter by Louis Favreau and William Ninacs present preliminary results from a study of CED projects in Quebec.

Themes

Timing of data collection, assessment, and reporting efforts is a continuum with periodic evaluation studies at one end and monitoring studies at the other. Monitoring forms of program evaluation involves the regular collection, analysis, reporting, and use of information throughout the life of a CED project. In contrast, periodic evaluations are conducted on an infrequent, interval, or once-and-for-all basis. For example, a CED program manager may decide to have the program evaluated, hire an evaluator, receive the results, and then not have any further evaluation work done for several years, if ever again. A problem with this periodic approach to program evaluation is that CED programs do not stand still. Favreau and Ninacs report that they inevitably change, both during and after the evaluation, and important new information needs are likely to go unintended, at least until the next evaluation is conducted. In contrast, an ongoing monitoring approach to program evaluation provides relatively continuous information about the operations of the CED program or project. Ideally, an ongoing evaluation system would be integrated with the record system in the CED program or project so as to avoid duplication of tasks. For example, background data on persons involved in the program, services provided, and changes the program or project attempts to accomplish, might all be collected and reported at specified times during program operations. In this way, a constant stream of data could be collected, analyzed, reported, and used to help focus program operations and improve program practices.

Kenneth Watson suggests that the type of evaluation implemented in a CED project or program is likely to be related to the way responsibilities for program evaluation are organized and managed. He describes a number of periodic evaluations of federally sponsored CED programs to serve the information needs of senior managers in the funding body, as compared to persons more directly involved in local projects. The evaluators were responsible to officials outside of local operations. This can lead evaluations to take on an external oversight flavour along with an emphasis on assessing long-term program impacts and effects. Concern with long-term program effects is likely to be less important to persons involved in local project operations. Their concerns are likely to be more focused on questions related to project implementation and decentralized responsibility for evaluation at the level of project management teams is likely to be preferred.

Evaluation Purpose

Two general approaches to the evaluation of CED programs run through these chapters. Watson reviews a number of evaluations giving rigorous emphasis to assessing program outcomes and effects—whether or not the program achieved a set of pre-determined objectives. The findings are then expected to provide guidance on the planning and delivery of services so that decisions concerning the maintenance, expansion, or termination of programs can be made on a more empirically justified basis. In contrast, Fontan and Shragge and Favreau and Ninacs describe an alternative evaluation strategy, one that aims at conducting evaluations for the immediate purpose of understanding operations. Here, the aim is one of looking at program processes or operations in order to learn more about the nature of the CED interventions and how they develop and change. Additionally, in the absence of clearly stated objectives at the inception of the program, focusing on program implementation may be of assistance in discovering and formulating program objectives. These two approaches can be seen as amounting to testing or verifying CED programs, as compared to discovering programs.

While emphasis on the evaluation of program outcomes may represent the preferred approach to meeting the information needs of policy makers and funders, it may not be useful in meeting the information needs of persons more directly involved at implementing the CED program or project. Their information needs may best be met by an evaluation strategy centring on the processes of program development and implementation, the manner and extent to which the program unfolds in the local action arena. Clearly, the two general approaches complement each other; the key considerations are the extent to which the CED program or project can meet the preconditions of each evaluation strategy and the information needs of designated decision makers.

A rigorous approach to the evaluation of CED program outcomes requires that several preconditions be met: program activities and operations are specified; program goals or objectives are stated in precise terms; and there is a clearly articulated and plausible rationale linking program activities with expected outcomes. Furthermore, an evaluation strategy aimed at testing CED program outcomes is based on the assumption that the program remains relatively stable throughout its cycle. Program staff are not allowed to introduce changes, and the program is required to hold still during the life of the evaluation. The critical question for any CED program is whether these preconditions can be met. If not, a test of program outcomes is useless for drawing inferences about the extent to which program activities achieved the intended results. Vaguely conceptualized program operations make it difficult to know what was evaluated; vaguely stated goals or objectives make the development of appropriate measurement indicators a guessing game; failure to articulate the program logic leaves open the implausibility of the program activities or interventions producing the planned results; and changes introduced into the program in mid stream raise questions about what the program was that produced the measured outcomes.

A strategy that aims at collecting information on program processes or program implementation will likely be aimed at meeting the information needs of program operators and persons most directly involved in program operations. The aim of such an evaluation is to modify and improve program operations, not stand in judgement. A collaborative relationship is called for between the evaluator and the evaluation stakeholders so that significant evaluation questions can be identified and prioritized in relation to the decisions to be made and the data collection procedures to be used, along with the expected content and timing of the reports to be produced.

Evaluation Stakeholders

Jean-Marc Fontan and Eric Shragge note that a number of different persons and organizations are often concerned with a CED program or project. All of them are likely to have some different interests and priorities with respect to the studies that should be conducted, questions to be addressed, the kinds of data to be collected and analyzed, and how the data should be reported and used. For example, in any particular CED program or project the following types of persons might be seen as having a substantial stake in the program or project evaluated:

- Program or project beneficiaries; citizens who may play a variety of roles, including those of advising and decision making;
- Program or project staff who may be interested in information about project operations and practices;
- Project supervisors who may be interested in how different types of project activities are being carried out;
- Program managers and administrators interested in obtaining information about the manner and extent to which services are being delivered, as well as their efficiency and effectiveness;
- Representatives of funding bodies interested in obtaining information about program effectiveness and efficiency.

These different types of stakeholders have different information needs and different questions they want the evaluation to address. Attention then has to be given to how they will be involved and efforts made to balance their concerns. This requires continuing interaction between stakeholders and evaluators. Involving stakeholders in the planning and implementation of CED evaluations can help ensure that the right information is collected within the constraints of the local situation and the available financial and human resources. Ownership of the evaluation results can be generalized to the various stakeholders with the enhanced probability of utilization. There are also disadvantages of involving stakeholders. Difficulties may be encountered in identifying the appropriate stakeholders to be offered an opportunity for involvement. Further, considerable evaluation resources may be required to solicit, reconcile and prioritize stakeholder views.

The CED Program or Project Evaluated

Kenneth Watson emphasizes the importance of defining the CED program or project to be subject to study. Ideally, evaluations can be used at the CED program design stage to guide decisions about goals and objectives, implementation activities, and required resources, as well as for monitoring program implementation and assessing program outcomes. CED often amounts to a black box for evaluation purposes or, in terms used by Watson, a non-replicable treatment. These chapters reflect general agreement with a view of CED as involving efforts to mobilize citizens directly affected by economic conditions into organizations to take action. But different writers place different emphasis on economic achievements, while others place more emphasis on social benefits. Clearly defining a CED project or program requires translation of abstract statements into specific CED processes to achieve specific goals.

One useful way to organize information about a CED project, and to arrive at a more precise definition, is to view the project as amounting to a set of resources and activities directed toward a common set of results. Three sets of elements make up the program structure: resources or inputs; activities, processes, or project/program operations; program results, outcomes or goals. Resources or inputs are things such as staff, persons served, equipment, facilities, and so on. Program activities, throughputs, processes, or operations are the means used to achieve desired results, the major work tasks performed or carried out in the project or program. Program or project processes or operations convert CED inputs to outcomes or results. Program or project impacts, effects, goals, or outcomes are the ends or results to be achieved; some of these may be intended results that relate to program or project objectives and goals, while others may be unintended effects or results, and these may be desirable or undesirable.

A related way to more precisely define CED programs is the logic framework analysis (LFA) developed originally by the U.S. Agency for International Development (Sartorius, 1991) and adopted for use by the Canadian International Development Agency (1991). This tool aims at clarifying the design of a development project by identifying project inputs or resources, intermediate and ultimate objectives, measurement indicators to be used in assessing progress at meeting objectives, as well as the set of assumptions seen as tying elements of program structure together. Evaluation can be geared into both the logic framework analysis and program structure and logic approaches by identifying specific measurement indicators used to provide information on the program in respect to the questions stakeholders want addressed. Ideally, the design of a CED project or program would be completed early enough so that stakeholder questions would be identified and data collection procedures implemented concurrent with program implementation. In addition to the measurement indicators included in the project design, and providing ongoing evaluation information, additional measures could be developed for more periodic types of evaluations to provide information about stakeholder questions for which it makes little sense to collect information on an ongoing basis.

Work at identifying the structure and logic of CED projects and programs amounts to viewing programs and projects as theories-in-action. That is, identifying the program resources to be used, activities to be carried out, results sought, and logical assumptions seen to link resources, activities and results. This is a very different view from the more common approach of using program labels as substitutes for detailed program specification. Labels give very little information about the services delivered, to whom they are delivered, and no clues about the causal relationships purportedly underlying the CED project or program. Using the same label, community economic development, to describe different programs and projects neither makes those program comparable in any meaningful sense, nor communicates anything about what the programs do or how they go about getting it done.

Evaluators can arrive at a more precise definition of the CED project or program by obtaining and reviewing program documentation and by interviewing a variety of stakeholders, including staff, program beneficiaries, funders, and others. Funding proposals, program descriptions, program narratives, and interviews provide data for a rough model of program structure and logic that identifies program resources, activity components and expected results, as well as the linkages between program resources and expected results. The draft version of program structure and logic should be provided back for review by the stakeholders. If necessary, a further set of interviews could be carried out with the stakeholders to address gaps in the model of program structure and logic and to obtain further information to help resolve conflicting views held by different parties.

Evaluation Questions

Each of the chapters note that the questions addressed in a CED evaluation are critical because useful evaluations answer specific, clearly defined questions that stakeholders want answered to make specific decisions. But, when asked what questions they want answered, stakeholders will often suggest a wide variety of vague questions that to be answered would require more resources than those available. Thus, attention must be given to clarifying questions, assigning priorities, and relating these questions to the always present constraints of time, money, and expertise available. The result of this clarifying and prioritizing work should be a list of questions about the project or program that stakeholders want addressed, with each question relating to clearly identified decisions.

Evaluation stakeholders for CED programs or projects could identify questions about any of the elements of program structure or logic—questions about resources, activities, or results. Questions about resources for a CED project or program might include:

- What are the key characteristics of the geographic community, including institutions, people, resources, problems?

- How many persons are involved in the project or program; what are their characteristics; how much time did they allocate to it; what are their needs and concerns?

- What are the resources and capacities of institutions to meet identified needs and concerns?
- What are the dominant forms of community power and decision making?

A variety of questions might be raised about the CED program or project activities, including:

- What activities and tasks are carried out by project staff when interacting with community members?
- Are community members provided with clear and consistent information about program activities and aims?
- How and to what extent did community members participate in the project or program; did they find it meaningful?
- Did community members take on leadership roles in the project?
- Which members of the community opposed the program or project and in respect to what issues?
- What individuals or institutions were helpful within the community and external to it?
- How were program or project staff perceived by community members?
- Did community leadership change or shift during the project?

Finally, questions might be raised about CED program results, including:

- Does the community have more ability to affect its environment as a result of the project?
- Have identified community problems been solved?
- Which projects have been successful and which have not?
- Did the CED objectives or goals change over time?
- Have citizens' knowledge and skills been enhanced as result of the project; how competent are citizens in organizing and planning as a result of the project; do citizens know where to look for help to carry out future development activities?
- What are the views and attitudes of community members about the program and has the program brought about changes in the way citizens look at their community?
- How permanent and wide spread have changes in the community been?
- Were there any unforeseen side-effects of the program, including the development of conflicts and divisions within the community, shifting leadership, or actual suffering by community members?

Measures and Data Collection Procedures

Three sets of concerns come out of the chapters regarding measures and data collection procedures:

- Identifying the specific indicators or measures to be used to provide information on the evaluation questions;
- Identifying the methods to be used to collect the measurement information;
- Specifying the frequency of collecting the information and the persons, samples, or groups from whom it will be collected.

The first of these involves translating or operationalizing each evaluation question into a measure or indicator on which information will be collected. Thorny program design issues come to the forefront. How much attention will be given to addressing social, as compared to economic program objectives? How amenable are these objectives to valid and reliable measurement? Is it feasible to estimate financial rates of return from a CED project and how difficult is it to assign a monetary value to the social benefits? The aim is to identify measures that can be used to provide valid and reliable information about the evaluation questions identified and prioritized by stakeholders.

The second concern is with the methods to be used to collect the indicators or measures on the stakeholder questions. A variety of quantitative and qualitative methods can be used in a CED evaluation, including existing social indicators; in-person, phone, and mailed surveys; group approaches such as focused group interviews, nominal group techniques, public forums and hearings; observational methods; and records. No single method is necessarily appropriate to all situations, each has advantages and disadvantages. The key to selecting the preferred collection method depends on the specific kinds of questions that stakeholders want answered, the amount and type of resources available for answering them, and the amount of evidence and degree of rigor required. Therefore, the challenge in evaluating CED programs is to propose a data gathering method tailored to the stakeholders' specific information needs, while taking into account factors such as the accessibility of data and time and other resource constraints. Inevitably, decisions have to be made that require trade offs between rigor, timing, physical and financial resources, and the expected use of the study results.

The third concern is with how often the measures will be applied and on whom. Will the evaluation involve repeated applications of measures to detect changes over time on a single case; will comparison or control groups be used to provide comparative information on those exposed to the program and those provided with an alternative service?

The decision requirements of stakeholders should drive the type of design implemented, not the converse, and CED evaluations should place high priority on timely information that is useful for making decisions. Rigorous outcome designs risk producing results after opportunities for their use has passed. Attempts must therefore be made to tailor the design and methods to be used to the local situation, available resources, and the nature and timing of project or program decisions.

Evaluation Implementation and Utilization

In putting the evaluation plan into action, attention needs to be given to any discrepancies between the expected or planned situation to be encountered in the conduct of the study and the situation that actually occurs as the study unfolds. Study plans often differ substantially from their actual implementation; thus, it is important that the ongoing course of the evaluation be monitored. Constant modifications are usually needed as the evaluation progresses and rarely will a study plan be implemented without the need for modification and alternation. The evaluator may need to make trade-offs in light of changing circumstances. The key consideration is to avoid violating the original spirit of the study plan, while at the same time not causing severe administrative problems. Evaluators need to exercise flexibility and creativity in working with persons involved in the program so as to not cause major disruptions in program delivery. Implementation of an evaluation plan will involve several key tasks: collecting the required data to answer stakeholder questions; analyzing the data collected; formulating conclusions from the data; developing recommendations for action by the stakeholders; and reporting the findings and recommendations.

The primary purpose for planning, conducting, and reporting evaluation information is to contribute to decision making about the program. The information reported may reflect the extent to which program objectives are being achieved by the CED program, serve to discover the theoretical premises underlying the program, or, when feasible, the relative contribution of program components to the attainment of different effects. For example, it may be discovered that program resources were not used as planned, that resources were inadequately translated into interventions, or that extraneous variables operated in such a way to mitigate the program's impact. The utilization of evaluation information may, therefore, have a dual thrust: measurement of possibilities of attainment and detection of impediments to that attainment. In both instances, the utilization potential of research findings will hinge upon the pre-planning carried out and the involvement of the evaluation stakeholders.

It has been said that the road to inaction is paved with research reports. The results of research, however, are only one of the number of inter-related factors taken into consideration in the decision-making process. There may be many reasons why evaluation findings are not used, including poor planning, communication breakdowns, and questionable commitments to appropriate utilization. Researchers have been accused of not making any suggestions for how findings should be used, of making them in terms that are too abstract and unrelated to practice, of making inappropriate recommendations that do not fit the systems studied, or of using their negative findings as hostile attacks against the program. Practitioners have been accused of being overly rigid, unresponsive to change, too easily threatened by any implied criticism, and overly concerned with their security within the program. Administrators have been accused of sponsoring research that they never intended to use, of using the research to subvert programs that they wished to get rid of, of being committed to the status quo, and of giving primacy to organizational needs such as survival and growth without regard to the adequacy of their service mission. The public has vacillated between being indifferent to research and endorsing any program modification that suggests change and implies hope. Funding agencies have been accused of only paying lip service to the need for program evaluation and being prone to seeking political justification for sponsored programs, rather than honest evaluation. Consumers of service, while gaining increasing voice in determining the kind and quality of services they receive, are still relatively infrequently consulted as program measures and are usually distant from evaluation procedures and the use of findings.

Evaluation findings should be seen as additional information that can be fed into the program development process. The very fact of being considered by decision makers may be a reasonable view of utilization. Expecting evaluations to have a determinate effect on program and policy decisions is probably not realistic and, in the final analysis, likely to be incompatible with democratic decision making.

PART 5

PARTNERSHIPS FOR COMMUNITY ECONOMIC DEVELOPMENT

17

Governments as Partners in Community Economic Development

Teresa MacNeil

Bold visioning, unlimited competence, and patience are prime requirements if CED is to have the benefit of genuine partnership. Three types of partnership structures are likely to accommodate government involvement in CED. First, partnership occurs within the public sphere through a vertical arrangement of various levels of government and the myriad of development-related agencies located in each level. Second, partnership occurs in the community through alliances with one or more local coalitions, usually for business purposes. Third, and most complex of all, partnership occurs through both vertical and horizontal arrangements where more than one level of government collaborates with coalitions of business and various citizen interest groups including small, independent business and organized labour. Partnerships tend to consolidate interests in economic development and reduce competing demands for attention to development needs. Partnership members invariably surrender some degree of autonomy as relations intensify and issues sharpen. Members of effective partnerships have an accurate, shared understanding of why the local economy is in trouble, the standard against which the community's failure is being measured, and the benefits and the costs of their development options. Canadians have had little experience, over the past generation or more, with participation either in complex partnerships or in CED. The prospect of successfully undertaking a combination of both is daunting. Nevertheless, this prospect holds promise as an approach to economic renewal. The challenge is to find models for achieving partnerships which will prove to be effective forces in CED.

The purpose of this chapter is to focus only on the role of governments as partners in CED. Attention, however, must be given to limiting the definition of CED. This is necessary because partnerships will be required to work in quite different ways if CED is viewed as development *in* rather than development *of* the community (Kaufman, 1959). If the objective is to change the way communities function, development *of* the community necessarily involves local interest groups in the partnership to a greater extent than would be required for economic development *in* the community. The goal of CED necessarily influences the composition and structure of partnership which fosters strategic alliances for CED.

Limiting the Definition of CED

The question of who is being served by local economic development should guide the determination of which interests are represented in partnerships. Transformation of the community's economic condition is the point but social mobilization of the community's population is one ingredient in the mix that generates economic improvement. It provides opportunity for people to understand their circumstances and the underlying causes of those circumstances before they can act to change them. Experience in Canada's development programs for economically disadvantaged regions shows that neither outside leadership (primarily political) nor outside capital encourages a local population to engage in social learning and assume responsibility for economic change.

Populations are generally aware of factors affecting their fragile economy but the citizens usually do not engage actively in altering the conditions which cause the economies of their communities to be forever insecure and reliant upon extraordinary measures. They view such work as belonging to government. Thus announcements of plans from above are the perennial expectation of a population that has learned to be helpless. Governments as partners in CED must take into account the current state of learned helplessness and follow processes to enable the population to see and take hold of ways to transform their community through its economy.

Development of communities, and especially less-advantaged communities, must follow a strategy that places responsibility for formulating and realizing change firmly in the hands of the people of the community who, in turn, learn to grasp and deal with that responsibility. Ideally, this approach involves all levels of the nation's governmental and corporate forces. First and foremost, it requires citizens to understand the facts of their economic circumstances and the causes of their underdevelopment. It then requires them to identify, choose, and act on their development options. To place responsibility more squarely in the hands of citizens does not mean that governments must abandon their responsibility for economic development. Rather, government is situated as a stage-setter, as an enabler, and as the sponsor of a process which will transform a community according to the choice and determination of its population. Government is the force to handle those functions and activities which are otherwise impossible for citizens to handle themselves. The role of specialists is shifted from being decision makers who specify development policy to being the major source of support for citizens who would determine the direction of development in their local economy. This is a formidable role shift.

That this approach is not well-established by governments is evident in a working paper of a Task Force on Regional Development Assessment (1987) produced by representatives of federal and provincial development departments. They expressed their preference this way:

> The biggest stakeholders in regional development are the Canadian public—workers, businesses, the unemployed, local communities. Unless the programs of governments have practical application at the local level they create more problems than they solve. There is a good deal of evidence that government programs are becoming administratively unintelligible and remote to the point where they are inaccessible or irrelevant. Whatever the causes, more programs are not the solution. It seems to us that the situation calls for much greater attention to program design and delivery, to public information and participation efforts, to as much decentralization of delivery responsibility as is feasible, and to more simplification of application and approval procedures. Policy and management control functions tend to be bureaucratically prestigious compared to the 'menial labour' of program design and delivery, and unchecked this tendency will be counter-productive to effective regional development efforts (p.64).

These are views of public servants who have no reason to be destructively critical of the system they run. They are seriously convinced of the need to relate the design and delivery of development programs much more strictly to local circumstances and to strive to shift responsibility in the direction of local participation and management. They treat this as neither a new or radical idea, just a difficult one to realize.

Three examples of collaborative opportunities are outlined in this chapter. Each represents one of the partnership types—intergovernmental collaboration, government-community collaboration, and comprehensive intergovernment-intercommunity collaboration. Attention will be given to the leadership role played by partners. The objective is to inform policy considerations regarding an effective role for governments as partners in CED.

Partnership: Corporatist or Incorporation?

Partnerships invariably bring together a diverse, conflict-prone array of interest groups around development issues. Partnership building is an enterprise of creating entirely new combinations of people to mold new ways of working and, at the community level, of living together. The word partnership is inadequate because it fails to convey such complex implications as the high level of sensitivity and singlemindedness required to succeed. New combinations of people and agencies assembling to build a local economy call for partnership members to behave as never before; to be different in their opinions, knowledge, skills, attitudes, and in most other respects than they were before they moved into new alliances. Effective partnership building is not a casual job. Audet and Rostami (1992) point out that each partnership project is unique by its circumstances. Such diversity detracts from the need to be precise about defining the essential elements of partnership. Consequently, the term tends to be used to refer to any combination of interests in a project. Critical components of partnership include an ongoing collaborative venture, mutual agreement, shared contributions, compatible with the objectives of each partner, addresses common issues, respects the needs of each, and encourages solutions acceptable to all participants (Audet & Rostami, 1991, pp.12–13).

Public-private partnerships are frequently formed as a means to achieve local development. Typical of this kind of arrangement is the role of the Scottish Development Agency in redevelopment of the City of Glasgow. Public funds leveraged large amounts of private sector investment to achieve a surge in service-sector employment (Judd & Parkinson, 1990). Usually this form of partnership is limited to arrangements between business and government. Often they are as short-lived as the time it takes to package and launch a business venture. Jezierski (1990) suggests that broader forms, such as neighbourhood organizations, develop as a response to the public-private partnership. Her review of partnerships in Pittsburgh reflects a gradual shift in the role of neighbourhood groups from reaction to the threat of public-private collaboration, to one where they became "less adversarial and increasingly technical and bureaucratic in order to participate" (p.237). The Pittsburgh model of development incorporates more than business, neighbourhoods, and government. Judd and Parkinson (1990) mention that the partnership also included nonprofit cultural, medical, and educational institutions. Jezierski observes that the "durability of partnerships for initiating and coordinating urban social change requires constant effort to institutionalize conflicting interests and construct legitimacy for development policy and for the partnership itself" (1990, p.218).

The theoretical constructs of corporatism and incorporation (Jezierski, 1990) provide convenient points of differentiation between the business-government and the broader-based forms of partnership. The corporatist approach combines the separate interests of state and private capital around a common goal of business development, leaving a population dependent and government as the high-paying but weak partner. This has been repeatedly found in Atlantic Canada where firms take advantage of financial incentives with little commitment to place. Incorporation theory would have broad-based coalitions catch the commitment of the state to represent their interests rather than allowing the state to be an entity that can act in its own interest.

Three Types of Government Partnerships

Examples of government participation in partnerships which relate indirectly to CED are plentiful because at all levels there is some responsibility for aspects of community well-being. Three illustrations of opportunity for government to collaborate as partners for local change are presented for the suggestions they generate about ways to effectively link public policy with local development. The examples are not specifically attuned to CED but each contains general implications for local economic change.

Government—Government

Haddow's (1992) analysis of corporatist policy-making in relation to Canada's Labour Force Development Strategy presents several suggestions about characteristics of intergovernmental partnerships. He notes features of the national board and examines the response in three provinces (Ontario, New Brunswick and Nova Scotia) to the new training agenda represented in the mandate of the Canadian Labour Force Development Board (CLFDB). Here is an opportunity for federal-provincial partnership building in the interest of joining, as Haddow puts it, the new international economic order. Haddow notes that at the national Board level, chances of achieving equitable involvement of the Board's two predominant co-partners (labour and business) were limited by Canada's pluralist nature and limited commitment to corporatism; ... "while business organizations agreed to sit on the CLFDB ... the hedged commitment of business to the board and its mandate partly reflects reluctance about this equality [with labour], so artificial in the context of Canada's broader pattern of social relations" (Haddow, 1992, p.9).

Haddow situates each of the respective responses of the three provinces along a continuum which has Ontario proceeding furthest in response to the labour force development agreement, New Brunswick making reasonable progress, and Nova Scotia being pathetically slow. He attributes these differences to three factors: (1) commitment of federal and provincial governments to reform which seems to relate positively to change, where Ontario has strong commitment, New Brunswick modest commitment, and Nova Scotia virtually no government commitment; (2) ability of main parties involved in corporatism to overcome pluralist dispositions seems to relate negatively, with Ontario experiencing considerable trouble around the notion of labour-business equity, New Brunswick also having trouble, and Nova Scotia, because of government inaction, having to rely on the joint effort of labour and business for any initiative; (3) federal-provincial relationships where, as federal-provincial agreements came up for renewal, Ontario had minimal interest in a formalized agreement, and New Brunswick and Nova Scotia were reluctant to risk loss of federal support for training by shifting the terms of previous formal agreements. Haddow's reasons for the differential response are summarized as (1) prospects for intergovernmental collaboration are positively related to their shared commitment to goals for CED; (2) prospects for intergovernmental collaboration are positively related to high levels of corporatism; (3) prospects for intergovernmental collaboration are positively related to the mutual independence of the governments.

Public—Private

In Nova Scotia, the initial impetus for a community mobilization approach to heart health came from Health and Welfare Canada in partnership with the Province's Heart Health Program. This was soon joined by the Nova Scotia Heart and Stroke Foundation and a university extension service (Health and Welfare Canada, 1992). This assembly of the main public and private agencies concerned with heart health, and a non-governmental agency to assist mobilization at the community level, was external to the community where the mobilization project was subsequently launched. No representative of the community was involved but it was anticipated that a strong local network would in time connect with the initial partnership. After four years, however, the partnership has yet to move beyond being a vertical arrangement of external organizations working in cooperation with a local organization. Commitment has yet to come from a range of community interests to function as partners. Neither the government partners nor the university community mobilization partner received support for the project from local staff of their respective organizations. The local county health unit, which serves the community where the heart health project is located, does not lend its support to the project, possibly because the project requires a shift from the way services are normally delivered. Resistance on the part of different professionals to meet partnership requirements for collaboration is significant when central agencies commit their support to local development. Too often the call for agency support at the local level is either not made, is not espoused, or may even be overtly opposed by local representatives of the agency who are feeling that the project is a threat to their professional expertise (Weiss, 1988).

Intergovernment—Intercommunity

The third example, the relationship between intergovernmental partnerships and Boston's linkage policy, is a demonstrated case of incorporation success. This two-phase case refers to 1960s federal and city collaboration to improve the economic fortunes of the city of Boston. The outcome was a strong public-private partnership which, by the 1980s, had become a thoroughly integrated, complex partnership of city government, powerful business interests, and strong local community interests. The primary force in Boston's economic revitalization was increased federal social spending in health care and education along with a federally financed urban renewal program during the 1960s (Dreier & Ehrlich, 1991). This evidence of firm collaboration between federal and city governments was strengthened by a powerful coalition of business leaders who mobilized resources to transform both business and residential districts. Later, in 1983 when circumstances brought Boston into fiscal crisis, local government took on the new linkage policy despite opposition from business and development communities.

Linkage policy involved a fee imposed, at first, upon the Boston Rehabilitation Authority to accommodate the impact of development by creating funds for housing programs. Later, a strong coalition of low-income housing interests achieved its goal to expand the program to all large commercial development projects. Linkage policies were added for job-training, minority business development, child care, theatre development, inclusionary housing, and linked deposit banking. The city administration "worked aggressively to establish the routine participation of community groups" (Dreier & Ehrlich, 1991, p.370).

This kind of political accommodation needs an expanding economy and therefore might not be appropriate in every city. Further, the linkage dollars are insufficient to finance Boston's housing and other social service needs. Nevertheless, the example provides strong and encouraging evidence that all members benefit when there is strong, multi-level, mutually shared responsibility for community economic advancement. Only the federal government can provide the billions of dollars to close the gap between the social services required by the city and what it is able to provide. Boston's strong model of incorporation may be most appropriate in an intergovernmental climate where the respective levels of government share commitment to social mobilization.

Which Is the Ideal Form?

Only vague and tentative suggestions may be drawn from the scant review of three cases. Those suggestions are:

- strong intergovernmental collaboration around CED requires each level of government to be deeply committed to local economic transformation, to be financially strong in their own domain, and to be able to behave in a corporatist way.

- vertical partnerships formed for the benefit of community change are ineffective without corresponding horizontal partnerships at the local level which will work collaboratively for change with the external partnership.

- the prospects for lasting change are increased by a highly integrated partnership which incorporates the range of public, private, and local community interests.

Among the significant factors affecting government's role in CED are the elements of time, trust, and program mandate. The community must be able to take as much time as required to understand the circumstances of citizens and to plan and implement change if responsibility for economic transformation is to be taken by citizens who are most affected by the change. Often the time needed to establish such a base extends well beyond the limits of government program funding. This impediment expands as more than one level of government is involved in the development. An element of trust is needed in every form of partnership. The ability of governments to establish a strong base of trust with the community is reduced by partisan politics, geographic boundaries, and competing staff expertise. Probably the greatest impediment to governments as partners in CED are the limitations of agency mandate. Limited departmental mandates prevent government development efforts from extending across the range of activities required to achieve solutions mutually acceptable to both government and community.

Partnership as Leadership for CED

Leadership becomes the most critical competence in the range of technical competencies which partnerships must possess when the goal of CED includes social mobilization. Other required competencies are ability to put together, finance, and sustain strong business deals. The challenge is to allow sufficient room for local participation without jeopardizing the development effort. But it can be quite unwise to identify a uniform cadre of leaders who are selected because of structural or professional roles in the community. For example, it would be convenient to assign leadership responsibility for promoting awareness and understanding of the development process to the chief administrators of municipal industrial development commissions. But in municipalities where the administrator is a very good judge of investments, but a poor promoter, this might be the least appropriate way to generate awareness and understanding. The need to attend to local differences cannot displace the requirement for leaders who can perform the respective development tasks. Attention to local differences removes the convenience of automatically assigning responsibility for leadership to an established role but it adds the burden of attending rigorously to the skills and dispositions that are required to get the job done effectively.

The role played by government in partnership for CED depends on how aggressive government chooses to be as a leader of the CED process. At least four leadership functions are required to assist the overall process of initiating and maintaining a system for community economic development: (1) visualize the development process with attention to the general purposes to be achieved; (2) initiate and sustain the development process; (3) provide training support for the development process; and (4) participate in the development process as a learner and an agent for change. These leadership activities can be performed concurrently and any member of a partnership may perform more than one of these functions. An assumption underlying each leadership function is that people who perform the function will have a great deal to learn. Learning is an imperative where social mobilization is the objective. There is no well-established practice to inform the respective leaders about the ideal way to proceed. There is not even the popular expectation that responsibility for CED belongs primarily with the local population. Popular acceptance for the approach must be established.

Learning is a continuous and purposeful part of the local development process and cannot be overemphasized.

Where does the initiative originate for establishing partnerships which promote incorporation of multiple interest groups, leadership, and continuous learning? What role is played by governments? Response from any serious-minded senior government official who has thought about goals for local development, invariably places responsibility with the state. If this is so, there is a gap between the rhetoric and the reality in Canada. Savoie observed that "by and large, these (regional development) efforts are planned and implemented outside the public view, so that one must turn to elected and to permanent government officials to gather the facts and to gain an appreciation of the circumstances under which the efforts were launched" (1986, p.IX). Some programs include functioning advisory councils and boards but their role tends to be more consultative and legitimating than initiating. Policies, as distinct from details of program implementation, are essentially finance-related and are the product of a relationship between government officials and established government processes.

> Usually those policies treat the region without attending to the respective development strategies of the provincial governments within that region. This has the effect of widening the distance between provincial and federal development approaches with resulting failure to integrate the provincial economies into a more coherent regional form which, in turn, will mesh with the directions being pursued in the federal economy (Savoie, 1986, p.153).

Responsibility for economic development has increasingly become a matter for intergovernment collaboration. At least that is the claim. To use one example from the perspective of a coalition of coastal communities in Nova Scotia, intergovernment collaboration is too often an exercise in old-time buck passing. A joint-meeting of federal and provincial agencies was convened to hear the coalition's proposal. Two of three federal departments indicated willingness to support, while no interest was shown by any of the provincial agencies. Where does the locus of responsibility lie? Who takes the initiative to build appropriate partnerships for CED? Who does the bold visioning and who builds the unlimited competence and patience which are the prime requirements for a partnership-based approach to CED? Perhaps the initiative must come from the local milieu. Wien (1991) refers to a claim that regions are reconsolidating their resources such that new alliances are being formed by enterprises so they can respond competitively to their competitive and rapidly changing environment. Perhaps they will be the force that will spur governments to belong to a private-public partnership. Wien believes that "we may see in Canada some rearrangement of federal provincial powers" (1991, p.114). When governments act in partnership to foster CED they have little choice but to take their clue from the milieu and to do everything possible to foster social mobilization through local leadership development.

18

The Corporate and Voluntary Sectors as Partners in Community Economic Development

Christopher R. Bryant

Community Economic Development is a process that is rapidly coming of age and attracting attention as a complement to the traditional activities of all levels of government, but particularly at the higher levels. CED, however, can never be carried out by government, although government can be an important contributory player for capacity-building, sources of information and expertise, and sources of capital for certain types of community initiatives. How does CED really get accomplished to make a sustainable and significant contribution to social and economic development in communities? A host of players—individual, institutional, and organizational—can be involved with a variety of roles. This chapter considers two broad categories of players, the corporate sector and the voluntary sector. A vision of CED and the functions and roles that groups or organizations can perform in CED are discussed as a prelude to understanding the potential of the corporate and voluntary sectors to contribute as partners to effective CED initiatives.

Vision of Community Economic Development

CED as Holistic, Inclusive, and Purposeful

CED is a holistic, inclusive, and purposeful process of addressing community needs through setting goals and objectives, identification of strategies, and implementation of appropriate initiatives. CED has evolved in Canada from two distinct origins (Bryant, 1991). First are initiatives oriented towards particular segments of the population usually in specific communities. Frequently, the population segments targeted in such initiatives have tended to be underprivileged in some way such as low income, high unemployment, low levels of education, and so forth. The segments can be defined by socio-economic and demographic characteristics such as women, street youth, and aboriginals, or they can be defined by geography, e.g., low-income areas within a particular urban environment. The second source that has contributed to CED in Canada is local economic development with a strong territorial base; this includes the extensive experience of municipalities and regional forms of local government in economic development which have become particularly important since the late 1960s (Bryant and Preston, 1987a; Douglas, 1989; Dykeman, 1990).

CED aimed exclusively at a particular marginalized or underprivileged segment (defined sectorially or thematically, whether in a particular geographic context or not) will tend to remain marginalized if the people are not included in broader decision-making processes. This provides a possible explanation for why so many of these initiatives remain as experimental projects dependent upon external sources of funding for long periods of time. Power relationships can be substantially modified and effective empowerment take place when such segments are able to reduce and eliminate dependency and/or become accepted as players in their own right. Organizing and implementing initiatives in the context of particular segments is a critical and essential part of the first stages of awareness and mobilization of a segment. The danger is that such CED initiatives will remain marginal unless it goes beyond that stage.

A second source of CED has been local economic development initiatives dominated by local and regional governments, or by the corporations that are usually intricately tied to local and regional government structures. These initiatives have tended not to be particularly inclusive or global in their efforts. Frequently, the planning processes involved have been controlled by a small group of people, often from within the municipal organization, and efforts to reach out into the community have been limited so that the integration of social and economic objectives and concerns has been little more than an aside.

All the community's needs and objectives as a whole are not addressed, in either case, but this does not mean that these movements have been unproductive. On the contrary, movements aimed at particular segments of the community have sometimes created a certain pride and cohesiveness within those segments that can be the basis for a broader participation in the community; and the second source has given rise to considerable experience of long-term planning in local development.

Recently there are signs that the two movements are beginning to become more integrated. First, there is increasing acknowledgement of the need for alternative and complementary approaches to those pursued during the 1960s, 1970s and much of the 1980s (Lamontagne, 1989; O'Neill, 1990). Second, there is greater recognition of the need to involve the whole range of segments in the community partly because of the democratic principle involved, partly in order to address the range of legitimate needs and objectives within the community more effectively, and partly to benefit from the greater levels of creativity and human resources that are assumed to arise from greater levels of participation (Bryant, 1992a). Third, more inclusive community-based processes with links to local government, but independent of it have developed in some rural and resource-based regions. Most notable in this respect is the Community Futures Program run under the auspices of Employment and Immigration Canada. Fourth, several urban areas have developed extensive local development programs structured around the industrial model of local development (Bryant, 1991, 1992b). Some cities and towns are becoming more open to reaching out to segments of the population that were not previously included in development efforts.

The new form of CED is placing greater emphasis on a purposeful process of strategic management and planning to achieve community goals and objectives as defined by the community and implemented through the community's own efforts. Its ultimate form does not involve centralized control over the process at the local or regional level by any particular group—governmental or otherwise. Rather, building on the fact that the community environment is characterized by a variety of legitimate interests and participants (individuals, organizations, formal and informal groups), this form of CED is characterized by participation, collaboration, cooperation and partnership-building in order to carry out effective CED initiatives. The evolving form of CED recognizes the reality of different institutions and organizations within the community and aims to build bridges among the various institutional and organizational structures so that there is communication between their planning processes and so that they work towards the same broad goals of community development (Beaudoin and Bryant, 1993). Identifying all the important segments of the community and involving them effectively in the CED process is a significant part and challenge in this process. The most difficult challenges include overcoming the inertia inherent in many organizations and institutions, getting the people that work inside them to recognize the legitimate rights of others to be involved in the CED process, and ensuring that collaboration between the important players does not become a process that excludes significant segments of the community.

The Functions and Roles of Players in the Community Economic Development Process

A framework that lays out the different types of functions that any group or organization can perform in CED is useful to consider the roles of the corporate and volunteer sectors. Four functions can be identified:

1. The *information* function involves providing and developing an adequate information base for decision-making, rather than trying to provide all possible types of information about a community.

2. The *integration* function involves three aspects: (a) integrating the community into the specific organization or group under consideration (through representation or the development of appropriate and effective channels of communication); (b) integrating the group or organization into the community by ensuring that it is credible and respected; and (c) integrating segments of the community which have not previously been significantly involved into the CED process.

3. The *planning* function involves collaborative and cooperative decision-making (making choices). Different groups, organizations and institutions will share ideas on objectives and ensure consistency in their respective decision-making processes.

4. The *action* function involves undertaking and being involved in projects and initiatives necessary to achieve the goals and objectives. Action can include initiatives in the information, integration and planning functions, as well as initiatives that have as objectives the achievement of tangible results (in conventional terms). This means that potential partners can be involved in initiatives in all four of these functions as well.

Groups and organizations can assume different roles, within these four functions. These range from relatively passive staff roles, in which support (e.g., human resources, financial resources, expertise) is provided to others, to much more intensive involvement in line roles. Line roles will involve the individual, group, organization, or institution in a much greater presence in the initiatives including ultimately directing projects.

Partnerships in Community Economic Development

The terms partners and partnerships have become very popular in CED. Unfortunately, the terms have been used loosely and often hide nothing more than traditional relationships between so-called partners structured along hierarchical lines of authority. Generally, partnerships in CED are founded upon:

1. joint management involving multilateral, equal, voluntary and non hierarchical relationships between partners. Equal does not mean that each partner is the same; partnerships characteristically involve joint action between partners who are complementary in the types of resources they can bring to the table, including financial, human, expertise, and other kinds of resources;

2. a dynamic organizational structure involving collaboration rather than opposition, the search for convergence rather than divergence, and action that fits into a broader process;

3. a common and agreed upon set of objectives between the different partners, with an emphasis on collective or community-based objectives;

4. sharing responsibility for success and failure, and sharing responsibility for evaluating the success or otherwise of the partnership; in true partnerships, there is no room for one way evaluations.

Different types of partnership can be related to different stages in the CED process and its management. Partnerships can be developed during the visioning, the analysis, the action, as well as the monitoring stages of strategic planning. In the broader strategic management process, partnerships can be developed to deal with information (analysis, monitoring, etc.), integration, planning and action functions. Process is more important in CED and its implementation through the strategic management and planning processes, than results defined in conventional terms. The process of involvement and participation is a prerequisite for getting results, such as greater equity of treatment of different segments, more equitable distribution of income and opportunities, more employment opportunities and so forth. Effective CED initiatives must include process-oriented initiatives as well as more conventional results-oriented initiatives. Different partners can become involved in five types of activities to further CED initiatives:

1. information analysis and communication activities;

2. the reduction of financial barriers to development;

3. the creation of greater community spirit and pride;

4. the development of a spirit of teamwork;

5. the creation of an entrepreneurial spirit (Bryant and Preston, 1987b; Coffey and Polèse, 1985).

There is no hierarchical authority between partners in a true partnership; these partnerships almost always represent a delicate equilibrium between the partners. Partnerships are examples of cooperation and collaboration but not all cooperative and collaborative situations represent true partnerships. It is essential to keep information flowing, to ensure that all partners are achieving their own objectives as well as the collective or common objectives. Anything that looks as if it would cause the initially agreed upon division of responsibilities and resources expected of each partner to change is addressed immediately.

Partnerships in CED usually involve a conscious effort on the part of one or more of the potential partners to search out and communicate with other potential partners. The objective of these first contacts is to feel the way and develop some common understanding. Partners, even in the context of CED initiatives, have their own agendas. Getting the potential partners to the table may involve stressing their interests and how these can be achieved more effectively by sharing resources and risks with other partners. These interests are not necessarily community-oriented at first and can include financial and economic interests, prestige, preservation of position in the community, and others. A partnership arrangement for community benefit is, however, fragile unless the broader collective or community objective is given a high profile in the longer term.

The Corporate and Voluntary Sectors: Their Characteristics

The actual and potential roles of corporate and voluntary sectors as partners in effective CED initiatives depends upon how the actors perceive their role (in relation to others) within each of the four different functions of strategic management and planning for CED and in relation to the particular segment or segments that they represent. Different types of actors present different characteristics as potential partners, making them more or less suitable to act in a true partnership. What are the particular interests and agendas of the different potential partners? Corporate and voluntary sectors often do not appear to be compatible. But the corporate sector is not only concerned with profit making and corporate image, and the voluntary sector is certainly not only motivated by making a contribution to improving the quality of life in the community.

The Corporate Sector

The corporate sector's involvement in CED initiatives is most obvious in relation to business development within communities where corporations have direct financial and economic interests and expertise. Corporate players can be expected to play an important line role in the development of sectoral plans in which their own corporation has a direct stake. The corporate sector also has an interest in the maintenance and development of a sustainable base of local employment in other sectors since this would, for example, reduce their moral obligation to the community. In this case, the corporate sector may take on line or staff roles depending on the level of intensity of involvement.

A line role might involve a corporation in taking a lead role in the development of a business support system for local business development in association with other partners; a staff role could involve the corporation only in the provision of some financial support or some expertise while the lead role is taken by other partners in the community. Staff roles are likely to dominate, apart from activities that involve the corporate sector's immediate and specific financial and economic interests. The corporate sector's contribution will most likely be support to the development of adequate information and contributing financial, human resources, and in-kind resources to the integration, planning, and action functions of other organizations involved in CED. This does not preclude more of a line role for certain individuals from within the corporate sector, but these people are often acting more in relation to their position within the voluntary sector than through their corporate affiliation.

The Voluntary Sector

The voluntary sector is likely to be more heterogeneous than the corporate sector in its relationship to CED initiatives. The voluntary sector includes various non-government organizations (NGOs) and individuals representing particular segments of the community or NGOs. CED process targeted to specific segments of the community has been heavily dependent on volunteer resources. CED that is more inclusive and territorially-based also moves forward largely on the basis of volunteer effort, but the difference is that it takes place in an atmosphere of a greater sharing or communication between the different segments of the community. NGOs at the local level are an essential set of players because they represent different segments of the population and can communicate with various governmental agencies at all levels in the CED process.

Maintaining interest on the part of the volunteers and their organizations partly depends on stressing their representation of particular segments of the community. This goes beyond simple representation, and involves having them first act as information nodes between the community as a whole and the particular segments they represent, and second, encouraging them to become involved in specific development initiatives within the respective segments. The challenge is to have these specific voluntary resources placed in a position from which they are able to exchange with those representing other segments.

The chances of this occurring are substantially greater when there is a holistic and inclusive process in place for CED, than when each segment operates on its own. This is even the case when there is substantial communication between the various social development agencies in a given region. A communication process is an important first step towards a coherent community development process. But even with communication, it is not evident that a common set of goals and objectives has been identified and that there is a purposeful process established aimed at achieving common community development goals. A common understanding of how economic and social development can be integrated and achieved is unlikely with communications alone.

Many of the voluntary sector groups and organizations occupy a line position because of the nature of their involvement in the CED effort. However, particularly in the social development area, the roles are often so line oriented in relation to a specific segment that their involvement becomes more fire-fighting and dealing with problems than putting their activities in the context of a broader CED process.

Conclusions

The corporate sector most often and appropriately plays a staff role in CED because of differences in representativity. The actors within the voluntary sector have a greater range of roles to play because they are more likely to represent a particular segment. They are critical to the information, integration, and planning functions within which they can play line or staff roles, but with a strong tendency towards a line role if they are to be effective in integrating their own segment within the broader CED process. Unfortunately, the link of the voluntary sector link is frequently stronger to the particular segment of the community which is represented than to the community as a whole; thus coherence of the more inclusive process remains elusive.

19

Community-Based Social Service Organizations and the Development of an Ecologically Sound Model for Sustainable Community Economic Development

David Challen and Dennis McPherson

The focus of this chapter is on the participation of social service organizations in the economic development of rural and remote communities in Canada. This approach taken to rural and remote communities provides a framework from which a revised model for CED is derived. This model of CED emphasizes the full participation of community members in the process of community change (Dykeman, 1990b; Boothroyd, 1991) and builds on the realities of the interrelatedness and interdependence of all interests and sectors in each community. While the focus of this chapter is on the role carried by social service organizations in rural and remote communities the perspective presented is also applicable to the many local communities found in larger urban settings.

The basis for the perspective is drawn from over two decades of experience working with rural and remote communities, from a review of current developments in CED, from applied research in the field, and from a review of the relevant literature (Coates and Powell, 1989; Johnson, 1980; Nelson, 1984; Nelson, Kelley & McPherson, 1985, 1986; McPherson, 1992; Ross and Usher, 1986; Nozick, 1992; Schumacher, 1974; and Wharf, 1984). This perspective has been directly influenced by a vision of the world that is based on a traditional Indian world view (McPherson and Rabb, 1991) and incorporates values, ethics, and traditions of the social work profession.

Very little has been written about the role of social service organizations in CED in Canada. Most CED literature is written from an economic or entrepreneurial perspective. This literature includes both general and specific references to social objectives and community development orientations but it does not incorporate principles of community development that have evolved in social work practice. Furthermore, the CED literature includes few references to perspectives and concepts derived from either the environmental movement or the wisdom of traditional native beliefs and the native way of life (Boldt & Long, 1986; Boldt, Long & Littlebear, 1986; Laronde & Harris, 1991; Littlebear, Boldt & Long, 1986; Lyons, 1986, 1991). Dykeman (1990) and Nozick (1992) are recent exceptions.

Nineteen-ninety-three was designated as International Year of the World's Indigenous People by the United Nations and endorsed by the Canadian government. A Department of Indian and Northern Affairs poster commemorating the declaration declares the beginning of A New Partnership (Canada, DIAND, 1993). This partnership means a respect for the culture, traditions, and history of the Native peoples of Canada. An ecological perspective could result from translating this into economic and community development. Native peoples' stewardship to conserve the earth and its many resources provide many lessons that might give direction to CED (Boothroyd, 1991; Zapf, 1991; Laronde & Harris, 1991). Two gaps in present knowledge are information regarding the form, nature and frequency of social service organizations' participation in CED and, second, the feasibility of integrating traditional Indian beliefs and practices in the pursuit of CED.

Rural and remote communities have lived in the shadow of overriding concern for the prosperity, development, and needs of larger centres (Coates & Powell, 1989; and Kirwin, 1991). Much of the attention on larger centres has been on the growth of capital and financial interests, and an infrastructure, rather than on the health and well-being of the urban centre itself. The downturn of global markets and the impact of recessions has created the need for many larger economic centres to address the broad effect of economic decline on communities as a whole. What has been experienced by the larger centres is similar to the boom bust cycle that many rural, remote, resource based communities have suffered time after time (Nelson, Stafford & McPherson, 1986; Reid, 1986; Uren, 1985).

The boom and bust scenario has been created by traditional approaches to resource based economic development that are susceptible to the direct effect of changing world markets and shifting national policies. The exploitive nature of a singular pursuit of wealth has failed to achieve either long-term economic benefits or social stability in these communities. Rather a negative impact has affected the people and the very survival of local communities (Glick, 1983; Lucas, 1974). There is need to rethink the goals and process of economic development to ensure more positive outcomes for communities, people, and the overall environment.

Both urban and rural, remote communities have had some common experiences in recent years. More attention has recently been paid to the development of healthy communities, including neighbourhoods and smaller communities within larger metropolitan areas (Dykeman, 1990;

Dare, 1992; Ministry of Community and Social Services, 1989 and Wharf, J. 1992). This small, but positive reorientation, has resulted in part from the realization that accepted approaches to development have damaged the world and have created a destructive physical and social environment (The World Commission on Environment and Development, 1987).

Financial and economic orientations have failed to produce growth or stability, and have not delivered the good life that was thought to be the promise of the study and science of economic theory. Local, national, and global practices exhibited in fiscal and monetary policy, economic forecasting, and corporate and political decision making have largely been ineffective in stabilizing and strengthening the economic world (Dykeman, 1990; Friedmann, 1992; Nozick, 1992; Seidman, 1987; The World Commission of Environment and Development, 1987). This situation necessitates a fundamental reorientation in the principles and practice of economic development to community based economic development (Dykeman, 1990; Nozick, 1992; Friedmann, 1992; Meehan, 1987; Tester, 1991; Turner, 1987).

A sound process and body of knowledge to support successful community based economic development (Bruyn & Meehan, 1987; Friedmann, 1992; Meehan, 1987; and Ross and Usher, 1986) will benefit communities, their people, their cultural context, the economic base, and the physical environments. The balanced goal of CED to achieve social, economic, cultural and physical growth needs to be more fully acknowledged and put into practice at the policy level. The notion of incompatibility of economic and social objectives is challenged. This challenge evolves from an appreciation of the close linkage between economic and social objectives and their compatibility for sustainable development (Boothroyd & Davis, 1991; Dykeman, 1990; M'Gonigle, 1991; Nozick, 1993). Emphasis on sustainable economic development moves away from a singular exploitive, profit making focus to an approach that seeks to reconcile economic growth with environmental protection, human growth and developmental needs, cultural and spiritual practices, capacity of renewable resources and their systematic rejuvenation, and conservation of non-renewable resources (DeFaveri, 1984; Laronde & Harris, 1991; Lyons, 1986; The World Commission on Environment and Development, 1987).

Definition of Community Economic Development

Originally CED was conceptualized as an economically driven approach to improve the physical, economic, cultural and social aspects of community living. The objectives for CED include development of an improved economic base upon which general community conditions and quality of community life can be improved. Measuring improvement in quality of community life or even defining quality of life is difficult. Similarly, it is also difficult to identify the key ingredients of CED that lead to improvement in

Figure 19-1
A Perspective on Sustainable Development

In its broadest sense, the strategy for sustainable development aims to promote harmony among human beings and between humanity and nature. In the specific context of the development and environment crises of the 1980s, which current national and international political and economic institutions have not and perhaps cannot overcome, the pursuit of sustainable development requires:

- a political system that secures effective citizen participation in decision making,
- an economic system that is able to generate surpluses and technical knowledge on a self-reliant and sustained basis,
- a social system that provides for solutions for the tensions arising from disharmonious development,
- a production system that respects the obligation to preserve the ecological base for development,
- a technological system that can search continuously for new solutions,
- an international system that fosters sustainable patterns of trade and finance, and
- an administrative system that is flexible and has the capacity for self-correction.

These requirements are more in the nature of goals that should underlie national and international action on development. What matters is the sincerity with which these goals are pursued and the effectiveness with which departures from them are corrected.

Source: United Nations Commission on Environment and Development, 1987 p.65.

quality of community life. Nevertheless, CED has both economic foundations and social development implications.

Two additional developments are relevant to CED. The first is the early notions of small-is-beautiful planted by Schumacher (1973). The second is the increasingly vocal and important environmental movement of the 1970s which culminated in the development of the World Commission on Environment and Development in 1983, and the subsequent publication of the Brundtland Report (World Commission on Environment and Development, 1987). The report envisioned a significant and important shift in thinking toward integration of social, economic, legal, cultural, physical, environmental and political objectives into global economic development. The interdependence of local community development with development at national and international levels was emphasized. The concept of sustainable development was elaborated and is summarized in Figure 19-1. Briefly, this encompasses an approach to community growth that incorporates concern for meeting peoples' basic needs with non-exploitive development while also ensuring ecological protection of environments, resources, existing cultures and social organizations (The World Commission on Environment and Development, 1987, pp.43–66).

Dykeman (1990) has identified important approaches in CED. His contribution applies economic, business, social, ecological, and developmental perspectives in the advancement of rural entrepreneurial communities and considers models of development and the process of strategic planning and action that leads to the achievement of sustainable communities. Ross and Usher (1986) provide an approach to development built on the natural strengths of the informal economy, mutual aid networks, and natural helping systems inherent in communities. Nozick (1992) provides the most recent Canadian addition to the review of community development perspectives. She promotes the relevance of ecology in guiding community economic development.

> Ecology is the study of relationships between living organisms and their living and nonliving environment, between plants and animals, between humans and nonhuman nature, and between humans and other humans. These interactive relationships form a multitude of systems, in which each system is self-contained like cells or organs in a body while at the same time, connected to and a part of larger systems. Ecology, then, is about more than trees, air and water—it is a complex of processes, relationships and natural systems of integration, which together make up a holistic model of human and non-human development (Nozick, 1992, p.72).

The application of ecological principles in CED practice leads to consideration of the definitive characteristics of communities, their component parts, functional processes, the natural interconnections of their existing internal and external systems, and the strengths and resources inherent in communities that may ensure their continued health and well-being. Consideration must be given to the roles of internal and external organizations and community based social service agencies in considering the future maintenance and developmental needs of communities.

A community can be presented as a natural component of human existence in which people live, feel nurtured, sustained, involved, and are stimulated (King and George, 1987 p.217). Community also represents an ongoing process of interconnection between people and the sharing of responsibility for the physical and spiritual condition of the common living space. This internal strength of the community forms the foundation and stability of larger societies (King and George, 1987). Dykeman proposes a comprehensive definition of CED:

> Community development is the process by which the efforts of people themselves are united with those of governmental authorities to improve the economic, social, and cultural conditions of communities, to integrate these communities into the life of the nation, and to enable them to contribute fully to national progress. This complex of processes is, therefore, made up of two essential elements: the participation by the people themselves in efforts to improve their level of living, with as much reliance as possible on their own

initiative; and the provision of technical and other services in ways which encourage initiative, self-help and mutual help and make these more effective (Dykeman, 1990, p.11).

Development must be redefined to include the concept of sustainability (World Commission on Environment and Development, 1987). Dykeman has also provided a definition of the sustainable community:

> Sustainable communities are those that aggressively manage and control their destiny based on a realistic and well thought through vision. Such a community based management and control approach requires that a process be instituted within the community that effectively uses knowledge and knowledge systems to direct change and determine appropriate courses of action consistent with ecological principles. The process must be comprehensive and address social, economic, physical and environmental concerns in an integrated fashion while maintaining central concern for present and future welfare of individuals and the community (Dykeman, 1990, p.7).

Sustainable development draws on local resources, local participants, and local skills in the community. An example of this is drawn from the experience of the Hemlo gold mining project at Marathon, Ontario. This project initiated a contract with the local Indian Band for the development of a pool of trained mine workers. The contract benefited the mine with a ready pool of trained workers, the Band who received an administrative/management and training fee, and the Indian workers who were employed on a basis that also allowed them to pursue traditional work and income from trapping, hunting, and fishing. One unexpected result was that trained workers wanted to remain in contracted employment as this was a financial benefit to them, given the opportunity to continue to hunt, trap, and fish (Reid, 1986; Uren, 1985; Ministry of Municipal Affairs, 1985).

A direct relationship exists between a community's economic base and all other sectors of the community's life (Bowles, 1981; Coppack, Beesley & Mitchell, 1990; and Cunningham, 1984). An interdependence exists between the realities of community living and the internal or external sectorial interests of economics, culture, social services, law, politics, government, and business. There is an interconnection that needs to be recognized and built into all efforts at community planning and development. This moves communities away from segregated and hierarchial structures of expert planning to full participatory involvement of members of a broadly construed constituency (Hammond, 1987; Kelly, 1977; Luther, 1990a & b; Nelson, Stafford, & McPherson, 1986; Plant & Plant, 1991).

Social Service Agencies in Economic Development Partnership

Social service organizations have a potential role to play in all phases of CED. Unfortunately social service agencies are rarely involved in the initial stages of economic and community development. Mainstream social services have not been regarded as an integral part of the social, economic, and community planning structure; rather, they have been primarily involved as an afterthought. The role erroneously assigned to more traditional social service agencies has been to deal primarily with human problems. This does not include providing input regarding social issues, community resources, or the purposes and perceived impact of community economic development. As well, a time lag has often occurred between the development of a social problem and the identification of negative consequences on the community. Social service organizations may be called upon to address the difficulty at this later stage. The unnecessary suffering experienced by the community and the late involvement of social agencies can be prevented by the participation of a full range of social agencies, planning councils, and organizations working with specific target populations in the initiation, planning, and progress of CED projects.

One of the fundamental principles for success in any enterprise involving people is to involve the people in the beginning who are affected by decisions. A strong focus of the social work profession in community work is the effective and broad participation of people from all walks of life in the decision making of their community. This premise holds true for social service interventions from policy making in complex organizations to direct counselling with individuals (Hogwood and Gunn, 1984). When people are involved they are committed to decisions and planning, invest of themselves, and work harder to achieve objectives (Germain and Gitterman, 1980). Social services agencies may act as a resource involving community members in economic development and as a resource by providing a link to potential participants including volunteers, professional staff, and clients.

Part of the rationale for involving community based social service organizations in CED is based on the pragmatic realization of the multifaceted function of social service organizations (Wharf, 1984; Whitaker, 1984; Bella, 1991). The history of social service agencies in Canada has evolved over the past one hundred and fifty years. Their mandate has been broadly defined as responding to identified social problems, social needs of community members, and specialized needs of targeted populations. The social purpose and objectives are to ensure that a formalized societal response exists to address individual and collective needs, to ensure the continued stability of communities, and to strengthen society as a whole (Hanton, 1978; Rubin & Rubin, 1986, 1992). There is a dual focus on individual needs and on the general well-being of communities and society (Carniol, 1991; Wharf, 1990a & b). This mandate and dual focus relates directly to the CED interest on the social well-being of communities.

Social service organizations primarily employ personnel trained in the profession of social work. Many larger agencies and organizations also employ staff trained in business administration, management, policy analysis, computer science and accounting. Some community based agencies carry specialized functions in social and community planning and thus employ staff trained and experienced in these disciplines. Thus, social service organizations provide a staff with a multidisciplinary base and with experience and skill in addressing individual and broad social problems from a variety of perspectives. This staffing arrangement presents a resource of knowledge and skills that is directly applicable to CED (Boothroyd, 1991; Dykeman, 1990).

In addition, social service and community based organizations have a history of community organization and development theory, skill, and practice knowledge important for CED. Community organization skills include community assessment and planning, identifying and networking with community resources, linking interest groups and other sectors, negotiation skills to resolve conflict and develop consensus, advocacy skills, and skills in resource development (Germain & Gutterman, 1980; Irey, 1980; Lecomte, 1990; Mayer, 1984; Wharf, 1984). Interpersonal skills are a particular strength of social work personnel and include focus on problem solving, resolution of conflict, and strengthening of relationships. These are also skills that are drawn on in achieving CED goals.

Several principles to guide social service involvement in CED can be identified including:

- recognition of the importance of participation of general community members, as full participants in decision making.
- inclusion and full partnership of social service and other community based organizations at the inception of any CED.
- clear enunciation of principles for economic development that include traditional native beliefs and practices of stewardship, conservation, and respect for the spiritual, cultural, social, and physical environment.
- recognition of the interrelationship and interdependence of social, cultural, recreational, educational, physical, legal, economic and political sectors in the health of the community.
- inclusion of all sectors of the community that are affected by development decisions.

20

Partnerships Conducive to Effective Community Economic Development: Summary, Policy Implications and Research Agenda

Nick Coady and Burt Galaway

The chapters by Teresa MacNeil, Chris Bryant, and Dave Challen and Dennis McPherson address the roles of government, corporate and voluntary sectors, and community-based social service organizations in effective CED partnerships. This chapter summarizes the common themes on CED partnerships, identifies implications for Canadian public policy, and suggests directions for future research.

Common Themes

The most striking general theme concerns the ideal nature and focus of CED partnerships. The authors promote a vision of long-term, collaborative partnership that includes a broad range of interest groups and focuses holistically on social, as well as economic development. Central to this vision is the social mobilization of marginalized segments of the community towards capacity building, empowerment, local control of resources, and sustainable development. The range of groups and organizations that must be considered for inclusion in such a partnership is vast and includes grassroots community groups, business and industry, government (including municipal and regional government), social service agencies, local planning councils, unions, financial institutions, private and community foundations, and tribal organizations and bands. A thorough understanding and respect for each partner's needs and potential contributions must be established to facilitate a stable, long-term collaboration of such diverse groups. The task of the CED partnership is to identify a common set of goals via collaborative assessment, identify and obtain needed resources and expertise, develop an action plan that clearly outlines the roles and responsibilities of each partner, and execute coordinated action toward the achievement of mutually acceptable solutions.

The difficulty in establishing and maintaining such an inclusive, holistically focused partnership is another theme running through these chapters. MacNeil discusses the difficulty in fostering local leadership given the state of learned helplessness in many communities. Bryant notes the common resistance in many organizations and institutions to acknowledging the rights to involvement and the potential contributions of marginalized segments of the population. Similarly, Challen and McPherson identify problems of excluding ordinary community members from the CED decision-making process and focusing on economic development, while neglecting social, environmental, and spiritual concerns. All of the authors acknowledge the difficulty presented by the disparate, often conflicting, interests of the potential partners and the lack of trust and acceptance among them.

The authors also provide ideas for how to address the range of difficulties that can be encountered in CED partnership development. Local grassroots participation in the initial stages of the CED partnership building process is to be actively encouraged. MacNeil stresses that governments need to help foster local leadership and social mobilization and support local initiatives. Challen and McPherson argue that local social service agencies need to be involved early in the CED process to facilitate the involvement of clientele and volunteers, and to contribute professional skill in conflict resolution and consensus building. Bryant suggests that an initial engagement strategy, of pointing out to each potential partner how their particular interests may be furthered through a partnership arrangement, can be followed with a subsequent strategy of educating partners about the interdependence of their goals. Potential partners may need to be lured to the negotiating table and then sold on the linkage between their seemingly disparate interests, including the linkage between economic and social goals.

Policy Implications

A number of public policy considerations, many of which are broader than the partnership theme itself, are raised. These policy considerations relate generally to the various functions that government can perform towards stimulating and supporting CED partnerships. To argue, as MacNeil points out, that there must be more community involvement in and control over economic and social development does not mean that government is absolved of responsibility. Government needs to promote and facilitate the development of local planning initiatives for CED activity and provide ongoing financial and informational support for such initiatives. Government, given the reality of limited funds, would be prudent to adopt a proactive strategy for identifying communities that are most in need of and conducive to CED initiatives. Government must be prepared to foster local leadership, either by identifying and supporting existent leadership or by cultivating new leadership through sponsorship of community organizing activity.

Initial support for CED initiatives will require government financial support for the community planning and partnership-building process, including tax incentives to encourage the formation of CED partnerships. Government can assist with the information and training needs of new CED initiatives by supporting and encouraging linkage with successful CED projects. In addition, government must be prepared to monitor the initial CED process to ensure broad-based participation that is inclusive of marginalized groups. Government, in supporting and monitoring CED initiatives, must recognize the need for CED policy to be culturally sensitive and locally oriented.

Government should explore ways to assure long-term financing of CED initiatives through exploration with potential partners such as credit unions, co-op organizations, and pension funds. Government needs to realistically assess the time-frame for CED self-sufficiency. A broad view of indicators should be used for evaluating the success of CED partnerships including social, as well as economic, indicators. The long-range economic impact of positive social change must be recognized. Government should consider shifting decision-making power and funding allocation for a wide range of social, economic, cultural, and environmental programs to the community level.

Research Agenda

There is a pressing need for research on both the process and outcome of CED partnerships. Qualitative, case study-based approaches to documenting the development of successful CED partnerships are important for developing a data base that can be used to maximize the likelihood of success for new initiatives. Research on the outcome of CED partnerships needs to combine quantitative and qualitative methods and to incorporate a multiple bottom-line. Such outcome research needs to focus on traditional, hard economic and social indicators, but must also consider softer information related to quality of life and sustainable development.

A research agenda focused on the theme of CED partnerships should include the following questions:

1. What are the structures and characteristics of successful CED partnerships and what were the processes and critical events that led to success?

2. What different types of CED partnership arrangements (e.g., comprehensive partnerships, coalitions, alliances, patronage) are best for different community conditions and problems?

3. What are the appropriate roles of various levels of government in relation to different CED partnership arrangements?

4. What are existing informal partnerships that occur within communities (including business and industrial sectors) that might provide opportunities for CED?

5. What methods and procedures are helpful in establishing and sustaining CED partnerships?

6. What methods and procedures can be used to increase participation of a broad range of local interests in CED partnerships?

7. What are the capital gaps for CED partnerships and how can credit needs be better addressed through traditional and alternative financing mechanisms (i.e., arrangements with banks, credit unions, co-op organizations, pension funds, and so forth)?

8. What are the effects of adequate and inadequate external funding on CED partnerships (e.g., does secure funding make for vitality or lethargy on the part of CED initiatives)?

9. What types of governmental and non-governmental CED partnerships facilitate progress toward self-sufficiency?

10. To what extent and in what time period do CED partnerships achieve various aspects of self-sufficiency (e.g., financial, technical, human resources)?

11. What are the effects (benefits, costs, unintended consequences) of CED partnerships on various social, economic, cultural, environmental, and political variables?

PART 6

URGENT AND SPECIFIC NEEDS OF COMMUNITY ECONOMIC DEVELOPMENT

21

Development Indicators and Development Planning: A Case Study

François Lamontagne

Judging from the continued vitality of CED initiatives in Canada, and the government support which it receives, one is inclined to believe that the CED movement is quite healthy. While CED enjoys a strong and growing support base, the development of technical instruments for CED practitioners has not kept pace with the flourishing of CED organizations and initiatives. CED practitioners have to improvise or rely upon development tools which are not designed specifically for the task at hand. Both the development of a conceptual framework and the development of useful, conceptually coherent tools has lagged behind practice.

The concepts of development indicators and development planning have, however, found their way into the arsenal of concepts and tools available to CED practitioners. These concepts are not new but their combination and application to the field of CED is relatively recent. Development indicators, originally conceived by sociologists more than thirty years ago, have not been widely disseminated in the area of socio-economic development at the local, regional, and national levels. Their application in Canada has been even more limited. By comparison, the concept of development planning--or the related concept of strategic planning—has been more broadly used and has been applied in government, regional, and business planning and management. These two concepts, while gaining increasing acceptance amongst CED practitioners, have usually been used independently; there have been very few attempts to utilize development indicators as a development planning tool for CED. This chapter takes a critical look at recent attempts to link development planning and indicators in the context of CED, reviews the use of these concepts in Canada, and assesses their practicality.

Development Indicators and Development Planning

Development Indicators

Development indicators refer to "statistics which measure socio-economic conditions and changes over time for various segments of a population" (Land, 1975). Indicators are distinct from statistics, which can be described as "measure[s] in [their] rawest, least processed form" (Rossi and Gilmartin, 1980: 18). The concept of a development index further refines this concept and involves the weighted combination of two or more indicators (Dawe, 1992: 22). Development indicators gained popularity in the early 1960s and have been applied in different areas of research and development. For instance, they have been used in the field of comparative research (Berger et al., 1987; Harbison et al., 1970; Lui, 1980; Shin, 1977; United Nations Research Institute for Social Development, 1972) and have also been utilized by governments as a tool for regional planning (Government of Canada, 1987; OPDQ, 1988). Development indicators can be distinguished from the more narrowly-focused concepts of economic indicators (Nichols Applied Management, 1983), social indicators (Eberts and Young, 1971; Rossi and Gilmartin, 1980; Wood, 1972), and health indicators (British Columbia Ministry of Health, 1992). By definition, development indicators provide a more holistic measure of development, accounting for its economic, social, cultural and political dimensions.

The development indicator concept has recently been applied in many countries and disciplines. One group of authors created the idea of a "social indicators movement" to describe the research begun in the early 1960s which aimed to provide yardsticks for better understanding and describing well-being and quality of life (Rossi and Gilmartin, 1980). The widespread diffusion of the concept took place over the following twenty years, fueled by social scientists interested in comparing regions and countries in terms of their level of development (Corporation for Enterprise Development, 1987; Harbison et al., 1970; Hicks et al., 1979; Organization for Economic Cooperation and Development, 1982; Shin, 1977). These attempts to construct and analyze development indicators have generally been focused at the national and international level and have largely bypassed the community.

The research in Canada is more recent and more limited. The Department of Indian Affairs and Northern Development (DIAND,1979) proposed three sets of development indicators—economic viability, social vitality, and political efficacy—to analyze the situation of aboriginal communities. This research is of particular interest because it uses both objective and subjective indicators. Objective indicators are based on counts of behaviours or conditions associated with a situation, while subjective indicators refer to personal feelings, perceptions, evaluations, and attitudes (DIAND, 1979, 14). The DIAND study is instructive because of its use of a broad range of indicators to account for the relationships between objective economic and social conditions, and people's subjective reaction to them.

Another important study was conducted by the Office de planification et de développement du Québec (OPDQ). The OPDQ (1988) presented results of a comparative analysis of Quebec's regional municipalities based on an aggregate index regrouping nine socio-economic indicators. This paper represents an attempt to use development indicators for regional planning purposes. In the same vein, a recent study done for the Economic Council of Canada examined the development level and growth potential of Quebec's administrative regions, using four composite indices grouping a total of sixty-four indicators (Lamontagne and Tremblay, 1989). This research built on the methodologies developed by the Corporation for Enterprise Development (1987) and by the OPDQ (1988). Other development indicators research in the Canadian context include studies by the Canadian Association of Single-Industry Towns (1989) and Dawe (1992). DIAND (1990), Nichols Applied Management (1983), and PJS Geach and Associates (1985) have also produced innovative Canadian research on development indicators in the context of aboriginal development. In Canada, aboriginal communities have a long CED tradition which has stimulated a great deal of research on CED concepts and practices including work on development indicators.

Development Planning

Development planning has not yet become a CED buzzword but the related concept of strategic planning has found widespread acceptance within the business community, government circles, and among CED practitioners. Part of the concept's attractiveness derives from its potential to give organizations and communities more control over their resources and socio-economic future. The difference between strategic planning and development planning is primarily one of scope. Development planning is defined as the application and broadening of strategic planning principles to include promotion of individual and community well-being. Thus, strategic planning can be applied to a process of development planning. Strategic planning, in turn, can be defined as:

> Fundamentally, strategic planning envisages a desired future, and realistically assesses present opportunities and constraints; then, through clearheaded decision-making, it indicates how you can move from where you are to where you want to be (Lewis and Green, 1992, p.3).

Organizations or communities engage in a strategic planning process for development purposes. The key word is process. The definition suggests that, in order to yield desirable outcomes, strategic planning must be based on active community participation on a continuing basis. Strategic planning is not a one-shot deal which can solve an organization's or community's problems.

Figure 21-1
Strategic Planning Stages

Clarification of a Vision
Mission Statement
Analysis of Internal and External Environments
Selection of Potential Development Strategies
Setting of Strategic Goals
Preparation of Action Plan
Implementation
Monitoring and Evaluation

Source: Adapted from Westcoast Development Group, 1992, page 7.

The definition also implies that strategic planning is comprised of a number of distinct but complementary stages. Figure 21-1 outlines some of the stages most commonly associated with strategic planning. The process of strategic planning usually starts with the identification of a vision. Clarifying the vision requires envisaging a desired future and, as a result, the setting of limits on what can and should be accomplished. The second stage, the mission statement, is meant to focus and generate commitment to the vision. It identifies, generally in a fairly concise form, the priorities and values underlying the vision. The third stage is referred to as the analysis of internal and external environments. This analysis serves to pinpoint strengths and weaknesses, and identify areas of constraints and development potential. The next stage is defined as the selection of potential development strategies and requires selection of a strategy or a mix of strategies that will create the necessary conditions for the fulfilment of the vision.

The next step is the setting of strategic goals. Goals are desired, specific outcomes derived from the strategic plan and taking place within a defined time frame—usually five years. They set the course of actions for specific areas of intervention and are constrained by the agreed upon time frame. Preparation of an action plan follows once strategic goals are defined. The plan includes the specific operational objectives and details of the required human resources and budgets. The action plan will include annual targets and budgets. The performance of the organization (or the community) can be monitored and evaluated, as the action plan is implemented, so that the whole strategic planning process can be reassessed on a continuous basis and, if required, periodically realigned. Performance is usually judged on the basis of how effective the organization or community is in meeting its strategic goals. Monitoring and evaluation activities are valuable because they provide inputs for adapting to changing needs and a changing environment.

Combining Indicators and Planning

The combination of development indicators and development planning within the CED framework is one of the most interesting outcomes of recent CED work. The Westcoast Development Group (1990; 1992) has pioneered a series of useful CED instruments which are used by organizations across the country. Research by PJS Geach and Associates (1985), DIAND (1990), and the Development Indicator Project Steering Committee (1991) has proposed innovative ways of combining and using development indicators and planning as a CED tool for aboriginal development. The work of PJS Geach and Associates (1985) is one of the few studies that provides a framework for integrating development indicators for development planning. This study discusses the merits and potential applications of socio-economic indicators, in the context of Aboriginal development planning, and describes how indicators can support every step of the planning process. The study is conceptual in nature and does not provide specific examples such as worksheets or other tools to be used for strategic planning purposes. Furthermore, Geach's underlying framework focused on economic development and not on the many other facets of CED.

The research note prepared by DIAND (1990) draws from an extensive review of the literature on development indicators and provides a conceptual framework for constructing and applying development indicators. The paper's focus on aboriginal development is relevant to CED, given that CED and aboriginal development share many of the same principles (such as an emphasis on using local resources, on enhancing local human resources, and on building local organizational capacity). This conceptual framework contains a number of key principles aimed at guiding the selection and design of development indicators. The indicators should

- be relatively simple to construct, maintain, use and interpret;
- account for the social, economic, spiritual and cultural aspects of life;
- measure market and non-market economic activity;
- group objective and subjective indicators to allow for consideration of community members' perceptions and feelings, and to facilitate prioritization; and
- be flexible enough to account for the various stages of development of the community and to serve the information requirements at every stage of the development process (DIAND, 1990, pp.29–30).

Figure 21-2
Planning Stages and Indicator Program Components

	PLANNING STAGES	INDICATOR PROGRAM COMPONENTS
1.	Definition of goals and priorities	Goal setting
2.	Assessment of local resources	Community inventory
3.	Identification of strengths and weaknesses	Vulnerability checklist
4.	Identification of potential and obstacles	Capacity analysis Opportunity analysis
5.	Identification of alternative strategies	Comparative assessment
6.	Preparation of action plan	Priority assignment
7.	Monitoring	Performance analysis
8.	Reporting	Accountability analysis

Source: Adapted from DIAND, 1990.

These principles have been applied to the design of an indicator program that outlines a series of steps required to match development indicators with the various components of the planning process. Each of these program steps, in turn, relates to a particular methodology and indicator design. Figure 21-2 illustrates the linkages between strategic planning stages and the indicator program components.

The framework presented in Figure 21-2 suggests that it is possible to design specific sets of development indicators adapted to various steps of the strategic planning process. For example, a vulnerability checklist can be utilized to help identify a community or an organization's strengths and weaknesses. The checklist is a set of indicators which were originally designed to help single-industry communities assess their economic vulnerability (Canadian Association of Single-Industry Towns, 1989). The attractiveness of this framework lies in the fact that it proposes a full range of data gathering and analysis tools in support of strategic planning. However, many of these tools have not been thoroughly tested and require a relatively high degree of commitment and technical expertise in order to be implemented.

Research and Guidebook

The research conducted by E.T. Jackson and Associates (1990) was part of a larger research effort undertaken by a group of Aboriginal representatives from across the country. This research was to look at the historical

Figure 21-3
Development Wheel and Planning Stages

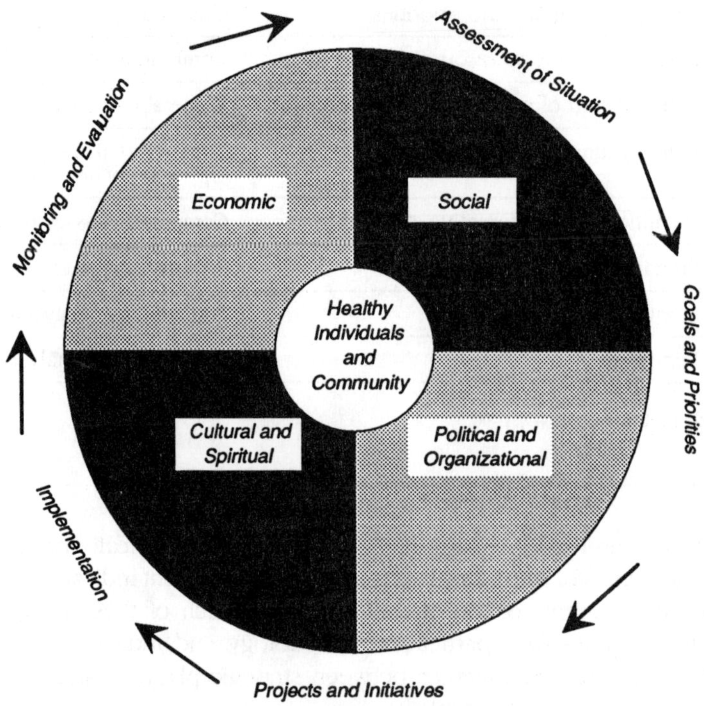

Source: Development Indicator Project Steering Committtee, 1991, p. 23.

background of development indicators, how they are applied in different environments, and their possible applications in aboriginal communities. The group developed a guidebook of tools and processes for using development indicators and for gathering data and analysis of information (Development Indicators Project Steering Committee, 1991).

This research work presents some unique and innovative features. Every step of the design was based on a collaborative effort. The research process involved a small team of technical advisors producing background material and drafts followed by working sessions of varying lengths (from a few hours to a few days) involving the larger working group. This process took place over the course of one year and resulted in a document which reflects careful consideration of the development needs and experiences of a broad range of organizations and communities. The guidebook specifically links development indicators to a strategic planning process, and contains a set of easy-to-use worksheets providing communities and groups with a framework and tools to keep track of their development efforts and progress. Development indicators have been used primarily for descriptive purposes—as a way of highlighting the socio-economic character of regions and nations, or for comparing, ranking and otherwise analyzing different territorial units on the basis of a limited set of socio-economic attributes. Applications of the development planning concept run the gamut from corporate decision-making to a set of community-based principles dictating the steps required to move along the development path. The Guidebook builds upon these two concepts: development indicators are fully integrated into the planning process and they play an important role in a community's or a group's efforts to improve its collective well-being.

The Guidebook is divided into three sections. The first explains the central concepts underlying the framework focusing on development indicators and development planning. It explains how development indicators can be used to measure the results of development activities. The second section defines how development can be divided into a number of stages and how development indicators can be used to help in the development planning process. The third section shows how development indicator worksheets can be used in day-to-day situations. The Guidebook conceptualizes development as a development wheel (see Figure 21-3) based on the North American Indian medicine wheel, which represents the four elements of personal and community life. The development wheel describes the social, economic, cultural and spiritual, and political and organizational areas of personal and community development. The ultimate goal of development is to foster healthy individuals and communities.

One of the challenges of the Guidebook project was to integrate this holistic notion of development within the more linear concept of development planning. The guidebook divides the development planning process into five stages:

- assessing the community situation,
- setting priorities and development goals,
- identifying activities to meet these goals,
- implementing the development activities, and,
- monitoring and evaluating the results.

These five stages represent the activities that a community or organization can undertake to improve its resources for long-term development and to promote well-being. Figure 21-4 groups these five stages of development planning into three general areas—strategic planning, implementation, and evaluation and monitoring—to understand how development indicators are integrated into this framework.

Development indicators can be utilized in the area of strategic planning to measure progress in meeting strategic goals. Strategic goals are measur-

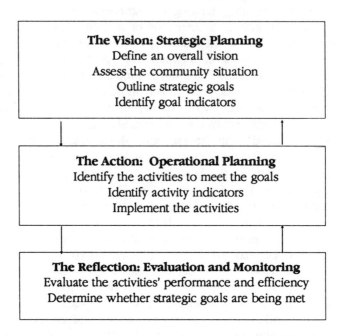

Figure 21-4
Development Planning and Indicators

The Vision: Strategic Planning
Define an overall vision
Assess the community situation
Outline strategic goals
Identify goal indicators

The Action: Operational Planning
Identify the activities to meet the goals
Identify activity indicators
Implement the activities

The Reflection: Evaluation and Monitoring
Evaluate the activities' performance and efficiency
Determine whether strategic goals are being met

Source: Development Indicator Project Steering Committee, 1991, p.24.

able targets that provide a basis for linking the vision of development and the activities aimed at achieving this vision. Goals can be defined for each of the four development quadrants—economic, social, cultural and spiritual, and organizational and political. The keyword here is measurable. The indicators designed to measure strategic goals—goal indicators—are effective only when the goals are quantifiable. An example of a measurable strategic goal in the area of economic development would be "to increase the level of self-generated income by 25 percent over ten years." Goal indicators would be relatively easy to define for such a target and could include ratio of earned income on total income or net annual profit generated from community enterprises. By comparison, finding an effective and unambiguous goal indicator for measuring a strategic goal such as "to increase employment" is difficult.

Development indicators can also be used in the area of operational planning to evaluate performance and efficiency. These activity indicators provide a measure of the effects of a development activity on achieving a given strategic goal, as well as a yardstick charting the performance and efficiency of this activity. A community investment fund might be the

Relating Strategic Goals, Their Indicators and Activities

	Strategic Goals	Goals Indicators	Activities
1	To increase the level of self-generated income by 25% over 5 years	ratio of transfer payments on total Band income	
		earned income derived from Band ventures	
2	To increase the use of traditional language among high school students by 15% over 5 years	number of students enrolled in traditional language, per school level	
3	To re-establish traditional leadership and government within 2 years	legal decisions on changes in government	
		number of programs/activities transferred to clan-based government	
4	To reduce alcohol-related deaths by 50% over 5 years	ratio of number of alcohol-related deaths on total deaths	
5	To increase the community housing stock by 10% over 3 years	number of new houses being built	
		number of new apartments being built	
		total number of dwellings (houses + apartments)	

appropriate development activity aimed at meeting the strategic goal of increasing the level of self-generated income by 25 percent over ten years. Activity indicators, such as the nature and size of the Fund's portfolio or the net return on investment, need to be defined to assess the performance and efficiency of the investment fund. The Guidebook proposes a series of six worksheets to facilitate the development planning process and the identification of appropriate development indicators. These worksheets provide an

Worksheet 2
Strategic Goal Worksheet

Strategic goal: Increase self-generated income by 25%.

	Goals Indicators	Data Needed	Methodology	Data Source
1.	ratio of transfer payments on total Band income	value of provincial and federal transfers to the Band (VPFP), by category of payment annual value of Band oncome from other sources (VBIO)	$\text{Ratio} = \dfrac{\text{VPFP}}{\text{VPFP} + \text{VBIO}} \times 100$	• Band office
2.	earned income derived from Band ventures	value of revenues derived from Band activities (VRBA) value of expenses derived from Band activities (VEBA)	Earned Income = VRBA-VEBA	• Band office

Worksheet 3
Activity Worksheet

Activity: Band-owned Development Funds

	Strategic Goals	Goals Indicators	Activity Goals	Activity Indicators
1.	To increase the level of self-generated income by 25% over 5 years	ratio of transfer payments on total Band income earned income derived from Band ventures	to provide loans to Band businesses to buy equity into Band businesses to provide counselling to Band entrepreneurs	nature and size of Corporation portfolio number of assisted businesses net profit of Band businesses

Worksheet 4
Activity Goal Worksheet

Activity goal: To provide loans to Band businesses

	Activity Indicators	Data Needed	Methodology	Data Source
1.	Nature of corporation portfolio	value of loans in primary sector (LP) value of loans in secondary sector (LS) value of loans in tertiary sector (LT)		
2.	Size of corporation portfolio	value of loans (VL) Value of loan guarantees (VLG) value of equity participation (VEP)	1) Share of loans: $$\frac{VL}{VL + VLG + VEP} \times 100$$ 2) Share of loan guarantees: $$\frac{VLG}{VL + VLG + VEP} \times 100$$	Corporation records

easy-to-use system for matching strategic goals with development indicators and development activities. Moreover, they facilitate the user's ability to understand the inter-relationships between strategic goals and development activities in all four areas of development. The Guidebook, while designed primarily by and for aboriginal groups and communities, can be used without modification by different groups and communities.

Conclusion and Future Directions

CED, as a field of research and practice, is still in its infancy but its support base is growing among the communities and groups which are implementing its principles as well as governments. The existence of federal and provincial CED programs is an indication that CED is viewed as a useful model for promoting the socio-economic well-being of Canada's citizens and communities. While CED has quietly proven its relevance to communities across the country, CED practitioners have pursued their development activities without the benefit of either a clear conceptual framework or a common set of tools to support their efforts.

Worksheet 5
Matrix of Expectations

Goals	Strategic Goals by Area of Development							
	Economic		*Social*		*Cultural/Spritual*		*Political/ Organzational*	
Activities	Increase income by 25%		Reduce alcohol-related deaths	Increase housing by 25%	Increase use of traditional language		Re-establish clan system	
Band-owned development funds	■							
Education program in traditional language					■			
Band committee on governmental affairs							■	
Health worker			■					
Training program in trades				■				
Financial incentive program for housing				■				

Worksheet 6
Matrix of Results and Impacts

Goals	Strategic Goals by Area of Development							
	Economic		*Social*		*Cultural/Spritual*		*Political/ Organzaitonal*	
Activities	Increase income by 25%		Reduce alcohol-related deaths	Increase housing by 25%	Increase use of trad. language		Re-establish clan system	
Band-owned development funds	■			▨				
Education program in traditional language					■			
Band committee on governmental affairs							■	
Health worker			■					
Training program in trades				■				
Financial incentive program for housing				▨				

KEY:	▨		▨		■		■	
	0-25% of expected impact		25-50% of expected impact		50-75% of expected impact		> 75% of expected impact	

The Guidebook is one of the more recent innovative tools that attempts to provide a simple yet comprehensive framework and related worksheets to put CED principles into practice. Work needs to be done in the area of creating flexible and effective CED tools. Training efforts and the establishment of a stronger national network for CED practitioners would be useful in disseminating existing knowledge about CED tools and otherwise providing support for them. More development work should be done to design CED indicator worksheets which could be used in a wide range of community environments. Research needs to be conducted to establish the validity of the development wheel concept in a wider range of community situations.

22

Training Needs for Effective Community Economic Development

Diane-Gabrielle Tremblay

Canada has gone through three major recessions since the 1960s (1974, 1981–82, and 1990–92) and many changes related to employment and economic development. Unemployment was 5% to 6% in the 1960s, passed the 10% mark in the end of the 1970s, and went up to almost 14% in 1982 and 1983. There was sustained growth throughout the 1980s but the unemployment rate stayed high. Over the last 10 years, Quebec has had on average an unemployment rate of 11%, a very high rate compared to Ontario during those same years, although Ontario's rate is now closer to that of the Canadian average. The social situation or social relations of production in the Canadian and Quebec situations are often different. Quebec has long been known for difficult labour relations. Until two decades ago, it came second, just after Italy, for the number of days lost due to strikes and other work conflicts. But the scene has changed over recent years; Quebec has evolved to what many see as the most consensual society in Canada, not to say in North America. CED has emerged in this context.

Quebec, like the rest of Canada and North America, is undergoing an important process of industrial and economic restructuring, which has translated itself in high unemployment, as well as the development of non standard and precarious forms of employment (Economic Council of Canada, 1987; Tremblay, 1990a). Macro-economic policy has not proven sufficient in the fight for employment and the efforts to control industrial restructuring, although the Canadian government has never really been committed to the objective of full employment. State intervention cannot, alone, solve all the difficulties and problems of given regions, localities, or industries. Temporary, occasional and contract work, as well as independent work, all of which are often characterized by lower wages and reduced or no marginal benefits, have become more and more important (Tremblay, 1990, Chapter 2). Polarization of wages and of quality of jobs (the good jobs, bad jobs debate) appears more and more important and calls for solutions which have been long to come. CED is one of the responses, but

CED actors often believe that too much is being expected of them, given the limits of their financial tools, governmental programs, and so forth.

In this context, training and human resources development are an important, if not determining variable, for CED as well as for most firms, small and large. Just as firms' efficiencies rest more and more on flexibility, work forces' training, and capacity to adapt to new demands, so CED's efficiency rests largely on flexibility, training, and capacity to adapt to new socio-economic situations. CED needs and efficiency must be considered in the context of consensus-building in Canada, as will be done here. This context plays an important role in defining today's CED needs, as do institutional realities. CED training needs in Quebec will also be identified in this paper. Contacts in the U.S., English Canada and France indicate quite similar needs. Finally, attention will be given to the way public policy should consider CED training.

CED, Entrepreneurship, and Employment

CED is often based on entrepreneurship and employment creation; Doeringer, Terkla and Topakian (1987) identify factors, in their study of the economic revitalization of Massachussetts, that need to be taken into account for an effective CED approach. The main elements are linkages to the local economy and community, as well as invisible labour market forces.

Cooperation between firms and linkages to the local community (business and others) are important for firms to be successful and for CED to be effective. The explanation of the revitalization of the Massachussetts region boils down to the provision of specialized products and services generated through niche-seeking strategies of specific firms, as well as community-wide business effects that reinforce these strategies by reducing production costs. Most noteworthy are agglomeration economies among local firms, through input-output relationships, and other forms of cooperation. Agglomeration economies based on input-output relationships are rarely based on visible cost competitiveness but are based on the ability, derived from physical proximity and cooperation, to participate in and respond rapidly to changing design and manufacturing practices. Proximity is an important factor in both flexibility of production as well as cost competitiveness. For many clusters of firms, proximity can reduce inventory costs through just-in-time deliveries which is important for the success of small and medium-size businesses. Proximity makes it possible for firms to consult with each other quickly to resolve quality problems over product specifications and the like (Doeringer, Terkla and Topakian, 1987). The present context of globalization of economies makes networks an effective instrument for international competition.

Second, the most important community-wide contribution to business competitiveness comes from labour market factors. The invisible labour market factors include skills, labour availability, absence of wage pressures, workers' attitudes that favour good productivity, and quality of labour-man-agement relations. These factors, which have traditionally contributed to the success of the local economy, are of paramount importance as the economy evolves towards specialized custom production. Changing technology, research and development, and patterns of business ownership did not appear as important in the Massachusetts context. To what extent is Quebec moving in a direction consistent with building linkages to local economies and communities and building invisible labour market factors? What future training is appropriate to move in this direction?

The Emergence of Consensus-Building: Or from Conflict to Cooperation

The invisible factors which can contribute to effective CED are niche-seeking strategies, agglomeration economies, flexibility in labour markets, cooperation and development of skills, and labour and management acting in concert. This section will concentrate on developments which have to do with flexibility and cooperation or consensus-building. The focus is on the Quebec situation as the Canadian situation seems distinct from that of Quebec in this regard. There are precedents for the recent evolution towards consensus-building, cooperation, and participation in Quebec (Tremblay & Noel, 1993), and these will be reviewed briefly here.

While it was in power, the Parti Québécois government held economic summits in Quebec; these were probably the first experiences of participation of different social actors in the definition of what should be done in terms of socio-economic development. The first socio-economic summits were organized in 1977 and 14 economic summits were held between 1977 and 1983 (Tremblay & van Schendel, 1991). Most were industry specific summits (food industry, textile-clothing industry, among others), but some were held on more general or national issues. Two of the major unions (the CSN and CEQ) often refused to participate in these summits, although the summits did represent the beginning of consensus-building process in Quebec. The FTQ, however, was rather open and participated actively in most of these summits; the president of the FTQ considered these summits as important moments in the development of labour management coopera-tion in Quebec (Gagné, 1992, p.5).

Starting in 1983, the PQ government organized regional summits, which had closer links to CED. Each region should have held a socio-economic summit every 5 years but the PQ lost power to the Liberal government in 1986. The Liberal government rejected the idea of national summits, and changed the nature of the regional summits. The regional summits had previously aimed at consultation and decision making; the new orientation was more limited (Stanek,1990) with the government itself defining the process as a "concerted planification" (Tremblay & van Schendel, 1991, pp.418–419). One third of the participants are from government, another third are elected municipal representatives, and another third are composed of representatives from regional community organizations. The idea of labour and management acting in concert may have developed and matured in these summits and some may actually have resulted in action and concrete realizations. Many critics, however, considered the summits more or less useless in terms of impact or change. The participants, other than the government representatives, thought they had too little influence on the definition and fundamental orientations of regional development, and that not enough new funds were injected in the process; most projects were being financed by old programs.

The National Table on Employment created in 1985 by the PQ government was another experiment which contributed to the more recent explosion of participation and cooperation. The objective was to develop a strategy for full employment in Quebec, through participation and cooperation of the different socio-economic actors. The election of the Liberal government brought this experiment to an end within a few months and, thus, it had little impact. The National Institute for Productivity was another structure of cooperation between unions and employers' representatives which was also abolished by the Quebec Liberal government. Many opposed the government's decision, and still consider this organization as one of the first places where participation and cooperation between unions and employers' organizations would have been possible.

New Initiatives for Employment in Quebec

Additional initiatives have developed over recent years without government participation. These include the Fonds de solidarité (solidarity fund) of the FTQ, the Forum sur l'emploi (forum on employment) and the Rendez-vous économiques (economic meetings) of the Quebec employers' council (CPQ). These various initiatives are important because employment issues are at the center of most forms of CED initiatives and are often an important source of financing.

The "Fonds De Solidarité" of the FTQ

In 1983 Quebec was just starting to recover from one of the worst recessions of its history and unemployment was still at a record high of 14%. Louis Laberge, then president of the largest Quebec union (FTQ), came forward with an idea that was to transform the image of his union over the next decade. Quebec unions had traditionally left management and investment to employers, but massive job losses in many industrial sectors gave rise to the idea that union members might invest in an investment fund which would support firms to maintain and create jobs. The project had been developed by Jean-Guy Frenette, economic counsellor at the FTQ, and received support from all the large FTQ unions. The other unions (CSN, CEQ) and the employers' council (CPQ) were originally not very favourable to the project. The FTQ Fund was, nevertheless, officially created on March 3, 1983. The "Fonds de solidarité" is like a mutual fund in which workers invest, except that the risk is somewhat higher since the fund must invest some 60% of its net assets in equity capital of Quebec firms which are in difficulty. The Fund does not invest in any firm that asks for support; firms are identified by the Fund, are the object of a serious financial analysis, and the Fund sets conditions for investment.

As the workers who invest, as well as those whose firms' are being helped, want to understand what's at stake, there is need for information in matters of economic development and employment. Group discussions help, but many social actors and CED representatives associated with projects feel at a loss when it comes to defining solutions to the company's employment problems and more so in legitimizing them. The Fund now imposes a condition that firms give 2 or 3 days for courses during which the firm's workers learn to read the firm's financial statements and to understand the firm's situation in its industry, its markets, and so forth. This training in economics and investment is delivered by people from the Fund; the objective is to create a better working environment, as well as to increase workers' confidence in themselves and in the employer, through a better understanding of the firm's financial situation. The Fund has developed a Foundation for economic education, financed in part by employers, in order to finance these educational activities. While some wonder whether this may not have a negative impact on workers' militancy, most consider that it helps the firms develop better labour relations and maintain jobs.

FTQ workers were the main contributors to the Fund in the beginning, but tax advantages have brought investment from other sources; FTQ workers now represent only half of the 110,000 shareholders of the Fund (Fournier, 1991, p.274). The return on investment has not been high over recent years, because the main objective of the Fund is to maintain and create employment, not to have high financial returns. People investing in the fund benefit from RRSP tax credits from Quebec and Ottawa; thus, the cost of the fund's shares comes out to about one third of the actual price paid. There have been critics of the Fund from other unions that argue it was not a union's role to invest in firms, as well as from financial analysts who considered the Fund not financially interesting. But most people from the business community, as well as from unions, now believe the Fund has had an important positive impact on labour relations and employment in Quebec. Some unions and businesses now want to benefit from the same type of fiscal advantages; the Quebec government's 1993 budget has actually limited the Fund's growth.

Over the years, the Fund has invested over 200 million dollars in about a hundred small and medium size businesses; these investments are estimated to have saved some 20,000 jobs. The Fund is an example of cooperation and can also be viewed as an example of CED; it is often involved in CED projects and its activities very closely resemble those of many CDCs. The Fund also plays an important role in community awareness of CED, and contributes to human resources development in many communities.

The "Forum Pour L'emploi"

Election of the Liberal Party in 1985 marked the end of the governmental initiative for full employment in Quebec but it did not mark the end of the social movement which had developed around this issue. Initiatives have been developing more actively over recent years, with little if any governmental support. The beginning of initiatives for full employment is related to the work of Diane Bellemore and Lise Poulin Simon (1986, p.54) who make a case for full employment by showing how unemployment is extremely costly for society, in terms of wages lost by workers, reduced profits and increased social charges for firms, and lost taxes and increased spending on social programs for governments. Bellemore and Simon (1986) also make the case for the adoption of a full employment policy through an analysis of Quebec and Canada's past economic policy and the economic strategies developed by Sweden, Norway, Germany, and Austria.

Preoccupation with full employment has not diminished in Quebec. As unemployment remains high, even through seven years of strong economic growth from 1983 to 1989, unions and community groups have become more and more preoccupied with this issue. Meetings were held in unions, community groups, and with some employers to initiate a process which lead to creation of the Forum pour l'emploi by a group of about 30 persons representative of different groups (unions, employers, the Desjardins cooperative credit unions movement, the Youth Council, the Quebec Women's Federation, and others) but excluding the federal and provincial governments. The first official meeting of the group supporting the Forum was held in February 1988, and the project was announced in May 1988. Some employers challenged the objective of full employment, and the initiative became a Forum for employment rather than full employment. Need for information and training in matters of economic development and employment was expressed by many CED actors present. Documents distributed by the Forum, and group discussions helped, but many social actors and CED representatives often felt at a loss at defining and legitimizing solutions to unemployment and development problems.

Some 2,500 persons participated in regional forums on the issue of employment held in 12 different regions of Quebec in the spring of 1989. In November 1989, a National Forum on employment was held in Montreal; 1,600 participants from business, cooperatives, unions, community groups and public service discussed various issues relative to employment, put forward solutions to the unemployment situation, and called for the adoption of a strategy for full employment (Forum pour l'emploi, 1991, p.256). Four basic principles considered essential to a full employment strategy were identified by the Forum—right of all to have access to employment, development of human resources and of the competitiveness of the Quebec economy, priority of employment in a good social and physical environment, and that all groups must work in common in order to develop employment (Forum pour l'emploi, 1991, p.220).

The Forum has defined its mandate as cooperation on various aspects of a strategy for developing employment in Quebec (think globally) and promotion and development of initiatives of local and regional cooperation for employment (act locally) (Forum pour l'emploi, 1991, Section 1). The Forum has had an important influence in the evolution of labour relations in Quebec, and, of course, the extremely difficult economic situation also played an important role in bringing employers to the same table as the unions to discuss issues of employment.

Participation and cooperation have flourished in Quebec because there were long hours of discussions and negotiations within and between the different organizations before any consensus was reached. The consensus which has been reached on occupational training and on the general objective of employment, but not full employment, may be fragile. There is certainly an agreement on the general objectives even if the means to be taken do not always get full support from all socio-economic partners. Building a consensus on issues such as taxation is not easy. The degree of consensus built over the last few years is, nevertheless, impressive, given the past trends in labour relations in Quebec. If consensus building provides a good answer to problems of economic development, then the Quebec economy should be on the right track for economic growth, employment growth and reduction of unemployment. However, the 1993 negotiations in the Quebec public sector were difficult, with the Treasury Board imposing wage cuts. Consensus may therefore prove to be fragile.

The "Rendez-vous Économiques" of 1991

A meeting organized in 1991 by the Quebec employers' council (Conseil du patronat du Québec) which called for a "Rendez-vous économique" was another important initiative related to consensus-building in Quebec. The employers' council (CPQ) was not originally associated with the Forum pour l'emploi (the Quebec Manufacturers' Association and individual employers were); later it became a member of the "comité de parrainage," a group of about 30 persons that supports the Forum and provides diversified representation. In the fall 1991, in the face of deteriorating employment and economic conditions, the employers' council decided to organize a meeting in order to put forward some concrete propositions which could rapidly create productive and permanent jobs. The meeting was restricted to some 20 groups including the Polytechnic university, four unions, Chambers of commerce of Montreal and of Metropolitan Montreal, Manufacturers' Association, Council for Cooperation, and a few other groups. Many of these were also members of the Forum, and the Forum itself was represented at this meeting. This was one of the first, if not the first, invitation addressed by the employers' council to unions and other community or socio-economic groups.

Over 60 propositions were discussed and 48 were agreed upon by all participants. Some had to do with industrial projects under discussion at the time, others were of a more general nature, a few even having to do with monetary and fiscal policy. Most were related to job creation programs, to investment, and to entrepreneurship; some had to do with technology transfers between the educational and research organizations and private business, with local investment funds, with support to exports, and even with the creation of an office for the management and rationalization of governmental programs and paperwork! The different organizations which presented the various propositions promised to ensure follow-up. In September 1992 the Forum pour l'emploi analyzed the proposals and offered support in the follow-up and realization of the various projects.

The Quebec Government's New Industrial and Employment Strategy

In 1992, six years after the Liberal government had abolished the various initiatives and structures created by the previous PQ government, the Liberal government came forward with two policy proposals which are clearly in line with the consensus built over recent years between unions and employers. These projects have not yet been implemented, but mark a recognition, by the government, of the importance of the consensus built up over the years by various socio-economic actors. CED actors should build upon these possibilities to develop their action. This implies specific training needs for these CED actors to be effective in this new context.

The New Industrial Strategy

The Industry and Commerce minister's new industrial strategy rests largely on consensus-building between employers and workers. This strategy was presented in December 1991, and is based on what the minister calls a new social contract (Tremblay, G., 1991). Quebec is to invest in 13 industrial clusters identified as groups of firms in the same industrial sector that should interact, compete, and cooperate in order to increase their competitiveness and accelerate their growth. Five of these industrial sectors are presently considered competitive on the national or international level; eight others are defined as strategic but need the proposed strategy to eventually become competitive. The competitive sectors are information technology, electric energy production, transportation and distribution equipment, metal and mineral transformation, aerospace, and pharmaceutical industries. The others include transportation equipment, textile and fashion, plastics, agribusiness, forest products, petrochemical industry, and others. Understanding this strategy and industrial economics becomes an information need for many CED groups in Quebec.

The medium term objective is to push the Quebec economy from mass production to value-added production, or to what many economists call diversified quality production (Sorge & Streek, 1987, p.37; Tremblay, D-G., 1991). This type of strategy requires qualified and informed human resources as participation of workers is part of the strategy. Unions used to be just as Fordist or Taylorist as their employers, generally rejecting any form of participation or job enrichment, but their attitude has changed over recent years. It now seems possible to get workers and their unions to adhere to such objectives as total quality of products, increased productivity through the introduction of new technologies, and redesign of job contents and work organization. A good understanding of all the aspects of this new competitive strategy is essential to CED. An understanding of industrial dynamics appears essential to the success of many CED projects, particularly in a long-term perspective.

Unions and employers adhere to the new industrial strategy but some union leaders doubt whether employers will be able to adopt the cooperative mentality necessary to the development of industrial networks. CED may have a role to play in this regard. Cooperative values cannot be developed overnight in an environment which has traditionally been characterized by competition. Some industries and firms may be more open than others and unions appear very willing to take that chance (Salvet, 1992). CED should play an active role in the development of such attitudes, especially among non-unionized firms.

The government has put little money in the project and does not seem to want to push private business into this strategy despite the support of unions and some employers. Most unions have a very positive attitude towards this industrial strategy as well as what it implies for labour in terms of better qualification (Tremblay, D-G., 1991) and more participation. Some unions (FTQ) have even gone as far as to tell members that they should take the initiative and go ahead in discussing issues of productivity, competitiveness, total quality, flexibility, and training with their employer (Salvet, 1992, p.10).

The Employment Strategy

Little has been done by the government since 1985 when it abolished all the structures created by the PQ in favour of employment although the labour minister has called for the exclusive jurisdiction of Quebec in matters of employment, including unemployment insurance and all manpower programs. These elements are part of an effective CED strategy and reflect themes on which CED actors should be knowledgeable; an understanding of employment strategies and labour economics appears essential to the long-term success of many CED employment projects. This second strategy has not received strong support but is considered innovative by most social actors. The strategy is based on the creation of a new regional and local level organization, the "Société pour le développement de la main-d'oeuvre," with offices in all regions of Quebec. Representatives from government, unions, and employers would establish economic development and employment priorities of the region. Union leaders insist on assurance from the government that this organization will have total autonomy as well as the necessary powers and funds. The degree of consensus on the proposed employment strategy is impressive. The main critique is that there is no clear engagement towards full employment.

Participation of CED groups is unclear but would be useful in many cases. Consensus-building on questions of employment may require the participation of community groups, particularly since unions only represent 40% of Quebec workers. Lack of recognition and of real participation of community groups is one of the main critiques which has been addressed to the various consensus-building initiatives such as the Forum pour l'emploi. Lack of training may have impeded the participation of some.

CED Training and Human Resources Development Needs

CED training content, objectives, and methods have been identified from a series of interviews done for the purpose of the development of a distance education course on CED, at the Télé-université (Open University) of the Université du Québec, an analysis of training needs done by the Institut de formation en développement économique communautaire (IFDEC) of Montréal, French documents from ADELS (Association pour la démocratie et l'éducation locale et sociale), and discussions with French specialists.

CED Training Content

Training about employment and economic development is essential to increase the efficiency of CED. Employment refers to elements of labour economics; sociology of work including matters such as labour data analysis; labour market analysis; employment policy; service economy; theoretical explanations of unemployment and employment development; sociology and economics of innovation and technological change; organization of work, skills and training; gender division of labour, employment and identity; human resources management; and labour legislation and industrial relations practices. Understanding the wider socio-economic context of CED action, from a theoretical as well as an empirical perspective is important. The objective is to understand the why and how of the present situation and to ensure attainment of social goals such as full employment and gender equity.

Economic development, which is different from simple economic growth, must also be viewed in a theoretical as well as an empirical perspective. Elements related to the theories of development; sustainable or durable development; socio-political and demographic influences on development; local, regional, and international development; multinationalization of firms and its impact on international economic development; theoretical differences between the concepts of growth and development, Keynesian and monetarist theories; and economic public policy are all subjects useful for CED actors. Understanding of various socio-economic indicators can also offer some insights as to socio-economic measures of the efficiency of CED.

Questions such as management of CED, entrepreneurship, financial management, business development, computer science, corporate and tax laws, housing development, land use, public relations and communications strategies are also useful if taught from the perspective of CED. Many of these subjects are the object of college or university courses, but these are generally not applied specifically to CED. In Québec, the IFDEC (1990, p.68) specifically calls for training in many of these fields and the Télé-université is presently developing courses in these fields.

CED Training or Human Resource Development Goals

The goals for CED training have been well defined by IFDEC (1990, pp.31–33). Four main goals were identified and two are most important and directly concerned with CED. The first goal is that of training leaders and managers, as well as employees and board members of CED organizations, to give them an integrated and democratic view of CED. The idea is to transfer skills and enable CED people to enter into effective partnerships. This is not easily obtained through normal schooling, as most educational programs and institutions are organized along disciplinary lines. CED agents must work together with specialists from different disciplinary backgrounds. Fields of action such as employment, employment training, urban revitalization, and entrepreneurship require an interdisciplinary, open, and integrated approach to be successful.

The second objective is to increase the efficiency of CED actions in the fields of employment, urban revitalization, housing, entrepreneurship, and so forth. This includes both increasing the efficiency of the different actions through development of CED concepts and strategies and the development of means to control and measure results of different actions. IFDEC indicates (1990, p.32) that an understanding of processes and strategies favours the full participation of all members of the organizations.

The third objective is aimed at the partners of CED organization members and is to initiate them to CED concepts, basic principles, and practices. The partners who should receive such training are representatives of social, economic, governmental, and community groups and organizations.

The fourth objective is to develop links with residents and entrepreneurs in the local communities and help them understand the basics of CED as well as its potential impact on the community. This has to do with increasing public awareness and understanding of CED and is a public relations function which should not be neglected. Human resource development should aim at developing knowledge which is transferable and at building a multi-purpose capacity to make CED more effective.

Methodological Propositions for Effective CED Training

What means will ensure that CED training reaches its objectives? CED training is advanced in France, where experimental CED training programs have been adopted since 1981. In France, as well as in Quebec, CED is often referred to as local development; the French expression puts the accent on the territorial or geographical dimension. The basic concept is "Formation-développement" or Training-Development (Senault, 1989, p.45) with training and development integrated in one unique action. Both training and development are closely interrelated in this pedagogical model. The concept of development is based on the postulate that, even in apparently empty lands, there exists resources which are either unexploited or badly exploited and which should be rediscovered. These resources are, for example, the physical resources which the dominant economy has ignored throughout the process of concentration due to competition in the New World Economy (Senault, 1989, p.48). But they can also be composed of know-how, innovative capacities, dynamism of the local population, and the like. Training can help identify developmental opportunities based on the articulation of human dynamism with the physical resources.

Training is considered from the point of view of the demand or need for training and only afterwards is any training proposition defined. The ideal situation is to develop all course content on the basis of needs expressed. The reality, however, is more often that trainees have considerable difficulty in identifying their needs and expressing them in terms that can find an answer in training programs. The idea of taking into account the needs of the public or clientele for training seems obvious but is in fact a rather recent preoccupation. Many public training programs are designed and offered to keep unemployed persons busy, and out of the unemployment statistics, without much consideration to the needs of the unemployed population. Only during the 1970s did consideration for needs of the target population start to emerge as a preoccupation in training and pedagogy (Senault, 1989, p.59–71). However, clientele remains an important consideration, all the more so since it is often related to the means which will be available to develop the course content.

Figure 22-1
The Three Phases of a Training-Development Protocol

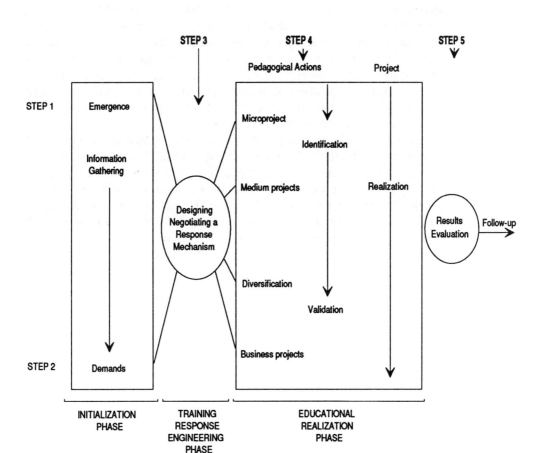

Another problem has to do with the concept of training needs or demands. A very sophisticated tool is required to be sure that CED actors all refer to the same idea when they express their needs. Marquart (1976) has gone as far as to say that the various methods of evaluation of needs of students or clienteles are a myth and serve only to justify and legitimate the teacher and the course content! In any case, it is essential to try to take these needs or demands into account and to try to identify the real needs of the individual CED actors as close as possible. It is also important to take into account the expectations of CED clients, as well as the orientation of the CED group, so that training can respond to collective as well as individual needs.

Figure 22-1 distinguishes three phases of a training-development proto-col. The first phase is divided in two steps—information and mobilization of the local potential for initiatives and, second, identification of needs, demands, and projects. The second phase, which corresponds to step 3, is when the training content is designed in response to the needs and demands expressed. Pedagogical actions take place in the third phase. Step 4 represents the training itself, while step 5 has to do with accompanying evaluation and follow-up. Training of this sort requires creation of some effective form of intellectual partnership which can bypass traditional institutional barriers. It is because of this that the concept of training-development is considered particularly efficient.

Training and human resource development is crucial for the future development of CED in Canada. Presently, most CED actors are training on the job, but more and more are expressing the need for a more complete and integrated vision of CED, as well as a better understanding of socio-economic issues relevant to CED. Training capacities are just starting to emerge and may be the beginning of a new field of specialization which will contribute to more effective CED in the future.

23

Training—An Urgent Community Economic Development Need

Flo Frank

Human resources are our most renewable and value added resource. With appropriate training they will allow movement into a new era of organization and production processes that can compete in the global market place. New economic initiatives will not be the major resource based projects of the past; they will be more technology based, often using telecommunications that will make distance from urban centres less relevant. These types of new industries fit well within the CED perspective. They can help minimize the current polarization between rural and urban communities and reduce the gap between wealthier and poorer communities. The emergence of CED as a distinct body of expertise and practice related to these transitions has brought with it urgent training requirements.

Training refers to a broad scope of activities from public awareness to specific skill development in individuals. It includes all aspects of learning, and can occur in many different venues using many different delivery methodologies. A wide audience is involved ranging from political or public stakeholders to community organizations or institutions such as Community Development Corporations and Business Development Centres. Practitioners and those who are involved in personal skill acquisition are key players in the process. Training provides a foundation for both social and economic development and is a critical component in any CED strategy. Social development, capacity building, and enterprise development each have separate human resource development requirements and are frequently in competition with each other. In addition, information sharing, governance skills, employment strategies, continuous or life long learning, and generational planning also have related training requirements. Appropriate resource allocation and good training will result in social, economic, and organizational benefit that are often the essential building blocks for community revitalization. Training is a critical need for governments, practitioners, and communities involved in revitalization through the CED process and has three aspects: (1) the need to increase awareness about

CED, (2) training as a component of the CED process, and (3) the evolving role of CED practitioners.

Community Awareness of CED

A trend toward community driven priority setting, increased local responsibility for planning and opportunity development, and decentralizing decision making is emerging across Canada. Governments are beginning to respond to the demand to make better use of dwindling resources and to be more inclusive in their policies and processes. The emergence of community-based training and economic development boards as well as aboriginal self government plans and training agreements has necessitated the cooperation and collaboration of a new mix of government officials, bureaucrats, and private practitioners. Education, business, industry and organized labour are becoming more involved in programming and policy related to employability training and economic development. Social development and economic growth are more clearly linked in the context of the training required for meaningful and long-term labour market attachment.

Community organizations sponsored by the public and private sector are affected as well. Business Development Networks, Community Development Corporations (CDCs) and Businesses Development Centres (BDCs) are identifying training and capacity building as a top priority in long-term economic or enterprise development. In many Canadian communities, CED has been primarily associated with job creation, business development, and financial or capital gathering initiatives for economic restructuring. Much of this has been on an ad hoc or project basis. The limitations of short-term job creation and project based activities are becoming recognized. Community plans with durations of five to thirty years are being developed with long range social, economic, and employment objectives. Training and human resource development at the community level are essential to develop, implement, and sustain these socio-economic strategies.

Partnerships, joint ventures, and community-based training plans connected to enterprise development require a new approach to community planning and government funding. Long-term commitments and continuity in priorities in aboriginal and rural communities have allowed a more comprehensive approach with respect to enterprise seed funding and human resource development strategies. Smaller communities are increasingly able to bring all the players to the table at one time to discuss socio-economic plans and potential financing. An excellent example exists in Rocky Mountain House, Alberta. Representatives of three levels of government (Federal, Provincial and Municipal) have been meeting with the Economic Development Group since 1985 to discuss long range plans for the area. The major focus of this group is social and economic well being and proactive well managed growth for the area. A plan is in place to encourage new industry and related businesses. There is a very specific training and employment strategy for those on social assistance, those who require retraining, and aboriginal people who live on neighbouring reserves. Included in the group are representatives from social agencies, local businesses, education, reserves, and government funders from social services and employment. Collectively they bring plans into reality by sharing resources and focusing on common goals.

Other communities have CDCs and BDCs which are starting to move beyond job creation into more elaborate CED strategies. Lloydminster's Community Futures program has completed its first generation of funding with successes in economic development, rural/urban/aboriginal programs, and a series of practical training initiatives tied to community based economic ventures. Lloydminster is acquiring knowledge and building capacity. Trainers are being selected from across the country to become delivery agents. Practical implementation tools are still needed, but this is an excellent first step to increase awareness of CED. The test will be whether communities take advantage of it.

Communities are insisting on increased local access to training and employment opportunities particularly for people who have barriers to the labour market. The 1988 Canada/Provincial Social Allowance Accords have allowed for five years experience with employability models, school/work connections, partnerships with business and industry plus numerous innovations in the area of employment and training at the local level. Each province across Canada has developed a variety of programs and services to combat the ever increasing numbers receiving government assistance. Hundreds of projects have emerged offering life skills, upgrading, career counselling, job placement, and various combinations of skill development. Some have been very successful and report placement into jobs or further education of 90% and higher. Others have had less tangible results. The assessment results of the past five years is mixed. People may have become social allowance recipients for shorter periods of time while regional economies shifted. With wage subsidy incentives, or even without government interventions, many of these people returned to the labour market. The value of the first few years of subsidy programs has been questioned because in subsequent years, social allowance clients have been less employment ready for a variety of reasons including the extended length of time they are receiving assistance. Projects have become longer in duration and more comprehensive in the training offered. It is within this context that a serious connection to community economic activities and partnerships has been made. Individualized and group community-based employability programs operate in all parts of Canada and range in size and cost from $2000 for a workshop to long-term agency contracts in excess of one million dollars. Larger urban areas could have as many as 60 or 70 projects operating at one time. Red Deer, Alberta (pop. 60,000) currently has 20 provincial, 25 federal and 20 jointly funded projects with a budget of approximately $1.8

million. Ultimately, placement in the labour market is the desired outcome, however communities are seeing these funds as providing an excellent opportunity to finance community-based human resource development strategies tied to local economic plans. Each community has a different approach to employment and training; across the provinces many successful models are in operation and should be documented and shared.

Employment, training, and labour market matters are as vital as economic restructuring, as governments re-establish their agendas related to poorer communities and revitalization. The Inter-governmental Accords have allowed ownership of labour market problems to extend beyond government. Gaps and barriers created by inter-governmental and inter-departmental policy have come to the forefront and partnerships with business and industry have become part of the training solution. An example of a training partnership exists in Sundre, Alberta, with Sunpine Forest Products Ltd. An agreement was made to train 40 people with severe labour market barriers (e.g., long-term social allowance recipients, and those with very low self esteem, criminal records, learning disabilities, or attitudinal problems). Some of the most difficult to place clients were brought into this demonstration project which was tied to the local economic development plan. The federal and provincial governments were asked to jointly fund the pre-employment training. Sunpine agreed to consider the trainees for permanent jobs after the training; however training on the job was not a feature of this project. The company was a partner in training plan development and the local community supported the project. Participants were encouraged by social workers, families, and the media. The results were that 38 of the 40 were hired into permanent positions. One year later 35 are still employed. Normally none of these local people would have been able to compete for positions with Sunpine. The company did not compromise its hiring standards and believes that graduates of the tailor-made training are some of the best in the company. Other employers are becoming more encouraged to participate and governments are increasing their funding for this type of model.

Central Alberta has several other excellent examples of governments working with increased cooperation and connectedness. An average of 60% of all employability projects are jointly funded by the federal and provincial governments. In the Red Deer area, decisions are made and priorities are set by local committees whose membership include community organizations, business, industry, and government representatives from municipal, provincial, and federal levels. There is a commitment to integrate funding into community planning and an effort is made to improve policy and program design. These communities face dilemmas defining their relationship to the various training/economic boards, finding qualified expertise to build capacity, and acquiring information and knowledge about new research, tools, or innovations from other communities. The institutional lag

Figure 23-1

EMERGING TRAINING NEEDS		
← SOCIAL		ECONOMIC →
H.R.D./Training (Existing/ not comprehensive)	Capacity Building (Existing/ becoming comprehensive)	Strategic Opportunities (Potential)
Examples:	Examples:	Examples:
Life skills, upgrading, job experience, welfare pre-employment programs	CDC's, BDC's, social agencies, Business Development Employment strategies, Community Futures LLFDB's, Pathways	Comprehensive CED strategies, potential to develop entrepreneurial partnerships and initiatives
Note:	*Note:*	*Note:*
Common in Aboriginal and Urban communities not usually connected to a CED strategy	Often part of CED strategy rarely in urban settings	Becoming a more viable long range approach to socio-economic development
Employability and Social Development	**Management Development/Job Creation, Business Development**	**CED and Improved Economic Development Strategies**
⇧	⇧	⇧
TRAINING FOUNDATION		

time between establishing government policy and designing programs is a major stumbling block, but the timelag is encouraging these communities to take the initiative for their own community economic development. As communities adapt to changing circumstances related to economic and labour market growth, a demand for CED practitioners, models, and training has emerged. CED is recognized as a specific strategy or discipline and is moving beyond job creation and business development. Figure 23-1 provides an overview of some of the emerging training needs.

Training as a Component of CED

Much of the success of the CED movement depends on the skills and abilities of community residents. Any aspect of resource, business or enterprise development, community planning, or employment based initiatives requires training. Communities are concerned with skill development as they recognize its importance and connection to quality of living. Long range training plans and requests to provide human resource plans for entire communities are increasing. Most CED practitioners recognize that there is no one model or approach for community-based human resource development. Successful strategies are tailor–made and combine a number of elements or components.

Labour Market/Skill Assessment

The labour force has changed as quickly and as definitely as technology has changed the workplace. Hiring people now requires training. Skills (or lack of them) in the market place have caused a new industry to be born related to employability and labour market development. Roles and occupations are blending or emerging in such a way that even a job description or training plan is not realistic. This situation highlights the need for human resource planning, training, career planning, and employment strategies attached to CED. The cost for not doing effective career and human resource planning is exceedingly high. The days of an abundance of skilled people looking for work are gone, and making the most appropriate use of what is available is critical. Communities must develop human resource inventories, know current skill levels, and anticipate the skills that will be needed for future initiatives. This assessment information is the base of a training plan design; the analysis will reveal whether significant skill gaps exist that could undermine the success of the CED plan.

Capacity Building

Communities must consider all areas of training associated with CED. This in itself demands particular skills and abilities. Priorities placed on the application of various tools and resources and the resources allocated to the different areas of need require a knowledge and understanding of human resource development, community development, and financial planning. Understanding training requires training. Communities have only recently insisted that job creation and/or employability projects be connected to meaningful and lengthy employment. Aboriginal communities are seeking skill development to manage a more complex set of community needs and the higher expectations related to self government. In Duffield, Alberta, an economically and socially needy native community has had four years of excellent results from planning. The community made a commitment to training connected to economic goals. As a result training in life skills,

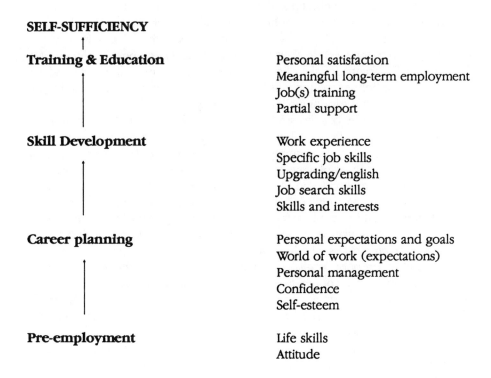

Figure 23-2
Employment Continuum

SELF-SUFFICIENCY
↑
Training & Education   Personal satisfaction
↑   Meaningful long-term employment
                                            Job(s) training
                                            Partial support

Skill Development   Work experience
↑   Specific job skills
                                            Upgrading/english
                                            Job search skills
                                            Skills and interests

Career planning   Personal expectations and goals
↑   World of work (expectations)
                                            Personal management
                                            Confidence
                                            Self-esteem

Pre-employment   Life skills
                                            Attitude

academic upgrading, and entrepreneurial initiatives has been initiated. Some of the results include over 75 graduates of upgrading (including in 1992 all elected representatives), ongoing life skills delivered by trained community people, several successful economic initiatives, reduced social problems, and increased pride and self governance capability.

Employment Development

Skilling up of individuals to take advantage of employment opportunities will result in stronger personal and community economies. Most successful training strategies start where people are and work into and along a continuum toward self sufficiency. Individuals and groups have been prepared for work in their communities by moving from personal management and academic upgrading into career planning and specific skill development. Figure 23-2 shows this as a continuum. The outcome is a more productive work force, closer balance in the labour market, lower social costs, more flexible and competitive economy, and better competitive edge.

In the Northwest Territories, a new initiative is connecting local residents to employment in the trades through capital works and housing projects. Three government departments (Housing, Public Works and Advanced Education) are developing a new curriculum for certification in pre-trades related to building. The model moves from core skills (life skills, safety, work standards) to transferable skills (use of tools, safety equipment, blue prints) to specific occupational skills (carpenters, electricians, plumbers, and so forth). Northerners will be assured of employment as this training is combined with a supportive local hire policy.

Other examples of successful innovations exist in Alberta's youth projects designed specifically for labour market attachment in local communities. Centres such as the Opportunity Zone in Edmonton and the Youth Services Centre (one-stop employment centre) in Red Deer combine all the related employment resources and services under one roof. Models based on peer advocacy or mentorship are built into projects to guide young people toward meaningful and interesting training or job options. Equally progressive is the proposed initiative in central Alberta to establish a reverse incubator. Would-be employees who have serious labour market barriers (e.g., mental disabilities or poor English language skills) are brought together in a community-based cooperative. Management and marketing expertise is purchased by the employee owned co-op: businesses such as janitorial, catering, and desk top publishing will be established. Profits from the business operations return in part to the employees, and in part to a fund for other entrepreneurial groups. These examples are useful to appreciate that the diversity of approaches go beyond traditional employment development.

Career Planning and Job Matching

Labour market changes in the past decade and shifting economies across the country have caused a rethinking of the value of having the right people in the right jobs with the right skills. Career planning for many individuals has been simply seeking employment at whatever jobs are around. An Employability Handbook, produced in Alberta, assists individuals entering the work force to over-come job search barriers. Readers are helped to present themselves in a positive and realistic way. The handbook is a tool for those who don't have access to employment counsellors or who want to use a do it yourself approach. This type of workbook is being duplicated and complemented with tapes and videos designed for various high need groups. Communities have always considered job creation as an important component of CED career planning and long-term success in the workplace have been lesser considerations. Community-based training strategies have had to take career planning into consideration in order to meet both social and economic objectives. It is increasingly difficult to make appropriate and satisfying career choices, and find work related to the chosen field.

Communities face a similar difficulty in creating employment opportunities and describing them in a way that people can make choices and demonstrate interest. The need for community capacity building in career planning, job analysis, and proper matching in the workplace is critical to CED initiatives.

Training Existing Community Employees

Rural and aboriginal communities must consider existing employees as a positive human resource asset. Band staff, community workers, recreation directors, social workers, and village office staff are the foundation for facilitating change. Often those in jobs are the last to be included in training, and are the first to burn out. Their roles are sometimes altered or changed by a CED strategy and their training needs are often neglected. Awareness about any community plan, and inclusion in the training, is paramount to developing support for the plan and to maintain competency in the functions. In Mayo, Yukon, a team of resource people assisted the N.N.D. Band with a five year implementation plan for self government. Emphasis was placed on existing band staff because their roles would change and an opportunity existed to plan the jobs properly to serve long range needs. This approach allowed for a proactive stance for the future and included the people whose jobs were going to be affected. The results included support for the planning from those on the inside and genuine excitement about the new roles and associated training.

Leadership Development

The role of politicians and leaders within communities has changed as much as the economy and the labour market. The way a community manages and governs itself, sets priorities, does its planning, hires and fires outside experts, makes decisions, and communicates ideas are all part of skill development and training. The need exists for both elected and non-elected community representatives from isolated native communities to downtown Montreal to become more skilled in use of new tools and innovative models for planning and development. Managing and promoting the development process and the linkages between social and economic agendas is a top priority. Leaders must concern themselves with a broad and changing knowledge base. Training such as communications, cross cultural collaboration, implementation planning, governance skills, environmental planning, and inter-national negotiations are appearing as training options in many post secondary institutions.

Communities need access to specific information on labour market, education, business, immigration, and economics so that they can plan strategically. Project Toward 2000 Together in Alberta, is bringing community leaders, politicians, business and industry, labour market, and economic specialists together to share ideas and information and to outline solutions to economic and community development. In 1990–1992, many communi-

Figure 23-3
Planning and Training Matrix

	Community Members (Labour Supply)	Staff and Administration (Workers)	Chief and Council (Politicians)
DO skill use application	• Practical Work Skills • Personal Career Planning • Stability and Confidence *Outcome:* Employment, Self-Sufficiency and Personal Satisfaction	• Effectiveness in the Workplace • Accredited Skills • Job Satisfaction *Outcome:* Human Resource Planning and Results	• Development of Strategies • Joint Ventures Partnerships • Interaction between Bands and other Communities *Outcome:* Community and Economic Development
LEARN skill development intermediate	• Communication, Coping Relationships Literacy, upgrading • Work Skills *Process:* Primarily classroom (Advocacy, Mentorship)	• Functional Skills • Basic for the job *Process:* Training on the job and courses (Consultant/Trainer)	• Leadership, Communication, • Planning and Management Skills *Process:* Workshops and Seminars (Coaching)
LOOK buy in entry	• Lifeskills, Career and Personal Development Social Growth *Goal:* Self-Esteem and Motivation	• Identify what's required and who has the skills *Goal:* Skilled and Satisfied Workforce	• Develop Attitude/Desire • Value Community: Social, Economic, Cultural Growth *Goal:* Political Stability

Design by F. Frank./78.

ties across Canada planned their political or leadership agendas on projects such as Vision 2020 in Red Deer. Entire communities were involved in charting out the preferred vision of the community in 30 years time. These exercises have assisted leaders and politicians to plan their own skill acquisition and has reaffirmed commitment to training. Figure 23-3 is one framework used for human resource planning in both native and non-native communities. All members of a community can be included in the learning, cultural, and training opportunities.

No community can participate in CED without considering people and their training needs and limitations. People are the most stable and often undervalued resource in a community. They must become as valued as natural resources and be given the same priority in terms of development. The balance between social and economic development requires a serious commitment to training for capacity building in community development organizations and for increasing the skill level and entrepreneurial spirit of a community.

CED Practitioners

The CED practitioner's role is in transition and is developing as an occupational field. Canadian CED practitioners seem to focus primarily on mechanisms to assist with economic restructuring. In other countries, however, CED is viewed more as a social development vehicle and is attached to job creation and training initiatives. Working within the same occupational cluster are specialists in community development, social work, human resource development, career and employment counsellors, industry consultants, trainers, educators, entrepreneurial or political development, and strategic, economic, natural resource or environmental planning specialists. Many of these occupations breakdown further into specialist activities such as visioning, assessment, data collection, strategic planning, venture capital development, evaluation, and testing. The CED arena is full of individuals who identify their skills or backgrounds as community-based and directed toward social or economic development. They may not see themselves as CED practitioners but would probably identify themselves as being within this discipline if the occupational field was more clearly understood. Practitioners are being brought together through training initiatives and an informal network is becoming a necessity. Community demand is creating a need for a more integrated approach and that alone is causing practitioners to collaborate on the design and delivery of training models. Often two or three separate companies will work on a common contract. In Alberta the Laingsbrough Resource Group and the Life Role Development Group are two companies that, like Westcoast Development Group of B.C., broker combinations of expertise and knowledge. Initiatives such as the implementation plans for self government agreements require coordination of expertise from several specialized fields such as law, economics, and human and natural resource management. Very few companies have networking and resource brokering as part of their activities, even though there is need for combinations of capable resource people to work on these and other CED initiatives. Governments are sponsoring training, the network is developing, and CED is evolving. Communities often have very limited access to this information and no formal way to connect with practitioners.

There is limited formal training or accreditation in the CED field. Diploma courses are being developed related to specific areas of the CED process, but there are currently few opportunities to acquire skills in a comprehensive and recognized program. Standards are being set through the evolution and experience of the CED movement, rather than by a conscious process managed by design. Both the issue of accredited CED training and standards require attention. Some of the integrated training needs of both communities and practitioners include employment and labour market dynamics, demographic influences, career planning and labour market development, values and attitudes about work, economics in general and specifically related to technological change, human resource and organizational development, labour and industrial relations, economic and financial growth models, and regional, national, and international trade.

Summary

Communities, governments, and practitioners have a common set of priorities related to CED training. CED is an emerging discipline and practitioners are becoming very active through networks and informal linkages. In addition human resource development and training are being accepted as vital elements of CED and require further understanding, commitment, and promotion. The agenda is to consciously take hold of the CED process and formalize its evolution. A combined effort is essential to identify present activity and further needs. Ways must be found to organize practitioners, develop the standards and training needed, structure research priorities, and link the collective learning to policy makers. Training in and about CED becomes an urgent need as Canada requires communities that are able to foster diversification, competitiveness, growing economies, and a good quality of life.

24

Promotion of Community Economic Development

David Pell

The current approach to learning how to develop sustainable communities appears to be very similar to the unsuccessful approach used by Winnie the Pooh. One day, while walking in the woods, Winnie came upon some mysterious tracks. The tracks of a strange animal presented this curious bear with a difficult problem. Who was in the woods? He decided the best strategy would be to follow the trail very carefully. With his friend Piglet, he embarked on a search for the answer to his question by keeping his head down so he could see the trail clearly, while very methodically retracing the steps taken by the strange creature that had walked before him. However, despite following the trail for a very, very long time, and with the greatest of care, Winnie and Piglet did not find their creature. In fact, their problem became more complex for there were now several sets of tracks to follow. Fortunately, Winnie's friend, Christopher Robin, had been watching and he was able to help. Christopher Robin pointed out that Winnie had been walking in circles and the tracks he was following were actually his own. Winnie had been so intent on solving his problem quickly, that he had not taken the time to stop, review his actions, and possibly try a different approach. Rather, he had been walking in circles and repeating the same mistake over and over and over again. As a result, his problem was getting more complex and difficult to understand rather than solved.

Community economic development is a new solution to an old problem.[*] How do we develop healthy sustainable communities? It is an idea which has not been fully accepted by governments and many research organizations, because, like Winnie, they are content to follow the old familiar course of action. CED, in its current form, has been around for approximately 20 years but is only beginning to be recognized as a legitimate planning strategy. Expanding the awareness of CED within communities and governments continues to be an important and ongoing task. Information needs to be developed explaining why CED should be considered as an alternative

---

[*] This chapter will use the definition of CED proposed by Boothroyd and Davis (1991, pp.8–13).

to existing conventional development strategies, the barriers inhibiting the creation of successful CED ventures, and the impact of successful CED initiatives.

During the past few years support for CED has increased in several jurisdictions. The federal government and provinces of Quebec, Ontario, and Saskatchewan are notable examples of senior governments supporting CED; the cities of Toronto, Montreal, and Winnipeg have demonstrated how municipal governments can support local CED programs. An increasing number of community organizations are adopting CED as a strategy for resolving local social and economic problems. Limited endorsements have come from several major research organizations including the Organization for Economic Cooperation (1990) and the Economic Council of Canada (1990). CED appears to be at a crossroads. Significant barriers to further development exists despite increased support from both governments and communities (Organization for Economic Development and Cooperation, 1990; Pell, 1991). Expanded research combined with public education programs are critical to the elimination of these barriers. This chapter will identify current trends in community economic development, examine current models and difficulties with project assessment, and suggest general directions for expanded research and public education.

Current Trends

Community-based economic development practice is changing in response to changes in social and economic conditions. Continuing levels of unemployment which exceed 10% (*Globe and Mail*, January 1, 1993, Section D, p.2), loss of traditional sources of employment in a variety of industrial sectors, and increasing concerns with environmental degradation are influencing how CED organizations plan and manage their programs. Further, the rate of change affecting Canadian communities is forcing CED organizations to conduct both operational and program reviews. Many are reviewing existing strategies and developing new plans and programs, examining alternative sources of funding and establishing community-oriented financing programs, and promoting an expanded role for municipal government. CED initiatives continue to focus on programs which address labour market problems. Community planning, support for small business, and skill training initiatives to assist the unemployed characterize CED work in Canada. In smaller communities, particularly in northern regions, community facilities and housing projects are also prevalent. However, in recent years, initiatives that respond to local environmental concerns are expanding. Scandinavian countries lead in this area but a recent exploratory study identified a significant number of projects in Canada (Pell & Tomalthy, 1992).

The ways CED organizations are funded are also changing. Increasingly, CED organizations are expected to be based on working partnerships between the community, government, and private sectors. Government assistance continues to be the primary source of funding. However, the conditions under which funding is available is changing from grants to contributions that need to be matched with funds from other sources, including the private sector and the community itself. There is also a trend towards establishment of financial institutions which support CED business activities. These new community-based organizations are considered essential to successful CED programs. Established financial corporations and new community finance corporations have been established to provide clients of CED organizations with access to debt financing and, on occasion, equity financing.

Further, there is a move towards an expanded role for municipal governments. Municipal governments in small northern and aboriginal communities are often directly involved in local CED initiatives, but other governments of municipalities usually are not. The reduction of available funds for development work from senior governments, combined with the shift towards broadly-based community partnerships, has resulted in requests from many CED organizations for an expanded role for municipal governments. Municipal governments are being encouraged to move beyond their traditional regulatory role and reliance on importing business and industries from other communities, to a pro-active role which supports local entrepreneurship with technical and financial support. Several municipalities have reacted favourably to these requests and are allocating municipal resources for CED programs.

Understanding Community Economic Development Work

There is little systematic information which analyzes and explains the impact of local CED projects even though the number of CED programs is expanding in response to the increased government and community support. Current support for CED is largely based on personal experiences and anecdotal information. As a result, it is difficult to substantiate the value of CED as a strategy for changing social and economic conditions. Existing information supporting CED describes successes in creating jobs, starting small businesses, and provision of housing or community facilities. However, there continue to be questions regarding the efficiency of CED programs and their impact on local social and economic conditions (Organization for Economic Development and Cooperation, 1990).

CED is not a well understood field of work. Only a relatively few studies have been conducted which systematically examine CED with economic indicators, project development indicators, or standard impact assessment criteria. Notable examples of program reviews and exploratory studies during the past 15 years include examination of Halifax Human Resources Development Association by the Atlantic Province Economic Council and Price Waterhouse study of Community Futures, and work of the Economic

Council of Canada. Canadian CED organizations have also been included in studies conducted by the Organization for Economic Cooperation and Development. These studies, although useful, do not adequately answer the critical questions regarding efficiency and socio-economic impact.

Webster's Dictionary defines efficiency as "the state or quality of being competent so as to accomplish or have the ability to accomplish a job with a minimum expenditure of time and effort" (1989, p.455). How to achieve optimum efficiency at the community or regional level is widely debated. Weisbrod (1988, p.38) argues that the unique role and contribution of non-profit sector, which would include CED organizations, will be compromised if classical economic criteria, including profitability, are used to determine the efficiency of their work. Also, Higgins and Savoie (1988, p.195) propose that neoclassical economics not be used to measure the efficiency of regional development policies and programs because an alternative approach which would involve a broader group of social and economic factors is needed.

The full impact of CED organizations on social and economic conditions is difficult to determine. For instance, very few CED organizations have been operating as established organizations for 10 years, the estimated time required to assess any long-term impacts of a local program. Also, CED organizations function in an environment where other local and external organizations also provide assistance to the same people served by the CED organization. As a result, it is very difficult to determine what specific contributions a CED organization has made to resolving a client's problem.

Current Models

The number of CED organizations is increasing despite the lack of systematic assessments and a thorough understanding of the CED process and its potential to facilitate change. The reasons for this growth are not clear. Perhaps, the apparent success of older CED initiatives such as the Nanaimo Community Employment Advisory Society, New Dawn Enterprises, and the Kitsaki Development Corporation, as well as better known CED initiatives in the United States, has encouraged supporters of CED to start new projects. The failure of conventional development strategies and increasing problems of unemployment and related social problems may have fostered a willingness in many communities to try something new.

The priorities and programs of CED organizations vary considerably, although facilitation of entrepreneurship has become a centre point of many. This focus reflects the larger international trend towards an entrepreneurial society where an expanding proportion of the labour force are either self-employed or work in small companies. Providing support for local entrepreneurship has been recognized as an effective strategy for local development by the Organization for Economic Cooperation and Development (1990). Similarly, the Commonwealth Foundation has encouraged member countries to develop community-based entrepreneurship programs to assist youth to be more employment self-reliant (Ball, 1991). CED organizations supporting local entrepreneurship have been developed in communities across Canada. In excess of 250 of these initiatives are supported by the federal government's Community Futures Program. Others receive financial assistance from provincial and municipal governments. The Cambridge Opportunities Development Association, Cambridge, Ontario, is an example of a CED organization which receives substantial support from the province, while the Community Business Centre/Newcomers Enterprise Centre, Toronto, is supported by a broad-base partnership which includes the municipality, provincial government, and private sector.

The Business Development Centre (BDC) has become the most popular program model adopted by CED organizations. These resource centres provide a range of small business counselling, training, and information services to clients who are usually unemployed. Community loan funds to provide start-up loans for clients are perceived as an essential complement to the technical services provided by the BDC. Many of the Business Development Centres operating within the Community Futures program have established loan funds and a smaller group of CED organizations, which are not part of this federal program, have also established loan funds for their clients. The lack of government funding and reluctance within the private sector to invest in this type of initiative has prevented many CED organizations from establishing loan funds.

Business incubators have also been established by several CED organizations. Business incubators provide selected entrepreneurs with work space, secretarial and office support, and business counselling during the tenuous first two years of a new business. The YMCA has operated nine incubators across Canada for more than six years. The incubators historically have served unemployed youth, although this has been changed to include anyone interested in becoming self-employed. Other community economic development organizations have established specialized incubator programs. The Toronto Centre for the Promotion of Fashion Design has developed an incubator for fashion designers. In Winnipeg, similar programs have been established for artists and craft persons.

Other types of CED programs include support for community businesses and cooperatives. Community businesses are business ventures which are sponsored and sometimes owned by non-profit organizations including community development corporations. Usually, they are established to assist groups, such as immigrants, with multiple barriers to entering the labour force. The Halifax Human Resources Development Association, a community development corporation, owns and operates several community business ventures which employ social assistance recipients. CJRT, a Toronto radio station which broadcasts entertainment and education programming across Ontario, is an example of how the community business model can be developed in the communications sector. Cooperatives have been established by artists, industrial workers, and farmers to ensure their businesses are viable.

Promoting Community Economic Development: Some First Steps

The future of CED work in Canada is dependent on the elimination of the barriers which inhibit further development of policies and programs. In addition, there must be recognition and acceptance of the potential of the voluntary sector, and the fundamental changes which are restructuring the Canadian economy. Peter Drucker (1990) and Burton Weisbrod (1988) have promoted the efficiency of the voluntary sector and its capacity to effectively solve many types of community problems. In their opinion, the voluntary sector should continue to be a provider of services when familiarity with local conditions and responsiveness to a diversity of community needs and adaptability are required organizational attributes. Weisbrod also believes that the non-profit sector is viewed as being more trustworthy than either government or the private sector and will more likely be supported by community members (1988, pp.25–28, 40, 41). Many problems detrimental to the social and economic conditions of communities have unique qualities and require specific almost tailored made responses as well as the active support of the community. CED organizations are well suited for mobilizing community resources to solve local economic problems. CED organizations are managed by community members who are familiar with local conditions and have better access to local resources than external organizations (Pell, 1990).

Canada, like other advanced industrial countries, has witnessed a decline in employment opportunities in manufacturing and resource productions industries. The country is no longer able to compete with many developing nations which have significantly lower labour costs and, in some instances, are rich in natural resources. Nuala Beck (1992, pp.36–41) believes Canada has entered the technology cycle in the evolution of modern economies. The technology cycle is moving Canada's economy away from the manufacturing and into an age dominated by cheap and accessible semiconductors (Beck, 1992, pp.27, 37).

One significant impact brought about by this evolution is the decline in manufacturing jobs and the significant increase in service sector employment. There is debate about the meaning of this trend and how it will affect the Canadian labour force. Some observers have suggested that the decline of manufacturing with its relatively high wage paying jobs will result in the decline of the middle class (Economic Council of Canada, 1990; Gershuny, pp.51–59) resulting in an increasing number of people finding themselves in low skilled service jobs which have low wages and few benefits. This pessimistic scenario is challenged by others who believe that the emerging service sector will be characterized by high paying jobs and that Canadian labour is in a good position to capture many of these positions. Both groups agree that retraining is critical to the future of the economy. Beck (1992, p.66) and Gershuny and Miles (1983, pp.240–245) argue that retraining should be in strategic areas where the economic growth is possible. These areas include computers, semiconductors, software and information services; medical care and diagnostics, pharmaceuticals, surgical and medical instruments and supplies; telecommunications services, guided missiles and space equipment, radio and microwave communications and entertainment; optical instruments and environment consulting and equipment. CED organizations must understand these changes and incorporate an analysis of opportunities and available resources for the local economy in their respective strategic plans. For instance, CED organizations should determine what location factors are pertinent to these emerging industries and whether their community would be an attractive location.

Understanding and removing institutional, legislative, and knowledge barriers to the future development of CED organizations is critical. A recent survey of barriers experienced by CED groups across Ontario identified several problem areas (Pell, 1990, p.9); discussions with CED practitioners in other regions across Canada indicated that these problems are not unique to Ontario. Most CED projects are forced to work with inadequate budgets. Funding usually comes from a government program, which is not set up specifically for CED work. Agreements are often limited to one year contracts and are on a one-time-only basis. Funds from private foundations, corporations, and religious organizations are usually tied to a specific project and cannot be used for ongoing operating costs. Funds for individual ventures are difficult to secure, because CED organizations are non-profit corporations with no previous track record for business development. Further, CED ventures are usually small, involve high risk ventures, or are located in communities which have serious economic problems. As a result, both private and public sector lenders are unwilling to provide financing.

Many CED organizations have not developed mission statements or mandates that are tied to specific problems and objectives. They simply reflect the goals of a government program or are very general. CED groups have also identified strategic planning, opportunity identification, and market research as areas which require assistance. CED organizations require a broad range of skills in business development, human resource development, business management, and strategic planning. A small organization cannot afford the costs of retaining the services of people with this type of expertise. As a result, staff often lack the required knowledge and expertise to operate a CED organization effectively. The social needs of a community cannot always be met by the short-term realities of business development. Resolving unemployment and other related social problems requires many years of successful development work and many compromises along the way. CED organizations may not have the necessary long-term perspective or the patience required for effective CED work.

In addition to operational problems, CED organizations do not function within an established policy framework and macro economic strategy. Thus, it is difficult for local CED organizations to develop plans which are integrated with provincial or national initiatives. CED organizations often do not have access to a province-wide resource network. Such a network would provide individual CED organizations with information and assistance to foster the development of mutually beneficial relationships with other CED organizations and resource groups.

Results of the Ontario study were summarized and used to inform potential supporters of CED. Information in the report and discussion groups that examined the information facilitated a process of education and action. The discussions have contributed to the development of several initiatives each targeting a specific barrier or group of barriers. The provincial government has approved plans for a financial assistance program which would support the establishment of community-based loan funds (Bill 40, Community Economic Development Corporations, Government of Ontario, November, 1993). The province and several municipalities are making changes to existing policies to enable the expansion of CED activities. Several coalitions and associations of CED organizations have been established for the purposes of information sharing and other forms of mutual aid and a newsletter is being published.

Conclusion

The structure of Canadian society is rapidly changing. Changes in the economy are particularly significant. The development of local economies for the purpose of creating jobs and maintaining services is becoming the responsibility of individual communities and regions. Traditional solutions to economic problems that affect communities and regions no longer appear to be relevant. A community can only sustain itself, if it adopts and successfully implements new approaches to development which reflect changing social and economic conditions. Although large corporations continue to be significant employers and strategically important to future economic growth, most new employment is created by small businesses. Entrepreneurship which creates new small businesses that employ local people is viewed as the means of creating new jobs and becoming more self-reliant. CED organizations can play an important role in fostering a process towards increased community self-reliance and entrepreneurship. The principles of CED encourage self-reliance and business development. CED provides communities with a planning and management process for solving a community's social and economic problems as an alternative to existing development strategies. Future development of CED, however, requires removal of barriers that are currently inhibiting its growth. Supporters of CED must bring government, business, and academia together with representatives of CED organizations to examine the barriers and identify solutions appropriate to their communities.

25

Summary, Policy Implication and Research Needs

Leslie Kemp and Mary Coyle

Six areas of urgent and specific needs have been briefly described and discussed in relation to a potential research and development agenda and to their implications for Canadian public policy. Four chapters have been presented under this theme. Diane Gabrielle Tremblay and Flo Frank focused on education and training for CED, David Pell on the need to promote CED, and Francis Lamontagne on development indicators for CED. These chapters provide the background for discussion of six areas of urgent and specific CED needs: linking CED with macro policies, financing, educating for CED, sharing information, evaluating CED, and CED promotion.

Themes

CED operates within a broader policy context and, thus, linking CED with macro policies is critical. Furthermore, CED encompasses many dimensions of public policy including social, economic, environmental, and cultural policy. CED occurs when these dimensions of activity are integrated within a community context; they cannot,however, be effectively integrated at a community level when public policy treats social, economic, ecological, and cultural aspects of development as desperate and unconnected. Individual CED initiatives are affected by income security measures, labour market and employment policies, economic development policies and practices, trade policy, investment policy, and policy related to education and training, to name a few.

Education and training is essential to ensure practitioners are given the understanding and tools to engage in various aspects of CED activity. Information sharing needs to be encouraged among CED practitioners, projects, and communities. Improved information-sharing among the CED sector will encourage learning from others' experiences, promote the evolution of new approaches, and build networks of mutual support.

Increasing communication about CED approaches can also be an effective way of building public support and recognition of CED as a viable development alternative. This will help strengthen CED activity by increasing the resources allocated to CED initiatives.

Implications for Public Policy

Financing is a critical issue in CED. Many CED initiatives fail because of inadequate financing mechanisms or insufficient funding. There is a need to develop pro-active policies such as tax incentives for community investment. Macro policies must be more integrated and governments must work more cooperatively toward common goals both within federal and provincial governments and between various levels government. Policy integration and coordination is needed to avoid duplication of effort and contradictory policies. An inside out approach to policy development is called for with macro policies influenced by CED, rather than the other way around. Those vested with responsibility for creating policy have an obligation to find out what is happening in communities, to consult with communities in the development of policy, and to put resources into greater information-sharing between communities.

Public policy should encourage retooling of educational institutions to ensure they are responsive to emerging needs. Policies should reflect a training culture in which life long learning is accepted and supported. Priority in funding should be on developing skills and education for CED.

Public policy should support an evaluation process that is community-controlled, encourages self-evaluation, and incorporates CED values, principles, and approaches. Much can be learned from evaluating processes. Caution is needed to ensure that unrealistic expectations are not created for CED, given the conditions under which CED is undertaken and the limited resources communities frequently have to accomplish CED objectives.

Research Needs

Research and development is needed to identify the linkages to other areas of policy and to determine the policies which enhance and those which inhibit CED activity. In addition, research is needed on alternative CED models and service delivery mechanisms as they relate to macro policy. Research on specific CED policies would help determine where policies have been created explicitly to encourage or support CED activity and what their effect has been. There is a need to document current education and training approaches, models, and tools as well as a need to assess the effectiveness of these. Identification of gaps in education is required and support for innovation in education and training is critical.

A range of CED financing models exist, many of which are experimental and not well documented. Testing these models is needed to ascertain their applicability in various contexts. Thus, increased documentation and testing of alternative financing models should be part of a research and development agenda. The regulatory environment is a major obstacle to financing CED. Investigation of regulations respecting community investment is needed to determine how policies can be more supportive of CED.

Evaluating CED is important for CED practitioners to determine if their goals were achieved, what success looks like, what makes CED successful, and to learn from what is not working. Additionally, it is important to evaluate CED for reasons of accountability; to whom is CED accountable? The issue of to whom CED initiatives are accountable needs to be addressed in CED evaluation. As a community process, CED programs should be accountable first and foremost to the community rather than to a specific program. This must be balanced, however, with a recognition that program funders have a need to ensure their dollars are being spent in a worthwhile manner. Evaluation can help demonstrate the value of CED approaches; this, in turn, will help garner public and political support and funding for CED. The question arises of *what* and *how* to measure CED. Different measures of success may be needed from those used in conventional economic development. Values and principles of CED are an important backdrop for evaluation. The focus of evaluation should not be centred on narrow issues but should be broad in scope, ensuring that the full impacts of a project are considered. The time frame for evaluating CED is critical and must recognize CED as a long-term process of change.

What are the best ways of measuring the effectiveness of CED? Evaluation should not be seen as a separate element but, rather, should be integrated into the context of particular approaches and initiatives. Self-evaluation is essential. Communities need to be involved in the process of evaluation and in determining what indicators of success are most appropriate to ensure that CED evaluation is community-driven rather than program-driven. Benchmarks are a useful tool for assessing the progress of CED initiatives. The CED process works best if it is responsive to emerging community needs and priorities; thus, flexibility is required in evaluating CED. Client satisfaction should be a strong consideration in evaluation. Stories and case histories are a useful way of demonstrating what happened, what worked, what didn't work, and why. Much can be learned through case histories because of their ease in contextualizing the CED approach used. Furthermore, stories of success can be used in helping communities to learn from other examples.

Caution is urged when doing comparative analysis because CED looks different in each community. The wide variance in CED projects makes it difficult to find a comparative basis for evaluation. Thus, trying to develop a common basis for evaluation will be misleading unless the evaluation considers variability among CED approaches. Similarly, statistical measures can be limiting in CED evaluation because, unlike case histories, they do not tell the whole story. And, more importantly, they do not explain what happened and why; they merely report one aspect of success.

Further, evaluation needs to consider the cost of *not* doing CED. CED initiatives are frequently undertaken in situations of underdevelopment and high unemployment and in communities undergoing severe structural adjustment. Conditions such as these are not optimal for any type of development. The evaluation might focus on assessing what would have happened if no action was taken. Research and development is necessary to develop appropriate CED measures of success that take into consideration the value base for CED, recognize the long-term nature of the development process, and ensure the social, economic, and ecological dimensions of CED activity are considered.

The case for CED must be made to secure widespread public support. But how best to make the case for CED? One strategy is demonstrating and communicating the effectiveness of CED through further research, evaluation, and case studies. Information on how CED is positioned in other countries would help support CED initiatives here. Formalizing and organizing CED practice might also provide more legitimacy. Making a case for CED requires being clear about the context; CED is undertaken in situations where underdevelopment, chronic unemployment, and industrial failure is high. Conventional approaches to economic and social development have often failed. CED represents a new way of doing things that promotes and builds community self-reliance and control, inclusion and broad participation, and deliberately attempts to involve those who are marginalized by existing social and economic policy.

Information-sharing should be a part of all research. Effective communication of research results takes resources, time, and commitment; funding of research should acknowledge the importance of this element. Research and evaluation has documented examples of success in CED. Awareness of this work is missing even among those in the CED sector. Better communication of research results will avoid a reinventing the wheel.

PART 7

FUTURE DIRECTIONS

26

Summary, Future Directions and the Research Agenda

Dal Brodhead and François Lamontagne

The community economic development field is evolving rapidly and its breadth of action and definition is not yet fully delineated. Nevertheless, the experience accumulated in the last two decades indicates the potential of CED for influencing public policy development in the future. This chapter summarizes key issues and recommendations found in this volume. A policy-driven research and development agenda is proposed. Recommendations are made for the direction of future policy in Canada. The material is organized along the lines of the five themes which were used for organizing the material in this volume:

1. The scope and characteristics of CED
2. Environments conducive to effective CED
3. Evaluation of CED
4. Partnerships
5. Urgent/specific needs of CED.

Given the integrative nature of CED, of necessity, each of the themes overlapped each other to some degree and thus this chapter will tend to do also. For the sake of clarity, however, the term *approach* refers to a broad framework for CED, *strategies* refers to more precise initiatives or models, *mechanisms* concerns the delivery or implementation of CED.

Scope and Characteristics of CED

The starting point for a consideration of the field of CED is with its definition. This is essential to promote an awareness of CED. Communication needs to be based upon a relatively solid understanding of what is meant by CED.

Summary of the Research Papers

There is a broad consensus that there is no one definition of CED, but that it must be defined in the context of the situation within which it is being undertaken. However, there is also considerable agreement that CED approaches share many similar characteristics which imply a set of values differing from those traditionally brought to bear in development policies and programs.

The importance of the strategies of community empowerment and autonomy, of community as well as individual entrepreneurship, and of a sharing of the benefits of development across the community are all to form part of a CED ethos. CED is not a panacea but rather a complementary strategy of particular relevance to marginalized regions and populations. Its strength lies in its community roots and its utilization of local knowledge and resources.

A number of different strategies were identified in the research papers, including growth equity, loan and technical assistance, employment development, as well as planning and advisory services. The importance of a multiplicity of strategies to fit the differing community situations must be stressed. Along with this variety of strategies, the chapters identified a number of CED structures which have been created. These include the community development corporation, community development finance institutions, and community land trusts, to name a few examples.

Research findings and discussions have stressed the crucial involvement of governments and the need to press for comprehensive and integrated development approaches. Joint action by key actors drawn from a wide cross section of sectors, such as social, cultural, economic and environmental, is fundamental to effective CED.

Future Directions for Policy

The impact of the regulatory environment in which CED operates, and the important role of networks that facilitate the sharing of CED experiences are identified as two areas where innovative policy initiatives need to be implemented. The need for comprehensive policy approaches and enabling legislation supportive of CED initiatives was recognized while their absence was noted. Examples were cited from American and European CED initiatives. Integrated approaches by governments to tackle underdevelopment in Canada are required to replace multi-departmental and narrowly focused development programs.

Regional, national and local CED organizations must be able to share experiences and build on their accumulated knowledge. Networks, seminars, exchanges and computer communications linkages will all become vital to increasing the competence and efficiency which CED projects will need to incorporate to compete in the global marketplace. Policy and programs to facilitate such initiatives and to utilize new communications technologies are required.

Research Agenda

Three broad areas were identified as forming the core agenda for CED research. These included documentation and the establishment of analytical frameworks; enabling legislation, policy and the role of governments; and approaches to human resource development and training.

Documentation of CED projects and practices is still fragmentary and a systematic and ongoing process must be initiated to analyze the past, present, and future experiences. A focal point (or points) for the collection, study, and storage of this material must be established and be accessible to CED practitioners and policy development persons. Research into strategies, the process of CED, best practices and instructive CED experiences is needed.

The development of criteria for success and benchmarks for the evaluation of policies, programs and projects will be important to any effort to create the analytical frameworks required to systematically document CED practice in Canada. Research into various ways of assessing the effectiveness and relevance of CED is essential. Systematic analysis of CED is needed but the flexibility of CED approaches and strategies must be safeguarded. Analytical frameworks must reflect the diversity of CED approaches.

Research efforts are also needed in the area of enabling legislation and policy. In several jurisdictions, CED-related legislation has been promulgated and tested. A comprehensive overview of legislation relevant to CED in Canada will be required if policy makers are to be encouraged to look at CED from a macro policy perspective.

A critical part of a comprehensive CED approach is played by governments, yet the role of the public sector in supporting CED remains to many quite unclear. A careful review of the role various governments, at the local, regional/provincial, and national levels have played will contribute substantially to the development of an effective CED policy. A review of the documentation on this issue and a synthesis of the experiences in other countries will be needed. The under-utilization of human resources in marginalized communities represents one of the critical problems to be addressed. The development of human capital requires training tailored to specific community circumstances and focused on long-term capacity building. An overview of relevant training approaches, institutions, and materials, and an assessment of their effectiveness would aid in the further development of the field. Research in this area would be welcomed by development practitioners.

Related to the training issue is the need to strategically equip CED practitioners themselves with a strong knowledge base and the skills to assess CED strategies and mechanisms. Research in this area should include the study of best practice models, approaches to training and effective delivery methods.

Environments Conducive to Effective CED

The potential for the success of a given CED strategy is not inherent in the structure or strategy of the CED initiative itself. Rather, successful CED strategies evolve together with the environments in which they are undertaken.

Summary of the Research

The environment within which CED operates is comprised both of factors that are under the control of the community and those which are outside of community control. Access to local human and financial resources, community mobilization and awareness, or the internal mechanisms available to face the pressures of a crisis (such as a plant closure) are all factors that may play a role in determining the parameters for a successful CED approach and are all influenced by the specific community situation. Each community is unique and this uniqueness ensures that the environments in which CED operates are not homogenous from one case to another.

Other elements of the CED environment are external to the community and thus outside of its control. These elements are not specific to a particular CED initiative but apply to all social and economic projects. They include, for example, the regulatory environment, the bureaucracy, the economic climate and the existing national or provincial government policies and priorities.

It is all too easy to undervalue the community dimension when considering the CED approach, yet it is this intangible dimension that the research repeatedly highlights as unique. Although defined in various ways, the definitions of community usually include reference to shared values, interests, a sense of security, expectations, trust, and a common commitment to foster cooperation.

A growing recognition of the economic value of a sense of community is emerging and terminology such as "partenariat, synergie, and concertation" and "joint venture," "partnership" and "collaboration",illustrates that fact in French and English respectively. In an era of rapid change, the capacity to cope and innovate is also related to a sense of community, especially in threatened or marginalized situations.

Effective CED is believed to be more likely to occur in a cooperative, socially cohesive environment; although conditions may be similar for both conventional and CED business ventures, the success of CED depends to an even greater extent upon community involvement and support. Advocates of CED see the approach as more than a business strategy. Success is judged not only in terms of economic profitability, but on benefits accruing to the community at large as well.

CED must also be seen to be integrative and inclusive of groups and areas which have been traditionally left out of the development process. Environments conducive to CED tend to recognize and factor in the perspectives of women, persons of colour and aboriginal Canadians (to name a few important groups). Research and CED practice by and with such groups is increasingly confirming their particular contributions and their differing priorities. The role that women have played, for instance, in maintaining community networks is important to understand when designing a CED approach.

The melding of social and economic objectives is seen as part of the uniqueness of CED in terms of its capacity to address underdevelopment. It also represents its greatest challenge. Experience indicates that achieving a duality of objectives, while laudable, is in practice a difficult and sometimes near impossible goal.

Future Directions for Policy

Public policy in Canada is seldom reflective of the holistic approach to community issues and crises that is embodied in the CED approach. Linking social, economic, environmental, and other development objectives in designing development policies goes well beyond the current focus on business promotion as the engine of growth and development. The creation of a supportive environment for more integrative development approaches should be considered in future public policy initiatives.

CED is a medium and long-term approach to community revitalization, yet all too often it has been utilized as an ad hoc response to communities in crisis. However, crisis environments, such as those precipitated by industrial plant closures, are seldom conducive to effective CED work. Government policy in Canada must differentiate between development approaches and strategies appropriate to crises and those designed to create a longer-term capacity to utilize untapped local resources.

Policies which reinforce a focus on community are conducive to CED. Such policies must seek to be inclusive of groups often marginalized by today's political and economic processes. The early and meaningful involvement of these groups (e.g., women, aboriginal people, visible minorities, and so forth) is fundamental to the creation of an effective policy environment for CED. The political will to support needed legislative and institutional changes supportive of such holistic and inclusive CED initiatives needs to be encouraged.

Research Agenda

Further research is needed on the experiences of integrating social, economic and other objectives into a CED strategy. Additionally, studying the contribution of CED strategies and mechanisms in assisting communities to cope with fiscal restraint is relevant. Documentation is needed on this topic. Comparative studies of approaches and strategies used to deal with community crisis situations and more long range problems would be instructive for future policy-making. Rethinking of prevailing local and regional development approaches has been called for by academics and practitioners alike. CED as an appropriate additional policy response needs to be considered and researched.

Evaluation of Community Economic Development

The use of formal evaluation methods for assessing the effectiveness of CED undertakings is an important and instructive aspect of CED research, practice and policy. The complexity of the CED approach and the environment in which it takes place has led to the need for a certain degree of retooling of evaluation methods.

Summary of Research

Evaluation of CED is a controversial subject which brings traditional, often quantitative methodology into conflict with other more qualitatively oriented assessment methods. There is the difficulty securing agreement on appropriate methodologies given the broad definition of what constitutes CED in Canada. As well, the scarcity of evaluations of a comprehensive nature which have credibility has hindered progress in this area.

There is consensus that a CED evaluation framework should be based on a holistic definition of development: one which reflects the interaction between economic, social, cultural, organizational, and political development. It is thus necessary to situate any evaluation of a CED initiative in the wider context within which it operates. The idea of social or full cost accounting when assessing or designing CED strategies and mechanisms is recommended in order to determine the social, environmental, cultural, and economic benefits of CED and other approaches.

A growing body of research has also emerged that emphasizes the value of and the need for integrated and cooperative approaches to development and its evaluation. Early and meaningful involvement of key stakeholders in the evaluation process has been identified as an important component of such cooperation.

Documentation of the CED approach particularly emanating out of Quebec (Favreau and Ninacs; Fontan) increasingly makes the distinction between community economic development and community development and the structures specific to each—the community economic development corporation (CDEC) and the community development corporation (CDC). The sharing of certain common goals and the differences in priorities are important and need to be understood when undertaking to evaluate their somewhat different contributions.

Future Directions for Policy

The contribution of the CED approach, its strategies, and mechanisms needs to be more fully understood by policy-makers and practitioners alike. As the trend towards decentralization of government services continues, it will become more and more essential to draw upon the capacity of communities to plan, manage and evaluate CED and other development approaches. Future evaluation policy must reflect this community potential and take into account the broader development context within which it is expected to operate.

A participatory evaluation approach has increasingly been developed and used in international development work such as that financed by the Canadian International Development Agency. The relevance of this approach to CED is becoming clear. An essential aspect of evaluation is its role in helping community groups learn from their experiences. This is in addition to the requirement that evaluation be competently undertaken in order to satisfy funding authorities. The cooperative and interactive nature of the participatory evaluation approach assumes that evaluation is not an objective or neutral process, but that it is undertaken for a defined purpose. A community group may wish to review its progress or a government may wish to examine the effectiveness of its expenditures. Evaluation is very much a political process and control of it is always an issue. Evaluation policy for CED must take this view into account.

Research Agenda

While a common definition of CED would be useful for evaluation purposes, a universally accepted one that could reflect the diversity of communities in which CED operates is unlikely to be found. However, further clarification of the characteristics and objectives of CED—what it is and what it is not—would be useful, especially if drawn from the practice to date. Such clarification would contribute to a greater awareness of CED and its replicability.

Studies of CED projects which encompass both social and economic objectives in their goals and their practice would aid policy makers and practitioners. An accounting of the full social and economic costs and benefits of undertaking CED projects would be desirable. Inclusion of the implications of the broader societal context, such as the functioning of the informal economy and of other factors (the cost of UIC and health care for example), is necessary in order to provide a complete picture of the integrative nature and cost-effectiveness of a CED approach. The elements of an environment conducive to effective CED would become more discernible as a result.

Continued work on the application and development of an appropriate framework and indicators to assess CED has been stressed by those involved in the field.

Evaluation of CED must take into account the variety of CED strategies and mechanisms (e.g., CDECs and CDCs) in order for researchers and policy-makers to fully comprehend the actual and potential contribution of the overall approach in tackling underdevelopment in Canada. Research into the nature and evolution of such strategies and mechanisms would further the understanding of CED.

Partnerships

The complexity of the challenges raised by the diverse needs of marginalized communities and by the realities of the current economic and policy environments has led to the need for a diverse range of skills, perspectives, financial resources and even of organizational/legal structures to begin to undertake successful CED. A high degree of community participation or buy-in is also vital. Partnerships have arisen to bring resources together and to promote ownership in the CED process.

Summary of Research

The theme of partnership is raised consistently throughout the research papers. The creation of partnerships is the primary strategy advocated for the mobilization of a broad cross section of the community for the purposes of community revitalization (economic, social, etc.) and capacity building. It is a critical ingredient in the creation of an effective CED approach. The formation of alliances and agreements among the various interests, sectors, and players appeared to increase the chances of success. Yet it is also as a result of the diversity of such partnerships that differences could emerge and threaten the viability of the initiatives.

The range of partnerships described in earlier chapters varies enormously and can be as simple as networking and information sharing or, conversely, as complex as formal joint ventures for the purposes of carrying out elaborate business arrangements. Their common denominator is the direct involvement of the marginalized populations in a significant role. The research papers identify partnership as crucial to the building of local capacity and the empowerment of the marginalized population.

Partnership is also a strategy used to obtain outside expertise and to generate enthusiasm, sometimes through the involvement of an external catalyst/organizer, to facilitate the community development process in a marginalized community or group.

Government participation in partnerships has been judged to be desirable and often essential. However, a delicate balance must be maintained in order to ensure that the relationship is indeed a partnership of equals. Such a balance is fundamental to the success of the partnership. The need for a redefinition of development roles and methods of delivery is important in this context.

Future Directions for Policy

The CED approach is an alternative approach available to governments to deal with marginalization and disparity. It goes well beyond employment creation as a strategy and enables communities to handle their own problems. As a complement to existing government efforts, it should be considered in its own right as a priority deserving funding and other forms of governmental support.

Partnership with governments should not mean simply the delivery of government programs through CED organizations. It must be a more cooperative arrangement. Joint planning and shared resourcing of CED initiatives is needed. Governments, however, will be expected to remain active in development issues through resourcing of CED, identification of communities in need of CED, and facilitation of local planning initiatives for CED activity. CED mechanisms deserve encouragement through the use of tax policy and supportive regulatory frameworks. Alternative capital mechanisms are an example of a pressing need.

Research Agenda

There is need for a systematic review of the structure and characteristics of successful CED partnerships. This includes an assessment of many of the elements of successful partnerships and the related legal and organizational structures involved. The scarcity of research related to this important aspect of CED warrants future attention.

In considering the most productive role for governments in promoting and participating in the CED approach, examples of relevant funding programs, technical assistance resources and capital investments should be documented.

The relevance of the CED approach for dealing with marginalized peoples and areas is evident from recent research. The obligation of governments to create inclusive partnership approaches involving such groups in all aspects of their development is still contested while initiatives to deal with abuse, poverty, and discrimination are being proposed. A CED approach speaks to these priorities and thus should be utilized in order to create more effective development policy. A review of the recent and current experience would enable governments to better design future CED and other development policy.

Urgent and Specific Needs of CED

The identification of urgent needs of CED surfaced throughout the book and specifically in chapters on the theme of urgent and specific needs of CED. These needs are priority recommendations which may serve to map out a direction for advancing the further development of CED policy and practice in Canada.

Documentation, Analysis and Communication

The field of community economic development remains insufficiently understood. It has often been subsumed under the rubrics of job creation or regional development, but an increased awareness of the uniqueness of CED as an approach for tackling underdevelopment and marginalization must be achieved.

Documentation and analysis of the experience to date must be expanded to maximize the potential benefits to be derived from the practice of CED. Research remains fragmented and is often narrative in style. Access to CED research and documentation is difficult given the absence of recognized information clearinghouses or networks. Informal and voluntary lines of communications exist, but have severe resource and personnel limitations. A more systematic gathering and distribution of CED material is needed if a greater awareness of CED is to be generated. An inventory of CED models, training options, tools and technical resources should be undertaken, in addition to a study of approaches relevant to the creation of a CED information exchange network.

A top priority is the design and implementation of a national CED support structure. The inclusion of a networking and clearinghouse function in such a structure would respond to a need voiced by CED practitioners and could also serve the needs of policy-makers.

Policy and Regulatory Environments

The absence of a legislative framework supportive of CED is a major barrier to the widespread adoption of the approach. The Provinces of Ontario and British Columbia have recognized this fact and are currently developing or adopting some of the required pieces of legislation. In addition, municipal governments in Montréal, Toronto, Ottawa, and Vancouver, have initiated CED strategies or projects. A supportive legislative framework for CED will be essential if its benefits are to be maximized.

Policy explicitly directed at addressing local and regional disparity, marginalization, inequity and poverty must include a substantial CED component. Promotion of policy-oriented discussions is necessary to create an awareness among community and government decision-makers of the potential of CED as a significant policy thrust.

Research linking CED with macro policies such as development, training, investment, and trade policies needs to be undertaken. A comprehensive overview of legislation relevant to CED approaches and structures should be undertaken to aid practitioners and policy-makers alike in the planning and design of comprehensive development policies targeted at the marginalized populations and areas.

Financing of CED

Paramount among the areas identified as requiring urgent attention are those related to financing—both the financing of CED infrastructure and the issue of access to capital for CED projects (i.e., alternative financing mechanisms). Potential initiatives in both the public and private sectors ranged from support for the development of community loan funds, to the creation of quasi-development banks such as the ShoreBank in Chicago. Supportive public policy will be essential in this area.

Given the importance of developing new financial mechanisms in support of the CED approach, the review of legislation noted above must include careful study of the relevant legislation and models developed in other countries. Appropriate financing for CED will require policy innovations and regulatory revisions in order to accommodate the specific requirements of alternative financing.

Training

Implementation of a CED approach calls for a combination of committed community volunteers, trained CED staff and managers, as well as competent and knowledgeable leaders. Training in CED is an essential and almost completely missing ingredient. Only a few organizations in Canada have the capacity and the curriculum materials to undertake effective practice-based CED training. A plan of action and research is needed to supplement the limited existing training capacity and to extend its breadth and depth to include such areas as development management and policy.

Awareness and Promotion

Publication and distribution of CED research papers is an important step towards increasing the awareness of CED as a useful approach to community development.

To maximize the benefits of the resources that have been invested in CED research, policy-makers would find seminars or workshops with CED resource persons informative and useful in terms of examining the practical, as well as the conceptual aspects of the CED approach. Sessions held at the regional level might provide the greatest access to key policy development persons and practitioners from across Canada.

Conclusion

There is a shared sense of urgency to get on with implementing a CED approach, particularly in regions of the country faced with rapid and destabilizing changes. Given the pressing needs facing many Canadian communities, innovative CED approaches are being developed to respond to increasing marginalization, and underdevelopment. Community economic development is playing a significant part in the process of revitalizing some of these communities. Its pragmatic orientation, while not well documented, is increasingly generating useful results. In fact, CED practice seems to be well ahead of the research. Its promise as a useful development approach is becoming clearer to policy-makers in spite of the often difficult environments within which it has to operate. Within a more supportive policy framework, CED appears to hold considerable promise for disadvantaged communities.

Community economic development is a concept fundamentally different from traditional development approaches. It is a value-based approach which emphasizes development from within the community, for the benefit of the community as a whole and the empowerment of its marginalized members. It seeks to build partnerships among various sectors and to create local capacity to achieve greater long-term local self-reliance. Relevant public policy in the development field will need to encompass CED concepts in the future.

References

- Alderson, Lucy, and Melanie Conn (1988). *More Than Dollars, A Study of Women's Community Economic Development in British Columbia*. Vancouver: WomenFutures Community Economic Development Society.

- Alfred, Diane (1989). *Labour Market Paper: Women*. B.C. and Yukon: Employment and Immigration Canada, Economic Services Branch.

- Annie E. Casey Foundation (1994). Community empowerment: Making human services a community enterprise. *AEC Focus*, 4(1).

- Armstrong, Pat (1984). *Labour Pains, Women's Work in Crisis*. Toronto: The Women's Educational Press.

- Asshe, J., and C.E. Cosslett (1989). *Credit for the Poor*. (UNDP Policy Paper). New York: United Nation.

- Association for Enterprise Opportunity (1993). *Opening Enterprise Opportunity: Expanding the Micro-enterprise Development Field*. Chicago, Illinois: Association for Enterprise Opportunity.

- Association nationale pour le développement local et les pays [ANDLP] and Institut de formation en développement économique communautaire [IFDEC] (1989). *Le local en action: rapport du colloque international sur le développement local (Montreal 1988)*, Paris: Les Éditions de l'Épargne.

- Audet, Beverley A., and J. Rostami (1992). *Partnership Strategies for Community Investment*. Montréal: The Conference Board of Canada Institute of Donations and Public Affairs Research.

- Ball, C. (1991). *Pathways to Enterprise: Lessons from Commonwealth Experience*. London: Commonwealth Secretariat.

- Beaudoin, M., and C.R. Bryant (1993). *Des outils pour opérationaliser l'administration stratégique des Comités d'aide au développement des collectivités (CADC)*. Montreal: Employment and Immigration Canada, Quebec Regional Office.

- Beck, N. (1992). *Shifting Gears, Thriving in the New Economy*. Toronto: Harper Collins.

- Bélanger, P.R., and B. Lévesque (1992). Le mouvement populaire et communautaire: de la revendication au partenariat (1963–1992). In G. Daigle and G. Rocher (eds.), *Le Québec en jeu: comprendre les grands défis* (pp. 713–747). Montreal: Les Presses de l'Université de Montréal.

- Bella, L. (1991). Doctors, social workers and nurses: Hyphenated liberals. In B. Kirwin (ed.), *Ideology, Development and Social Welfare: Canadian Perspectives*. (Second Edition), (pp.181–204). Toronto: Canadian Scholars' Press.

- Bellemore, D., and L. Simon (1986). *Le défi du plein emploi*. Montreal: Éditions Saint-Martin.

- Bellemore, D., and L. Simon (1983). *Le plein emploi pur qui?* Montreal: Éditions Saint-Martin.

- Bennington, J., and M. Geddes (1992). Local economic development in the 1980s and 1990s: Retrospect and prospects. *Economic Development Quarterly*, 6 (4) 454–463.

- Berger, M., Blomquist, and W. Waldner (1987). A revealed-preference ranking of quality of life for metropolitan areas. *Social Science Quarterly, 68* (4), 761–78.

- Bhérer, H., and A. Joyal (1987). *L'entreprise alternative: mirages et réalités.* Montréal: Éditions Saint-Martin.

- Blakely, E.J. (1989). *Planning local economic development: Theory and Practice.* Newbury Park, California: Sage Publications Inc.

- Boisvert, Michel (1993). Les zone d'entreprise et leur applicabilité à Montréal: *Canadian Journal of Regional Science.* Vol. XVI, No. 1.

- Boldt, M., and J. Long (1986). Tribal traditions and European-Western political ideologies: The dilemma of Canada's native indians. In M. Boldt, J. Long, and L. Little Bear, (eds.), *The Quest for Justice. Aboriginal Peoples and Aboriginal Rights* (pp. 333–346). Toronto: University of Toronto Press.

- Boldt, M., J. Long, and L. Little Bear (eds.) (1986). *The Quest for Justice. Aboriginal Peoples and Aboriginal Rights.* Toronto: University of Toronto Press.

- Bolton, Roger (1992). Place prosperity vs people prosperity revisited: An old issue with a new angle. *Urban Studies, 29* (2) 185–203.

- Boothroyd, P. (1991). Community development: The missing link in welfare policy. In B. Kirwin (ed.), *Ideology, Development and Social Welfare: Canadian Perspectives* (pp.101–136). Toronto: Canadian Scholars' Press.

- Boothroyd, P., and C. Davis (1991). *The Meaning of Community Economic Development.* U.B.C. Planning Papers: Discussion Paper # 25. Vancouver: School of Community and Regional Planning, University of British Columbia.

- Boudon, R. (1984). *Les méthodes en sociologie.* Paris: PUF.

- Bowles, R. (1981). *Social Impact Assessment in Small Communities: An Integrative Review of Selected Literature.* Toronto: Butterworths.

- Brodhead, Dal (1994). Community economic development in Canada. In Burt Galaway and Joe Hudson (eds.), *Community Economic Development: Perspectives on Research and Policy.* Toronto: Thompson Educational Publishing.

- Brodhead, P.D. (1990). Lessons from Canadian case studies of community self-sustaining growth. In M.E. Gertler and H.R. Baker (eds.), *Sustainable Rural Communities in Canada,* (Proceedings of Rural Policy Seminar #1, Saskatoon, October 11–13, 1989, pp. 42–49). Saskatoon, Saskatchewan: The Canadian Agriculture and Rural Restructuring Group.

- Brodhead, P.D., F. Lamontagne, and J. Peirce (1989). *The local development organization: A Canadian perspective* (Local Development Series Paper No. 19). Ottawa: Economic Council of Canada.

- Brody, R. (1982). *Problem solving: Concepts and methods for community organizations.* New York: Human Science Press.

- Bruyn, S.T., and J. Meehan (eds.) (1987). *Beyond the Market and the State. New Directions in Community Development.* Philadelphia: Temple University Press.

- Bryant, C.R. (1992a). *La participation communautaire et le développement local: la voie de l'avenir.* Les Cahiers du Développement Local *1* (1) 5–7.

- Bryant, C.R. (1992b). Community development and changing rural employment in Canada. In Bowler, I., Bryant, C. R. and Nellis, D. (eds.), *Contemporary Rural Systems in Transition, Volume 2: Economy and Society* (pp. 265–78). Wallingford, Oxon: CAB International.

- Bryant, C.R. (1991). *Sustainable Community Development, Partnerships and Winning Proposals.* Sackville: Rural and Small Towns Research and Studies Program, Mount Allison University.

- Bryant, C.R., and C.R. Preston (eds.) (1987a). *Local Initiatives in Economic Development. Papers in Canadian Economic Development. 1.* Waterloo: Economic Development Program, University of Waterloo.

- Bryant, C.R., and R.E. Preston (1987b). A Framework for Local Initiatives in Local Development. *Economic Development Bulletin*, No. 1.

- Canada Department of Indian Affairs and Northern Development (1983). *International Year of the World's Indigenous People*.

- Canada Employment and Immigration (1990a). *Evaluation of the Community Futures Program—Overview Report*. Ottawa: Program Evaluation Branch.

- Canada Employment and Immigration (1990b). *Report of the Community Futures Review*. Ottawa: Community Development Employment Policies Section.

- Canada Employment and Immigration (1989). *Report of the Business Centre Funding Structure Review: Community Futures Program*. Ottawa: Community Development Employment Policies Section.

- Canada Employment and Immigration (1981). *Evaluation of the Community Employment Strategy*. Ottawa: Program Evaluation Branch.

- Canadian Association of Single-Industry Towns (1989). *The Vulnerability Checklist: A Tool for Community Self-Assessment*, Local Development Series Paper No. 10, Ottawa: Economic Council of Canada.

- Canadian International Development Agency (1991). Management of bilateral project evaluations. Ottawa.

- Carniol, B. (1991). Schools of altruism. In B. Kirwin (ed.), *Ideology, Development and Social Welfare: Canadian Perspectives*. (Second Edition) (pp. 229–246). Toronto: Canadian Scholars' Press.

- Centretown Community Health Centre (1984). *A Third Way*. Ottawa: Centretown Community Health Centre.

- City of Montreal (1990). *Partenaires dans le développement économique des quartier*. Montreal: Mimeographed document.

- Clamp, C. (1987). History and structure of the Mondragon system of worker cooperatives. In E.M. Bennett (ed.), *Social intervention: Theory and Practice*. Lewiston, N.Y.: Mellen Press.

- Coates, K., and J. Powell (1989). *The Modern North: People, Politics and the Rejection of Colonialism*. Toronto: James Lorimer and Company.

- Coffey, William J. (1991). Comprehensive bases for locally induced development. In D. Otto, and S. Deller, (eds.), *Alternative Perspectives on Development Prospects for Rural Areas* (pp.51–78). Portland, Oregon: Western Rural Development Center.

- Coffey, W.J., and M. Polèse (1985). Local development: Conceptual bases and policy implications. *Regional Studies*, *19* (2) 85–93.

- Coffey, W.J., and M. Polèse (1984). The concept of local development: A stages model of endogenous regional growth. *Papers of the Regional Science Association*, *55*, 1–12.

- Coffey, W.J., and M. Polèse (1982). Local development: Some policy options. Occasional Paper No. 9, Institute of Public Affairs, Dalhousie University, Halifax, Nova Scotia. Also published in French, Les politiques de développement local: éléments définition. *Études et documents*, *No. 34*, INRS-Urbanisation, Montréal.

- Compton, B., and Galaway, B. (1994). *Social work processes* (Fifth edition). Pacific Grove, California: Brooks/Cole.

- Conseil des affaires sociales (1992). *Un Québec solidaire: un rapport sur le développement*. Boucherville, Quebec: Gaëtan Morin, éditeur.

- Conseil des affaires sociales (1991). *Agir ensemble, rapport sur le développement*. Boucherville, Quebec: Gaëtan Morin, éditeur.

- Conseil des affaires sociales (1989). *Deux Québec dans un: un rapport sur le développement social et démographique*. Boucherville, Quebec: Gaëtan Morin, éditeur.

- Coppack, P., K. Beesley, and C. Mitchell (1990). Rural attractions and rural development: Elora, Ontario case study. In F. Dykeman (ed.), *Entrepreneurial and Sustainable Rural Communities* (pp. 33–56). Sackville, New Brunswick: Rural and Small Town Research and Studies Programme, Dept. of Geography, Mount Allison University.

- Corporation de développement communautaire des Bois-Francs (1987). *Fais-moi signe de changement: les actes du colloque provincial sur le développement communautaire* (Victoriaville 1986).

- Corporation de développement économique de l'Est (1992). *Rapport d'activités de CDEST.* Montreal.

- Corporation for Enterprise Development (1987). *Making the Grade. The Development Report Card for the States.* Washington:

- Côté, Marcel (1992). *By way of advice: Growth strategies for the market driven world.* New York: Mosaic Press.

- Cottrell, L. (1976). The competent community. In Burton H. Kaplan (ed.), *Further Explorations in Social Psychiatry* (pp. 195–209). New York: Basic Books.

- Crombie, D. (1992). *Regeneration: The final report of the Royal Commission on Toronto's waterfront.* Toronto.

- Cunningham, A. (1984). *Socio-economic impact assessment, development theory, and northern native communities.* U.B.C. Planning Papers: Studies in Northern Development, #4. Vancouver: University of British Columbia, School of Community and Regional Planning.

- Dare, W. (1992). The community development program of the Somerset-West Community Health Centre. Master of Social Work Program, Term Paper. Ottawa: School of Social Work, Carleton University.

- Dawe, S. (1992). *Rural Community Indicators: An Approach To Description and Information for Small Town and Rural Planning and Development.* Thesis presented to the Faculty of Graduate Studies, University of Guelph.

- de Rudder, V. (1987). La peur et le ghetto. *Politique d'aujord'hui,* 2.

- Decter, M., and J. Kowall (1967–1977). Manitoba's Interlake Region: The Fund for Rural Economic Development Agreement.

- DeFaveri, I. (1984). *Contemporary ecology and traditional native thought* (pp. 1–9). Source unknown.

- Development Indicator Project Steering Committee (1991). *Using Development Indicators for Aboriginal Development – A Guidebook.* Ottawa.

- Dewey, J. (1933). *How we think* (revised). New York: Heath.

- Dobson, R. (1993). Land and people. *City Magazine, 14* (2), 43–44.

- Doeringer, P.B., D.G. Terkla, and G.C. Topakian (1987). *Invisible Factors in Local Economic Development.* p. 34. New York: Oxford University Press.

- Douglas, D. (1989). Community economic development in Canada: A critical review. *Plan Canada, 29* (2) 28–46.

- Dreier, P., and B. Ehrlich (1991). Downtown development and urban reform: The politics of Boston's linkage policy. *Urban Affairs Quarterly, 26* (3) 354–375.

- Drucker, P. (1990). *Managing the Nonprofit Organization.* New York: Harper Collins.

- Dykeman, F.W. (1990). *Entrepreneurial Communities.* Sackville: Rural and Small Towns Research and Studies Program, Mount Allison University.

- Dykeman, F. (ed.) (1990a). *Entrepreneurial and sustainable rural communities.* Sackville, New Brunswick: Rural and Small Town Research and Studies Programme, Dept. of Geography, Mount Allison University.

- Dykeman, Floyd W. (1990b). Developing an understanding of entrepreneurial and sustainable rural communities. In F. Dykeman (ed.), *Entrepreneurial and sustainable rural communities* (pp.1–22). Sackville, New Brunswick: Rural and Small Town Research and Studies Programme, Dept. of Geography, Mount Allison University.

- Eberts, P., and F. Young (1971). Sociological variables of development: Their range and characteristics. In George Beal, et al. (eds.), *Sociological Determinants of Domestic Development*. Ames: Iowa State University.

- Economic Council of Canada (1990). *From the Bottom Up*. Ottawa: Ministry of Supply and Services.

- Economic Council of Canada (1990). *Good Jobs, Bad Jobs: Employment in the Service Economy*. Ottawa: Ministry of Supply and Services.

- Economic Council of Canada (April 1990). Local Development Paper No.18. Ottawa.

- Economic Council of Canada (1987). *Innovation and Jobs in Canada*. Ottawa.

- *Economics and Labour Market Research Group* (1993). The displaced workers of Ontario: How do they fare? Toronto: Ontario Ministry of Labour.

- Edwin Reid and Associates (1982). A model for the community employment program. In *Evaluation of the Community Employment Strategy in British Columbia*. Vancouver.

- Employment and Immigration Canada (1988). *Canada Employment Centre: Programs, Services — Employer's Guide*. Ottawa: Supply and Services Canada.

- Epstein, L. (1988). *Helping people: The task-centered approach*. Columbus, Ohio: Merrill.

- Fairbairn, B., J.M. Bold, M. Fulton, L.H. Ketilson, and D. Ish (1991). *Co-operatives and Community Development: Economics in Social Perspective*. Saskatoon, Saskatchewan: Centre for the Study of Co-operatives, University of Saskatoon.

- Favreau, L. (1989). *Mouvement populaire et intervention communautaire de 1960 88à nos jours — continuités et ruptures*. Montreal: Le centre de formation populaire et Les éditions du fleuve.

- Favreau, L., and W.A. Ninacs (1992). Le développement économique local et communautaire au Québec. *Coopératives et développement, 23* (2) 115–123.

- Favreau, L., and Y. Hurtubise (1993). *CLSC et communautés locales: la contribution de l'organisation communautaire*. Sainte-Foy, Quebec: Research laboratory, École de service social, Université Laval.

- Fontan, J.M. (1993). Case Study: A-Way Express. In Jean-Marc Fontan, Michael Lewis, and Stewart Perry (eds.), *Revitalizing Canada's Neighbourhoods: A Research Report on Urban CED*. Ottawa: National Welfare Grants.

- Fontan, J.M. (1993). *A Critical Review of Canadian, American, and European Community Economic Development Literature*. Vancouver: Westcoast Development Group.

- Fontan, J.M. (1993). *Revue de la littérature en développement local et en développement économique communautaire*. Montreal: Institut de formation en développement économique communautaire.

- Fontan, J.M. (1992). La démocratie économique communautaire. *Possibles, 16* (1) 53–64.

- Fontan, J.M. (1992). *Les corporations de développement économique communautaire montréalaises: du développement économique au développement local de l'économie*. Ph. D. thesis, Montréal: Institut de formation en développement économique communautaire.

- Fontan, J.M. (1991). *Initiation au développement économique local et au développement économique communautaire*. Montreal: Institut de formation en développement économique communautaire.

- Forum pour l'emploi (1991a). *Les actes du Forum pour l'emploi*. 5 et 6 novembre.

- Forum l'emploi (1991b). *Le Québec à l'ouvrage*. Document de base pour le colloque des 5 et 6 novembre.

- Fournier, L. (1991). *Solidarité Inc. Un nouveau syndicalisme créateur d'emplois*. Montréal: Québec-Amérique. 274.

- Friedman, J. (1992). *Empowerment: The Politics of Alternative Development*. Cambridge, Massachusetts: Blackwell Publishers.

- Friedman, M. (1962). *Capitalism and Freedom*. Chicago: University of Chicago Press.

- Gagné, P. (1992). *Le difficile compromis de la concertation*. In *20 ans de stratégie syndicale*. Special issue of the paper Le Devoir. May 1.

- Gallup Canada Inc. (1990). *Evaluation of Community Futures: Survey of Clients, Participants, Facilitators and Managers*.

- Gareau, J.M. (1990). *Le programme économique de Pointe-Saint-Charles 1983–1989: La percée du développement économique communautaire dans le sud-ouest de Montréal*. Montreal: Institut de formation en développement économique communautaire.

- Germain, C., and A. Gitterman (1980). *The Life model of Social Work Practice*. New York: Columbia University Press.

- Gershuny, J. (1983). *Social Innovation and the Division of Labor*. Oxford: Oxford University Press.

- Gershuny, J. (1983). *The New Service Economy*. London: Francis Pinter Publishers.

- Giarine, Orio (1980). *Dialogue on Wealth and Welfare*. London and New York: Peragmon Press.

- Glick, I. (1983). Resident perceptions of community well-being in a resource town. *Canadian Journal of Community Mental Health*. Special Supplement, 1(Winter) 39–44.

- Government of Canada (1987). *Report of the Federal-Provincial Task Force on Regional Development Assessment*. Toronto.

- Greffe, X. (1984). Territoire en France. *Economica*. Paris.

- Grémion, P. (1987). L'échec des élites modernisatrices. *Esprit*. 11.

- Haddow, R. (1992). *The political economy of labour market policy reform in Ontario, New Brunswick and Nova Scotia*. Paper presented at the meeting of the Atlantic Political Science Association Conference, Halifax, N.S.

- Hammond, J. (1987). Consumer cooperatives. In S. Bruyn and J. Meehan (eds.), *Beyond the Market and the State. New Directions in Community Development* (pp.97–112). Philadelphia: Temple University Press.

- Hanton, S. (1978). A case for the generalist social worker: A model for service delivery in rural areas. In *Effective models for the delivery of services in rural areas: Implications for practice and social work education*. Proceedings of the Third Annual National Institute On Social Work in Rural Areas (pp. 192–101). Morgantown, West Virginia: School of Social Work, West Virginia University.

- Harbison, F., J. Maruhnic, and J. Resnick (1970). *Quantitative Analyses of Modernization and Development*. Princeton, New Jersey: Princeton University Press.

- Health and Welfare Canada (1992). *Heart health equality: Mobilizing communities for action*. Cat. H39–245/1992E. Ottawa: Minister of Supply and Services.

- Heroux, (ed.) (1990). *Community Development: An Interprovincial Forum*. Toronto: Intergovernmental Committee on Urban and Regional Research.

- Hicks, N., and P. Streeten (1979). Indicators of development: The search for a basic needs yardstick. *World Development*, 7(6) 567–79.

- Higgins, B., and D. Savoie (1988). *Regional Economic Development*. London: Allen and Unwin Inc.

- Hogwood, B., and L. Gunn (1984). *Policy Analysis for the Real World*. New York: Oxford University Press.

- IFDEC (1990). *Les besoins en formation des organismes de développement économique communautaire de la région de Montréal*. Montréal.

- Indian and Northern Affairs Canada (1990). *Development Indicators in the Context of Aboriginal Development—An Overview*. Ottawa: E.T. Jackson and Associates.

- Indian and Northern Affairs Canada (1979). *Socio-Economic Impact Model for Northern Development*. Ottawa: Sandy Lockhart.

- Institute for Cooperative Community Development (1992). Working Networks. Internal working paper for a grant application to Housing and Human Services of the U.S. Department of Housing and Urban Development, under Section 4.03 — Transfer of International Innovations.

- Irey, K. (1980). The social work generalist in a rural context. An ecological perspective. *Journal of Education for Social Work.* Vol. 1, 36–42.

- Jacobs, J. (1985). *Cities and the Wealth of Nations: Principles of Economic life.* New York: Vintage.

- Jacquier, C. (1993). La citoyenneté urbaine en Europe. "Ville, exclusion et citoyenneté" Entretiens de la ville II sou la direction de Joël Roman. *Esprit.*

- Jacquier, C. (1992). A propos due développement social des quartiers: les référents de l'action. Paper presented to the Délégation interministérielle de la Ville (DIV).

- Jezierski, L. (1990). Neighborhoods and public-private partnerships in Pittsburgh. *Urban Affairs Quarterly, 26* (2) 217–249.

- Johnson, H. (ed.) (1980). *Rural Human Services: A Book of Readings.* Itasca, Illinois: F. E. Peacock Publishers, Inc.

- Judd, D., and M. Parkinson (1990). Urban leadership and regeneration. In Judd and Parkinson (eds.), *Leadership and Urban Regeneration: Cities in North America and Europe,* (pp. 13–30). Newbury Park, California: Sage Publications.

- Julien, P.A. (1991). Le rôle des institutions locales et le contrôle de l'information dans les districts industriels: deux cas québécois. *Revue d'Economie Régionale et Urbaine, 5,* 654–665.

- Kaufman, H.F. (1959). *Team Leadership: A key to development.* (Applied Series 1) Jackson: Mississippi State University, Social Science Research Centre.

- Kelly, R. (1977). *Community control of economic development: The boards of directors of community development corporations.* New York: Praeger. King, M., and George, S. (1987). The future of community: From local to global. In S. Bruyn and J. Meehan (eds.), *Beyond the Market and the State. New Directions in Community Development* (pp. 217–229). Philadelphia: Temple University Press.

- Kerr, C., J. Dunlop, F. Harbision, and C. Myers (1964). *Industrialism and Industrial Man.* New York: Oxford University Press.

- Kilby, P (1971). Hunting the heffalump: In P. Kilby, *Entrepreneurship and Economic Development.* New York: Free Press.

- Kirwin, B. (ed.) (1991). *Ideology, Development and Social Welfare: Canadian Perspectives.* (Second Edition). Toronto: Canadian Scholars' Press.

- Ladouceur, L., and P. Konoshameg (1986). Evaluation of the Local Employment Assistance and Development Program (LEAD). In Canada Employment and Immigration. Ottawa: Program Evaluation Branch.

- Lamontagne, F. (1990). *Development Indicators in the Context of Aboriginal Development – An Overview,* Ottawa: Indian and Northern Affairs.

- Lamontagne, F. (1989). Le développement des régions canadiennes: la nécessité d'une approche alternative. *Revue Canadienne de Santé Mentale Communautaire, 8* (2) 41–60.

- Lamontagne, F., and C. Tremblay (1989). *Development Indices: A Quebec Regional Comparison.* Ottawa: Economic Council of Canada.

- Langlois, R. (1990). *S'appauvrir dans un pays riche.* Montréal: Centrale de l'enseignement du Québec and Les éditions coopératives Albert-Saint-Martin.

- Laronde, M., and J. Harris (1991). The Temagami stewardship council. In C. Plant and J. Plant (eds.), *Putting Power in its Place: Create Community Control* (pp. 104–109). The New Catalyst Bioregional Series. Gabriola Island, B.C.: New Society Publishers.

- Lecomte, R. (1990). Connecting private troubles and public issues in social work education. In B. Wharf, *Social Work and Social Change in Canada* (pp. 31–51). Toronto: McClelland and Stewart Inc.

- Lemelin, A., and R. Morin (1991). L'approche locale et communautaire au développement économique des zones dévaforisées: le cas de Montréal. *Cahiers de Géographie du Québec*, 35 (95) 285–306.

- Lemieux, V. (1982). *Réseaux et appareils: logique des systèmes et langage des graphes.* Québec: Edesern.

- Lévesque, A., and J. M. Fontan (1992). *Initiation au développement économique local et au développement économique communautaire.* Montreal: Institut de formation en développement économique communautaire.

- Lévesque, B., and M.C. Malo (1992). L'économie sociale au Québec: une notion méconnue mais une réalité économique importante. In J. Defourny and J.L. Monzon Campos (eds.), *Économie sociale: entre économie capitaliste et économie publique/The Third Sector: Cooperative, Mutual and Nonprofit Organizations* (pp. 385–446). Brussels: CIRIEC and De Boeck-Wesmæl, Inc.

- Lévesque, B., A. Joyal, and O. Chouinard (1989). *L'autre économie — une économie alternative?* Proceedings of the 8th Annual Symposium of the Association d'économie politique.

- Lewis, M., and F. Green (1992). *Strategic Planning for the Community Economic Development Practitioner.* Vancouver: Westcoast Development Group.

- Lewis, Mike (1994). The Scope and Characteristics of CED in Canada. In B. Galaway and Joe Hudson (eds.), *Community Economic Development: Perspectives on Research and Policy* (pp. 48-57). Toronto: Thompson Educational Publishing.

- Lewis, Mike (1990). *The Development Wheel: A Workbook to Guide Community Analysis and Development Planning.* Vancouver: Westcoast Development Group.

- Lipsey, M.W. (1993). Theory as method: Small theories of treatments. *New Directions for Program Evaluation. 57,* 5–38.

- Little Bear, L., M. Boldt, and J. Long (1986). *Pathways to Self-Determination. Canadian Indians and the Canadian State.* Toronto: University of Toronto Press.

- Lockhart, A. (1991). Northern development policy: Hinterland communities and metropolitan academics. In T.W. Dunk (ed.), *Social Relations in Resource Hinterlands.* Thunder Bay: Centre for Northern Studies, Lakehead University.

- Lockhart, A. (1990). Northern Ontario and economic development theory. Occasional papers, Institute of Northern Ontario Research and Development. Sudbury: Laurentian Univ.

- Lockhart, A. (1989). Finding a common voice. In P. Kariya (ed.), *Native Socio-Economic Development in Canada: Change, Promise and Innovation,* Vol. 2. Winnipeg: Institute of Urban Studies.

- Lockhart, A. (1987). Community-based development and conventional economics in the Canadian north. In E.M. Bennett (ed.), *Social intervention: Theory and Practice.* Lewiston, N.Y.: Mellen Press.

- Lockhart, A. (1985). Northern development policy: Self-reliance versus dependency. In *Strategies for Canadian Economic Self-Reliance.* Ottawa: Canadian Centre for Policy Alternatives.

- Lockhart, A. (1982). The insider-outsider dialectic in native socio-economic development: A case study in process understanding. *The Canadian Journal of Native Studies, 2* (1) 159–68.

- Lockhart, A., and D. McCaskill (1986). Toward an integrated, community-based, partnership model of native development and training. *The Canadian Journal of Native Studies*, 6 (1).

- Lovins, A. (1991). *City Magazine. 12* (2).

- Lucas, R. (1974). *Minetown, Milltown, Railtown: Life in Canadian Communities of Single Industry.* Toronto: University of Toronto Press.

- Lui, Ben-Chieh (1980). Economic growth and quality of life: A comparative indicator analysis between China (Taiwan), U.S.A. and other developed countries. *American Journal of Economics and Sociology, 39* (1) 1–21.

- Luther, J. (1990a). Participatory design vision and choice in small town planning. In F. Dykeman (ed.), *Entrepreneurial and Sustainable Rural Communities* (pp. 33–56). Sackville, New Brunswick: Rural and Small Town Research and Studies Programme, Dept. of Geography, Mount Allison University.

- Luther, V. (1990b). Learning from successful communities: Rural case study research. In F. Dykeman (ed.), *Entrepreneurial and Sustainable Rural Communities* (pp. 193–200). Sackville, New Brunswick: Rural and Small Town Research and Studies Programme, Dept. of Geography, Mount Allison University.

- Lyons, O. (1991). Land of the free, home of the brave: Iroquois democracy. In C. Plant, and J. Plant (eds.), *Putting Power in its Place: Create Community Control!* (pp. 70–75). The New Catalyst Bioregional Series. Gabriola Island, B.C.: New Society Publishers.

- Lyons, O. (1986). Spirituality, equality, and natural Law. In L. Little Bear, M. Boldt and J. Long (eds.), *Pathways to Self-Determination. Canadian Indians and the Canadian State* (pp.7–13). Toronto: University of Toronto Press.

- M'Gonigle, M. (1991). Our home and native land? Creating an eco- constitution in Canada. In C. Plant and J. Plant, (eds.), *Putting power in its place: Create community control!* (pp. 49–58). The New Catalyst Bioregional Series. Gabriola Island, B.C.: New Society Publishers.

- MacLeod, G. (1992). *The Community business concept.* Sydney, Nova Scotia: Tompkins Institute, University College of Cape Breton.

- Maillat, Denis (1992). La relation des enterprises innovatrices avec leur milieu: In D. Maillat and J.C. Perrin, *Entreprises innovatrices et développement territorial.* EDES Neuchâtel (Switzerland).

- Maillat, Denis (1990). Innovation and local dynamism: The role of the milieu. *Sociologia Internationalis, 28* (2) 147–159.

- Marquart, F. (1976). L'analyse des besoins éducatifs. *Éducation permanente.* 35. Paris.

- Martin, Fernand (1987). Encouraging entrepreneurship in small less-developed regions: An evaluation: In *Local Development: The Future of Isolated Cultural Communities and Small Economic Regions*, W.J. Coffey and R. Runte, Nova Scotia: University of St. Anne's Press.

- Matthews, R. (1983). *The Creation of Regional Dependency.* Toronto: University of Toronto Press.

- Mayer, N. (1984). *Neighborhood Organizations and Community Development: Making Revitalization Work.* Washington, D.C.: The Urban Institute Press.

- McGranahan, D.V., C. Richard-Proust, N.V. Sovani and M. Subramanian (1972). *Contents and Measurement of Socioeconomic Development.* New York: Praeger Publishers.

- Mcpherson, Dennis (1992). Rural field trip to Armstrong, Whitesands and Gull Bay: A collection of student papers. SW 3313. Rural Social Work Practice. Thunder Bay: Department of Social Work, Lakehead University.

- Mcpherson, D., and J. Rabb (1991). *Indian from the Inside: A Study in Ethno-metaphysics.* Thunder Bay: Department of Social Work, Lakehead University.

- Medard, J.F. (1969). Communauté locale et organisation communautaire aux États-Unis. *Cahier de la Fondation nationale des sciences politiques,* p. 58.

- Meehan, J. (1987). Working toward local self-reliance. In S. Bruyn and J. Meehan (eds.), *Beyond the Market and the State. New Directions in Community Development* (pp.131–151). Philadelphia: Temple University Press.

- Ministry of Community and Social Services (1989). *Better beginnings better futures: An integrated model of primary prevention of emotional and behavioural problems.* Toronto: Queen's Printer for Ontario.

- Ministry of Health, Government of British Columbia (1992). *Health Indicator Workbook – A Toll for Healthy Communities.* Vancouver.

- Ministry of Municipal Affairs (1985). *Hemlo impact study update.* Toronto: Ontario Ministry of Municipal Affairs.

- Morris, D. (1982). *Self-Reliant Cities.* San Francisco: Sierra Club Books.

- Mumford, L. (1938). *The Culture of Cities.* New York: Harcourt, Brace, and Javanovich.

- Nawaz, R. (1992). The official "green" plan for the city of Ottawa. *City Magazine, 14* (1), 41–43.

- Nelson, C. (1984). Management practices in rural social service delivery: A case study. In W. Whitaker (ed.), *Social Work in Rural Areas. A Celebration of Rural People, Place and Struggle* (pp. 129- 147). Proceedings of the Ninth National Institute on Social Work in Rural Areas, Orono, Maine: Department of Sociology and Social Work, The University of Maine.

- Nelson, C., J. Stafford, and D. McPherson (1986). *Hemlo human services update 1985.* Thunder Bay: Centre for Regional Development.

- Nelson, C., M. Kelley, and D. McPherson (1985). Rediscovering support in social work practice. Lessons from Indian indigenous human service workers. *Canadian Social Work Review* (pp. 231–248).

- Nichols Applied Management (1983). *Economic Indicators for Indian Reserves – The Development and Maintenance of a Data Base.* Ottawa: Indian and Northern Affairs Canada, Alberta Region.

- Nicholson, J.P., and P. Macmillan (1986). *An Overview of Economic Circumstances of Registered Indians in Canada.* Ottawa: Indian and Northern Affairs Canada.

- Ninacs, W.A. (1991). L'organisation communautaire en milieu semi-urbain/semi-rural. In L. Doucet and L. Favreau (eds.), *Théorie et pratiques en organisation communautaire* (pp. 257–272). Sillery, Quebec: Presses de l'Université du Québec.

- Northern Women's Task Force (1977). *Northern British Columbia's Women's Task Force Report on Single Industry Communities.* Vancouver: Women's Research Centre.

- Nozick, M. (1992). *No place like home: Building sustainable communities.* Ottawa: Canadian Council on Social Development.

- Nozick M. (1991). Community land trusts: Addressing the urban land question. *City Magazine, 13* (2), 18–25.

- O'Neill, T. (1990). *From the Bottom Up: The Community Economic Development Approach.* Ottawa: Economic Council of Canada.

- O'Neill, Tim (1994). Differences between regional development, local economic development, and community economic development. In B. Galaway and Joe Hudson (eds.), *Community Economic Development: Perspectives on Research and Policy.* Toronto: Thompson Educational Publishing.

- Office de planification et de développement du Québec (1988). *Québec à l'heure de l'entreprise régionale—Plan d'action en matière de développement régional.* Québec:

- *Ontario Leads Gain as Exports Creat Jobs* (1993). *Globe and Mail.*

- Ontario Ministry of Municipal Affairs (1992). *International Forum on Community Economic Development Proceedings.* Toronto: Intergovernmental Committee on Urban and Regional Research.

- Organization for Economic Development and Cooperation (1990). Implementing change. Paris.

- Organization for Economic Co-operation and Development (1982). *The OECD List of Social Indicators*. Paris.

- Pagano, M., and A. O'M Bowman (1992). Attributes of development tools: Success and failure in local economic development. *Economic Development Quarterly*, 6 (2) 173–186.

- Paquet, P. (1992). De la formation des adultes à l'adaptation de la main-d'œuvre. *Possibles*, 16 (4) 15–34.

- Pecqueur, Bernard (1989). *Le développement local: mode ou modèle?* Paris: Syros, Alternativs.

- Pell, D. (1990). *Community Economic Development in Ontario: A Proposal for the 90's*. Toronto: Community Business Centre.

- Pell, D., and R. Tomalthy (1992). *Cities and Sustainable Development: Current Initiatives*. Ottawa: Institute for Research on Environment and Economy, University of Ottawa.

- Pell, David (1991). *Community Economic Development: A Roundtable Discussion*. Toronto: Community Business Centre.

- Perlman, H. (1957). *Social casework: A problem solving process*. Chicago: University of Chicago Press.

- Perry, S. (1993). Case study: HRDA. In Jean-March Fontan, Michael Lewis, and Stewart Perry (eds.), *Revitalizing Canada's Neighbourhoods: A Research Report on Urban CED*. Ottawa: National Welfare Grants.

- Perry, S. (1987). *Communities on the Way: Rebuilding Local Economies in the United States and Canada*. Albany: State University of New York Press.

- Perry, Stewart E. (1987). *Communities On The Way: Rebuilding Local Economies in the United States and Canada*. Albany: State University Press of New York.

- PJS Geach and Associates (1985). *Band Planning Handbook on the Use of Socio-Economic Indicators*. Ottawa: Department of Indian Affairs and Northern Development, B.C. Region.

- Plant, C., and J. Plant (eds.) (1991). *Putting Power in its Place: Create Community Control*. The New Catalyst Bioregional Series. Gabriola Island, B.C.: New Society Publishers.

- Point, Susan (1992). "The Shaper," Acrylic on Canvas.

- Polanyi, Karl (1957). *The Great Transformation*. Boston: Beacon Press.

- Power, A. (1991). *Housing Management: A Guide to Quality and Creativity*. Longman: London.

- Price Waterhouse (1990). *Role Review and Community Impact Analysis of the Community Futures Program*. Ottawa.

- Project Mayday (1985). *Mayday in the Community—A Research Study on Women's Experience in North Shore Single Industry Towns, Manitouwadge, Marathon, Schreiber, Terrace Bay*. Project Mayday.

- Provost, M., and M.A. Deniger (1991). Pour une politique familiale holistique orientée vers la lutte à la pauvreté. Mimeographed document by the Montréal Office of the Canadian Council on Social Development submitted to the Youth Task Force.

- Québec (1991). *Partenaires pour un Québec compétitif. Énoncé de politique sur le développement de la main d'oeuvre*. Québec: Ministère de la main-d'oeuvre, de la sécurité du revenu et de la formation professionnelle.

- Ranney, D., and J.J. Betancur (1992). Labor-force-based development: A community-oriented approach to targeted job training and industrial development. *Economic Development Quarterly*, 6 (3) 286–296.

- Reid, L. (1986). Ghost town/boom town. Marathon, Ontario. *Equinox*, (Fall, 1986) pp.90-95.

- Reid, W. (1978). *The task-centered system*. New York: Columbia University Press.

- Rich, Michael (1992). Local economic development in the 1980s: Editor's introduction. *Economic Development Quarterly, 6* (2) 148–149.

- Rodriguez, P. (1991). *Enterprises d'insertion projet de développement.* Montreal: Boulot Vers.

- Ross, D., and P. Usher (1986). *From the roots up: Economic development as if community mattered.* Canadian Council on Social Development Series. Toronto: James Lorimer and Company.

- Ross, David, and Peter Usher (1985). *From the Roots Up, Economic Development As If Community Mattered.* Ottawa: Canadian Council on Social Development.

- Rossi, R., and K. Gilmartin (1980). *The Handbook of Social Indicators: Sources, Characteristics, and Analysis.* New York: Garland STPM Press.

- Rostow, W.W. (1960). *The Stages of Economic Growth.* Boston: Harvard University Press.

- Rubin, H., and I. Rubin (1992). *Community Organizing and Development.* (Second Edition). New York: Macmillan Publishing Company.

- Rubin, H., and I. Rubin (1986). *Community Organizing and Development.* New York: Macmillan Publishing Company.

- Salvet, J.M. (1992). L'embryon d'une politique de plein emploi. In *20 ans de stratégie sydicale.* Special issue of the paper Le Devoir, May 1.

- Sartorius, R.H. (1991). The logical framework approach to project design and management. *Evaluation Practice,* 12 (2) 139–147.

- Savoie, D.J. (1986). *Regional Economic Development: Canada's Search for Solutions.* Toronto, Ontario: University of Toronto Press.

- Schumacher, E. (1974). *Small is Beautiful: A Study of Economics as if People Mattered.* London: Abacus.

- Seidman, K. (1987). A new role for government: Supporting a democratic economy. In S. Bruyn and J. Meehan (eds.), *Beyond the market and the state. New directions in community development* (pp.185–216). Philadelphia: Temple University Press.

- Senault, P. (1989a). *Formation et territoires: la formation-développement.* Paris: Syros Alternatives.

- Senault, P. (1989b). Caractéristiques principales des formations- développement. In P. Senault, *Formation et territoires: la formation-dévelloppement.* Paris: Syros Alternatives.

- Shin, Eul Hang (1977). Socioeconomic development, infant mortality and fertility: A cross-sectional and longitudinal analysis of 63 selected countries. *The Journal of Development Studies, 13* (4) 398–412.

- Sorge, A., and W. Streek (1987). *Industrial relations and technical change: The case for an extended perspective.* Discussion paper no IIM/LMP 87- 1. Berlin: WZB.

- Stanek, O. (1990). *Le développment régional et les conférences socio- économiques.* Enquête GRIDEQ-AQORCD. Université du Québec à Rimouski.

- Steering Group on Prosperity (1992). *Investing Our Future: An Action Plan for Canada's Prosperity.* Ottawa: Minister of Supply and Services.

- Swack, M., and D. Mason (1987). Community Economic Development as a Strategy for Social Intervention. In E. Bennett (ed.), *Social Intervention Theory and Practice.* Lewiston, N.Y.: Mellen Press.

- Task Force on Program Review (1987). *Service to the public: Job creation, training and employment services, local employment assistance development.* Ottawa.

- Tester, F. (1991). Local power versus global profits: The odds against. In C. Plant and J. Plant (eds.), *Putting power in its place: Create community control!* (pp.10–18). The New Catalyst Bioregional Series. Gabriola Island, B.C.: New Society Publishers.

- Tremblay, D-G. (1991). Computerization and the Construction of New Qualifications in the Context of Product and Process Innovation in the Banking Sector. In Nurminen, editor. *Computer Jobs and Human Interfaces*, Amsterdam: Elsevier Science Publishers. 113–123.

- Tremblay, D-G. (1990a). *L'emploi en devenir.* 119. Québec: Institut québecois de recherche sur la culture.

- Tremblay, D-G. (1990). *Économie du travail: les réalités et les approches théoriques.* 544. Montréal: Éditions St-Martin et Télé- université.

- Tremblay, D-G., and A. Noël (1993). Concentration in a high unemployment Society. *Inroads* 2 (Spring 1993) 74–85.

- Tremblay, D-G., and van V. Schendel (1991). *Économie du Québec et de ses régions.* Montréal: Éditions Saint-Martin et Télé-université.

- Tremblay, G. (1991). *Vers une société à valeur ajoutée.* Québec: Ministère de l'industrie et du commerce.

- Turner, C. (1987). Worker cooperatives and community development. In S. Bruyn and J. Meehan (eds.), *Beyond the market and the state. New directions in community development* (pp. 64–78). Philadelphia: Temple University Press.

- United Nations (1989). *Guidelines for social protection policies and programs aimed at development in the near future.* New York: United Nations Information Department.

- Uren, J. (1985). Born to die? The plight of one industry towns in Canada. *Canadian Heritage.* (October/November).

- *Vancouver Sun.* "More women in the labour force." (March, 1993).

- Vancouver Task Force on Atmospheric Change (1990). Clouds of change. Vancouver: City of Vancouver.

- Vidal, A. (1992). *Rebuilding Communities: A National Study of Urban Community Development Corporations.* New York: Community Development Research Center, Graduate School of Management and Urban Policy, New School for Social Research.

- Vieillard-Baron, H. (1990). Le ghetto, un lieu impropre et banel. *Les Annales de la recherche urbaine,* 49 (December).

- Waring, Marilyn (1989). *If Women Counted: A New Feminist Economics.* New York: Harper Row.

- Wein, F. (1991). *The Role of Social Policy in Economic Restructuring.* Halifax, N.S.: The Institute for Research on Public Policy.

- Weisbrod, B. (1988). *The Nonprofit Economy.* Cambridge, Mass: Harvard University Press.

- Weiss, J.A. (1988). Substance verses symbol in administrative reform. In C. Milofsky (ed.), *Community Organizations: Studies in Resource Mobilization and Exchange.* New York: Oxford University Press.

- Werrier, V. (1993). *The Winnipeg Free Press,* January 23.

- Wharf, B. (1992). *Communities and Social Policy in Canada.* Toronto: McClelland and Stewart Inc.

- Wharf, B. (1990a). Lessons from the social movements. In B. Wharf, *Social work and social change in Canada* (pp. 144–180). Toronto: McClelland and Stewart Inc.

- Wharf, B. (1990b). *Social Work and Social Change in Canada.* Toronto: McClelland and Stewart Inc.

- Wharf, B. (1984). Toward a leadership role in human services: The case for rural communities. In W. Whitaker (ed.), *Social work in rural areas. A celebration of rural people, place and struggle* (pp. 9- 37). Proceedings of the Ninth National Institute on Social Work in Rural Areas, Orono, Maine: Department of Sociology and Social Work, The University of Maine.

- Wharf, J. (1992). The healthy community movement in Canada. In B. Wharf, *Communities and social policy in Canada* (pp. 151–180). Toronto: McClelland and Stewart Inc.

- Whitaker, W. (ed.) (1984). *Social Work in Rural Areas. A Celebration of Rural People, Place and Struggle*. Proceedings of the Ninth National Institute on Social Work in Rural Areas. Orono, Maine: Department of Sociology and Social Work, The University of Maine.

- Wiewel, W., and C. Hall (1992). Local economic development: A review of the British and U.S. comparative literature. *Economic Development Quarterly, 6* (4) 396–405.

- Wilmott, P. (1984). *Community in social policy*. Policy Studies Institute, Discussion paper No. 9. London:

- Wolfe, A. (1989). *Whose Keeper? Social Science and Moral Obligation*. Berkeley: University of California Press.

- Wolman, H., and G. Stoker (1992). Understanding local economic development in a comparative context. *Economic Development Quarterly 6* (4), 406–417.

- Women for Economic Survival (1984). *Women and Economic Hard Times: A Record*. University of Victoria, Extension Division, British Columbia.

- Women's Research Centre (1979). *Beyond the Pipeline: A Study of the Lives of Women and Their Families in Fort Nelson B.C. and Whitehorse, Yukon Territory*. Vancouver: Women's Research Centre.

- Women's Unemployment Study Group (1983). *Not For Nothing, Women, Work and Unemployment In Newfoundland and Labrador*. St. Johns, Newfoundland.

- Wood, K. Scott (1972). *Social Indicators and Social Reporting in the Canadian North*. Halifax: Institute of Public Affairs. Dalhousie University.

- World Commission on Environment and Development (1987). *Our common future*. New York: Oxford University Press.

- Yaron, J. (1991). Successful rural finance institutions. *AGRAP* (World Bank), *1*.

- Zapf, K. (1991). Ideology and geography: The Canadian north. In B. Kirwin (ed.), *Ideology, Development and Social Welfare: Canadian perspectives* (Second Edition) (pp. 65–99). Toronto: Canadian Scholars' Press.

- Zdenek, R. (1987). Community development corporations. In S.T. Bruyn and J. Meehan (eds.), *Beyond the Market and the State* (pp. 112–127). Philadelphia: Temple University Press.